THE SKEPTICAL JUROR

AND

THE TRIAL OF CORY MAYE

SECOND IN A SERIES

BY

J BENNETT ALLEN

ALLEN & ALLEN SEMIOTICS, INC.

LONG BEACH, CALIFORNIA

First Edition, July 2010

ISBN 978-0-9842716-7-2
Published by Allen & Allen Semiotics, Inc., www.semiotics.com

Cover design by Ed Lewis, www.edlewisdesign.com
Cover design © 2010 Ed Lewis

Printed on acid-free paper in the United States of America

TABLE OF CONTENTS

PRELUDE
Thursday, 26 December 2001

"I got stopped one night. They said I had crack. I didn't have anything. They hit me. Said they were taking me to jail. Mister Ron Jones showed up later. Asked me if I was okay, and told them not to take me in. He was a good guy. He was a good cop." -- Resident of Prentiss, Mississippi

As are many rural areas in the country, the small town of Prentiss is suffering a surge in drug-related crime. According to Henry McCullum, Sheriff of Jefferson Davis County, drugs are now the major industry in an otherwise depressed economy. The steady supply of crack, marijuana, and meth enriches the few at the top, sustains those in the middle, and consumes those at the bottom. The illegal drug trade is our nation's deadliest pyramid scheme.

Perhaps fifty percent of the male population in Jefferson Davis County will spend time in prison before reaching their twenty-first birthday, mostly for drug-related crimes. The homicide rate will exceed that of Detroit.

Unfortunately, the drug economy is but one constituent of the pall that hangs over the small town of Prentiss, and over the county named for the president of the Confederate States of America. The population of Prentiss is primarily white, as is the town's five-man Police Department. The population of Jefferson Davis County is primarily black, as is the county's five-man sheriff's department. The issue of race is omnipresent.

Ron Jones has, for the last four years, worked to solve both the drug and race problems. He has earned the respect of those he serves and protects, regardless of skin color. Among the black community he is known as one of the good ones, perhaps the only good one. Among the drug community, he is known as the K-9 officer, the one with the drug-sniffing dog.

Now, in the waning hours of this first day after Christmas, Ron Jones is prepared to lead his motley team of officers into a darkened duplex to serve yet another search warrant for drugs. He is there based on the word of the town bigot that a large quantity of drugs is stashed inside.

As the rear door is breached, Ron is the first to enter. His announcement that he is a police officer, there to execute a search warrant, is interrupted by gunfire. Ron is struck in the abdomen, just below his vest.

"I'm hit," he says, making his way back down the steps. The bullet has punctured his aorta. He will bleed to death within minutes. He falls to his knees.

"Get me to the hospital, I've been hit." He collapses to the ground.

"Good Lord, help."

INTRODUCTION

The story you are about to read is fact. It is also fiction. It includes a fair amount of speculation. Allow me to explain, so that you will be able to orient yourself.

When writing of the trial testimony in the case of Mississippi v. Cory Maye, I have used the words of the witnesses, the attorneys, and the judge as I found those words in the trial transcripts. I concede that I have abbreviated much of what they had to say because attorneys tend to ramble and witnesses tend to stumble. I concede also that I have repaired some of the grammar and redacted many of the annoying speech mannerisms, for unedited transcripts are fearsome to behold. Despite this editorial license, I tried to preserve the integrity of the testimony as it occurred. To the extent I have been successful, the trial testimony portions of this book are factual.

When writing of events taking place within the jury room, I leaned on my four separate experiences sitting in judgment of fellow citizens, each of them charged with a felony, one charged with first-degree murder. The jurors are my creations. I am entirely responsible for their conversation and their behavior. I have no insight into the deliberations of the actual jury. The jury deliberations presented in this book are fictional.

When writing of an alternate scenario for the events of the tragic evening in Prentiss, on the day after Christmas in 2001, I suffer from imperfect knowledge. There was clearly more to the drug-raid-gone-wrong than was revealed at trial, more than could be inferred by a jury intentionally deprived of crucial information. The witnesses, though, left behind inadvertent clues in the trial transcripts, clues that today cast substantial doubt on the story they hoped the jury would accept as fact.

As a skeptical juror, indeed as The Skeptical Juror, I am troubled by portions of the trial testimony of which other jurors take no notice. I am troubled as well by information withheld from the actual jurors, specifically by the warrant documents and the autopsy report. These troublesome aspects cause me to visualize the events of that evening differently than the law enforcement community of Jefferson Davis County would want.

After the trial, the jury deliberations, and the verdict, I will present my version of the events surrounding the shooting of Officer Ron Jones. I will dare to speculate about what I cannot possibly know as fact. I will leave it to the reader to determine which version of events is more reasonable.

<<>>

You will read frequently of a small yellow duplex located on Mary Street in Prentiss, Mississippi. I do not have (and therefore cannot present) the photos of that duplex as entered into evidence during the trial of Cory Maye. I have constructed a 3D computer model of the small yellow duplex, and offer several images from that model to help you visualize the scene.

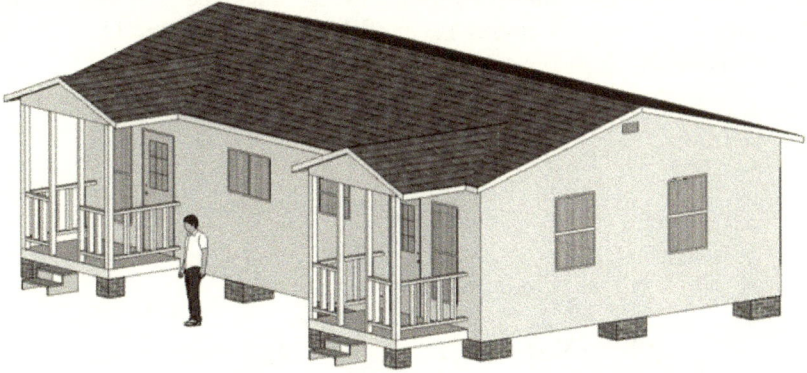

From the front-quarter view, Cory Maye's apartment would be the one on the right. The gentleman standing in front of the building is there for scale purposes only. He represents no party in this case.

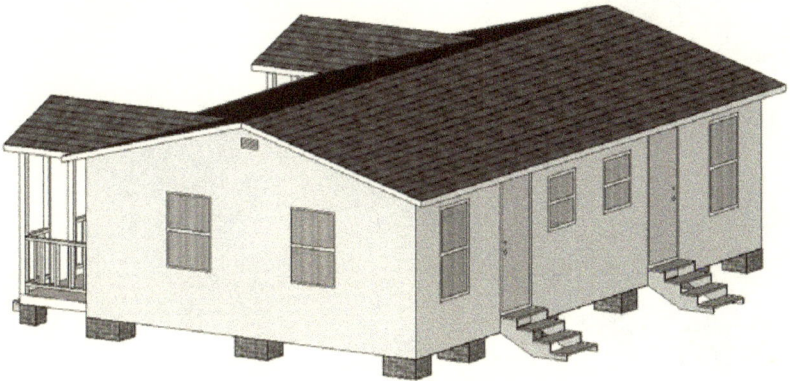

From the rear-quarter view, Cory Maye's apartment would be the one on the left. When referring to the apartments as left or right, it is important to mention the frame of reference, lest someone should become confused.

The cut-away interior view of Cory Maye's apartment shows only those items within that have any significance to the story about to unfold. Cory Maye was sleeping in the living room chair when the drug raid began. He had been lulled into unconsciousness by the television.

Cory Maye's fourteen-month-old daughter was sleeping in the bed in the back bedroom.

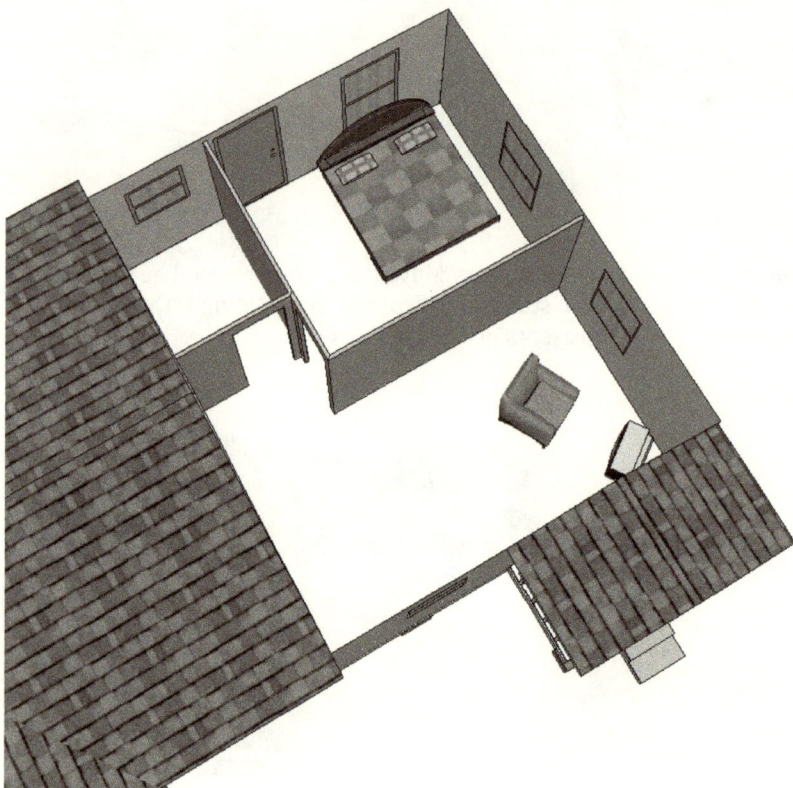

The bed had a larger headboard than the one portrayed in the sketch. On a shelf high on the headboard, well out of reach of his daughter, Cory Maye kept his unloaded pistol at the ready. He kept an ammo clip nearby.

JURY ROOM: MISSISSIPPI v. MAYE
Friday, January 21, 2004

The last of the jurors is just now entering. Once that door is closed, it will separate us from the rest of you who pass judgment on fellow human beings merely for sport. In here, passing judgment will literally become a matter of life or death. We are to decide if Cory Maye is to die for killing Ron Jones.

It is only through an odd set of circumstances that I find myself sitting in judgment of Cory Maye. I moved to Columbia, Mississippi just a little more than six months ago for family issues, planning to stay less than a year. Apparently that was sufficient time for Mississippi to identify me as a potential juror and randomly select me from the voter registration rolls, their drivers' license database, or from wherever they pick their jurors.

That odd circumstance alone would have been insufficient to place me among this jury. The killing of Officer Ronald Jones occurred in Prentiss, the county seat for Jefferson Davis County. The defense apparently requested and was granted a change of venue, so twelve of us from Marion County now sit in judgment.

Throughout the trial, brief as it was, I suspected it wasn't in the cards that I would be selected as jury foreperson. Being new to the region, my accent and mannerisms peg me as an outsider.

There's another factor weighing against me.

Angela.

She secured the seat at the head of the table the first time we entered this room. That was three days ago, right after voir dire. Two days ago, one of the other jurors got in the room first during a break and thoughtlessly sat there, right at the head of the table. The glare Angela gave him raised him to his feet like a revival preacher raising the crippled to walk. Only with less forgiveness.

Angela herself is a small compact woman, who dresses in tidy shirts and A-line skirts, with conservative pumps and a bubble of inhumanly blond hair that could withstand a Force 4 hurricane without mussing a strand. Her thin lips are habitually pursed. Her personality matches perfectly her no-nonsense style. After a few hours of watching her campaign for foreperson, I started thinking of her as a force of nature. Hurricane Angela.

She's been glad-handing everyone, telling them about her previous (single) experience as a juror and how she led that jury to a unanimous (and quick) verdict of guilty. I would declare her behavior shameful had I not previously engaged in similar shenanigans. You'll have to take my word for it, however, that I was considerably more subtle.

Not surprisingly, she speaks first.

"My experience tells me that we should elect a foreperson. To move things along, I'll put my own name forward. If anyone else would like the job, speak up now and we'll let the entire jury decide."

She looks quickly around the table, making direct eye contact with me in the process. I'm sitting at the far end of the elongated table, directly across from her. She knows I've been a juror in four previous criminal trials, serving as the foreperson in three of them. We've already compared notes and sized each other up. I sit quietly, content to let events run their course.

To everyone's surprise, Kyle speaks up.

"I think I could do a pretty good job."

Kyle is a nervous man of modest stature and modest demeanor. Other than being seriously over-dressed for the occasion (he has worn a suit, power tie, and matching pocket handkerchief for each of the three days of the trial), he manages to make himself disappear into the surroundings. I can't recall hearing him initiate a single conversation. I do, however, recall him taking voir dire so seriously that he gave overly-detailed answers and several times asked to speak privately at sidebar with the judge and attorneys.

Angela will have him as a snack.

"Okay, Lyle. Step on up here."

"It's Kyle."

"Sure. Anybody else."

Not bloody likely.

"All right then. Here's what we'll do. Lyle and I ..."

"Kyle."

"... sure, Kyle and I will turn our backs, and then I'll give you a chance to vote for which of us you prefer as foreperson."

Angela uses the fingertips and thumb of each hand to grasp Kyle gently by the shoulders and rotate him such that his back is to the jury. Then she turns her back to the jury and calls for a vote. It takes me back to grade school when I so badly wanted to be room monitor.

"Okay. How many of you would prefer that I act as foreperson?"

Seven people raise their hand, eight if you count Angela herself.

"Was that a majority?"

Doris, Angela's incipient second-in-command, answers for the rest of us.

"Yep, eight votes. Looks like you're it."

Angela, generous in victory, throws Kyle a bone. She pivots him ninety degrees so that they are facing one another and says: "If it gets to be too much for me, it's good to know you're there."

Kyle thanks her, returns to the seat to my left, and nearly disappears. It's almost as if the seat is occupied by nothing more than a reddish umber necktie and a matching kerchief.

Angela gets the ball rolling.

"I think we should begin by taking a preliminary vote, just to see where we stand. How many believe ...."

"Excuse me."

That's me interrupting. I have my hand up too. Not way up; that would be gauche. Just kinda up.

"Point of order," I continue, though I have no intention of arguing a point of order. It merely sounds good when I say that.

"Yes."

"I think it would be good to work around the table and introduce ourselves. I know some of us talked during meals and sometimes in the evening, but I haven't had a chance to meet all of you."

Angela hesitates. That's a mistake. I take the lead.

"Good. I'll begin."

I tell them my first name, then admit I'm foreign to these woods. That sparks a few smiles, a "Could have fooled me" and a "No shit!" from one of my earthier colleagues.

"I moved here six months ago, maybe a bit longer, to take care of some family business. I'm scheduled to be here for only one year, but no telling what will happen. I find Columbia to be a peaceful place. I like the pace of life here.

"My background is in the airplane business. I'm a self-proclaimed recovering engineer, but my wife assures me that I'll never be able to rid myself of my engineering ways. And that's about it for me. How about you, Kyle?"

Kyle sits up more rigidly in his chair, though I wouldn't have thought that possible a moment ago.

"My name is Kyle, with a K. I'm an actuary for an insurance company. I shouldn't mention which one. My job is to assess risks. I guess that's why I thought I would do a good job as a foreman."

His voice trailed off near the end of the last sentence. He has yet to recover from his crushing defeat.

The young lady sitting next to Kyle senses he's done and speaks up.

"I'm Cathy. I'm a student at SMCC. That's Southwest Mississippi Community College. I haven't picked a major yet. I'm thinking about journalism, maybe. Maybe communication."

Cathy is an effervescent, buxom young woman who frequently tucks her naturally-blonde, medium-length hair behind her ears. Each time she agrees with a head nod or disagrees with a head shake, all her hair-tucking comes to naught.

"I'm Bonnie. I'm a stay-at-home mom."

"I'm Vera. I'm a stay-at-home grandmother."

That gets a few chuckles.

Bonnie looks something like her namesake Bonnie Raitt, mostly because of her red hair, flushed skin tone, slender build, and modest stature.

Vera is one of only two black members in the jury. Normally, jury duty for me has been color blind. I have yet to personally witness any evidence of racial bias by prosecution or jurors. This is, however, Mississippi. Cory Maye is black, as is his attorney. While two-thirds of the people in Marion Country are white (and that makes the change of venue interesting all by itself), two jurors out of twelve seems low for a supposedly randomly-selected jury.

Vera is tall and cushy and comfortable, just as a grandmother should be. She smiles a lot and listens more than she speaks. When she does speak, it's usually to make someone feel a little better.

"Uh. I'm Webbie. I, uh, work at, uh, I'm a mechanic."

Though it is nearly impossible to be underdressed as a juror these days, Webbie took a stab at it. From the ground up, he's wearing work boots, work pants of some sort, and a clean white V-neck T-shirt.

That brings us to the top of the table.

"I've already talked to each of you several times. Anyway, I'm Angela. I'm the office manager for a large, a very large construction company."

"I'm Doris. I work at the Humane Society. We're always looking for good homes, so if any of you want a wonderful companion, we'll fix you up."

Doris is a practical dresser. I presume it's simply habit from hours at the shelter. Doris has attached herself to Angela like a metaphorical remora fish, though she is larger than her host.

"I'm Marion. I'm a dispatcher for the Post Office."

No surprise there. Marion had her post office shirt on the first day of voir dire, as if she had come straight from work. She's the other black member of this jury pool. Her hair is tied in long cornrows which she has braided together in some elaborate fashion I can't quite figure out. Maybe if I were a topologist I'd be able to understand how she does it. Fighting the mundane influence of her post office apparel, her hair gives her a wonderful, exotic appearance.

"Yes. My name is Raymond. I'm a pharmacist."

Think of Fred McMurray with glasses, a few wrinkles, and a white coat. Then remove the white coat and add a few more wrinkles.

"Hello everyone. I'm Joyce. I teach second grade and Sunday School."

She's not much older than community college Cathy, and somewhat more petite. She's barely larger than Angela. She speaks with a soft voice and a gentle smile. I'm sure the children adore her.

And finally, just to my right ...

"Name's Jerry. Welder. Mostly pipelines, but I'll weld anything to anything else. Got my own little company."

Jerry's welding claim energizes Webbie, who seems to take it as a challenge of some sort.

"Can you weld aluminum to lead?"

"Yeah, I can. You have to clean everything real good, and use an electron beam welder. You gotta pre-heat and use a faster weld speed, but you can do it. Mostly I'd recommend a good adhesive bond.'

"How 'bout stainless to titanium?"

Jerry seems a bit exasperated.

"That too. It's tricky, but I can do that with an electron beamer."

"How 'bout pewter to molybdenum?"

"How 'bout I weld your head to the table?"

Angela steps in.

"Now, now boys. No need for that. I'm sure Jerry's a very good welder."

There we go. Two new friends for Angela.

So that does it for the jury. Looking from the top of the table, the jurors are arranged as:

Angela (office manager)

Webbie (mechanic)	Doris (humane society)
Vera (grandmother)	Marion (post office)
Bonnie (mother)	Raymond (pharmacist)
Cathy (student)	Joyce (teacher)
Kyle (actuary)	Jerry (welder)

Myself

Angela is a quick study. She's learned not to pause. As soon as she's done fanning the flames of hatred between Jerry and Webbie, she's back to the task at hand.

"Okay. Good. Now I think we should take a quick vote just to see where we stand. How many . . ."

"Excuse me."

It's me again. My hand is up again.

Now Angela seems exasperated.

"Yes?"

"I think we're supposed to discuss the evidence before we decide our verdict."

Angela makes it simple so that I will understand: "It's not a final vote. It's just a preliminary vote, to see where we stand."

I explain my position.

"Where we stand right now is twelve votes not guilty. The judge explained that when he read us our jury instructions. You have a copy of those instructions right there." I point to the box the bailiff dropped off in the room. "Innocent until proven guilty. Discuss the case as a group. Rely on our collective memory. It's all in there. We took an oath. We haven't discussed anything as a group, except our names. Based on the discussion so far, Cory Maye must be not guilty."

Webbie: "It's not how we do it down here."

Doris: "It's just a preliminary vote. It's not a final vote. It will just let us see where we stand. That's all."

Angela: "How many think he's guilty?"

Five hands are up like a shot: Angela, Doris, Webbie, Raymond, and Jerry. Three hands come up a bit more slowly: Marion, Bonnie, and Joyce.

Angela counts the hands for us: "Okay. Eight guilty, four not guilty."

"I don't think that's necessarily a correct assumption," I say. "There may be abstentions."

Angela: "Fine. How many think he's not guilty?"

Two hands start up: Vera the stay-at-home grandmother and Cathy the community college student. Her hand is about half way up when she sees I'm refusing to vote. I suspect she hasn't noticed that Kyle has also declined. She drops her hand. Cathy, surprised to be the only one voting Not Guilty, sheepishly drops her hand.

Angela: "I see." She sounds like a saddened Captain Bligh speaking to a mutinous crew. "Look. It's nearly lunch already. After we're done here, we still have to go back in there and listen to the evidence for the penalty phase. Then we have to deliberate that. If we don't get going, we're going to be sequestered the entire weekend. I don't know about you, but I've just about had my fill of that."

I raise my hand, sort of.

"Yes?"

"It sounds like you're assuming we will find him guilty of capital murder. We don't go back for the penalty phase unless we find him guilty of capital murder."

"Okay. Fine. Assuming we find him guilty of capital murder, then we will have to -- the point is that these distractions threaten to keep us sequestered over the weekend. I can't imagine anyone wants that."

Various people murmur and mumble agreement.

"So if we can just get on with it. Please."

She looks at me and I nod my head in agreement. We should be getting on with it. I haven't the heart to tell them we may very well be sequestered over the weekend. I take no joy in it. I miss my family. I hate my dingy hotel room as much as the next person hates his or hers. I long for my computer, for a newspaper, and for a television set. I want to take a long walk, shoot a few hoops. I detest being held hostage by the State of Mississippi, but I'm not going to decide the defendant's fate based on a clock or a calendar.

Angela, ecstatic that I agree we should get on with it, forges ahead.

"Here's what we'll do. We'll work around the table and each discuss the evidence that is most incriminating. Then we'll vote. I'll go first."

I put my hand up. Angela's deep sigh sucks most of the oxygen out of the room.

"What now?"

"We're supposed to discuss all the evidence. All the evidence, not just the parts we think make him look guilty, not just the evidence that is the most incriminating. I think you'll find that in the jury instructions as well. They're right there, in the box, just behind you, to your right. Maybe it would be good if you were to read them to the entire jury."

Another deep sigh.

"The judge read them," she says. "I'm sure you remember that. We all heard him read -- we'll take a vote. How many of you want me to re-read the jury instructions?"

Two hands: mine and a seemingly disembodied one from my left.

"There. Happy now? Everyone remembers the instructions. Jeez, Louise!"

It's time for Doris to intervene.

"Look, the jury elected Angela to be the foreperson and you're doing nothing but obstructing things. Let her run it the way she wants. I think she's doing a good job, so if we can all just shut up and get on with it."

I avoid the obvious opportunity for sarcasm. We can't get on with it if we all shut up.

"Doris, it's Doris, right? I simply want the jury to discuss all the evidence, not some of the evidence, all the evidence in an unbiased fashion. Then I would like to weigh that evidence, in light of our discussions, against the elements of the crime that the State must prove to us beyond a reasonable doubt. I think it's a reasonable position, and I agree with Angela. We should get on with it."

Angela's turn. "What do you mean by all the evidence?" She emphasizes the word "all."

"I think we should consider the testimony of each witness, in the order they testified."

"What the fuck? That'll take forever."

It's Webbie. He's a delicate flower.

Angela doesn't seem all that excited to have Webbie as an ally. Maybe it was the profanity. She cuts him off. "Look, we were all there. We all heard them. A lot of 'em just kept saying the same thing as the previous guy. I don't see why we should waste time discussing what is essentially the same testimony over and over. I'm serious, everybody, if we don't get things going here, we're going to be stuck the whole weekend. So here's what we'll do. We'll discuss the closing arguments. Both sides had a chance to summarize their case, it's the last thing we heard, and so it will be fresh in our minds. So I ..."

I cut her short. I don't even raise my hand.

"Closing arguments aren't evidence. It says so right there in the instructions."

I helpfully point to them once again, in case she forgot where they are since I last pointed them out.

"I know everyone is in a rush to get this over with. I suggest the fastest way to get through this is to begin discussing the evidence, as a group, as a jury. I suggest we get started. First witness was Stephen Jones, as I recall."

Angela is near the breaking point already. Her fists are beginning to clench, as is her jaw. Her face is redder than it was a bit ago. She's forcing herself to remain calm, but it seems to be unnatural behavior for her. I'm sure if I worked for her at her large, very large construction firm, I would have been terminated by now.

Angela recognizes, however, that as a foreperson she has a problem. She must see to it that all twelve jurors are happy campers. Any single juror has the power to withhold his vote until satisfied he has fulfilled his oath. That assumes, of course, that the juror will be able to withstand the group pressure to conform. The pressure will be substantial. Right now, I'm held in low regard by almost everyone in the room. I'm a troublemaker, and an outsider to boot.

Angela folds. "Sure. Why not? Let's discuss Stephen Jones."

Quickly, I think back to Stephen Jones' testimony. Was it really only two days ago?

TESTIMONY OF STEPHEN JONES
Two Days Earlier: Wednesday, January 21, 2004

"Would you state your name for the jury, please." >> Stephen Jones.

Stephen Jones is examined by District Attorney Claiborne McDonald. When Claiborne introduced himself to us during jury selection, he avoided mentioning his first name. He gave instead his nickname. "I'm Buddy McDonald," he said, "and I'm the District Attorney. If you can't hear me, you probably really have a hearing problem."

He was certainly right about that. He speaks in a loud, booming voice; a down home, country voice; a friendly, "I'm one of you" voice. I'm surprised he allowed me on this jury.

"And Mr. Jones, were you or are you any relation to Ron Jones, who's the deceased in this case?" >> No, I am not.

"Were you on the 26th of December, 2001, a law enforcement officer in Jeff Davis County, Mississippi?" >> Yes, I was.

Actually it's Jefferson Davis County, a long-standing affront to the 60% of its population who happen to be black. Why the hell would the defense ask for a change of venue from Jefferson Davis to Marion County?

"Who were you a law enforcement officer for?" >> The Town of Prentiss.

Prentiss is the county seat of Jefferson Davis County. There are only two towns in the county, Prentiss and Bassfield. The population of Prentiss is slightly over a thousand, while the population of Bassfield is well under a thousand, so Prentiss ended up as the county seat.

"On that evening, were you on duty?" >> No, I was not. I was called in to conduct a search warrant.

"Did you meet with Ron Jones prior to the service of those search warrants?" >> Yes, I did. He had two search warrants. He told me that they were for the duplex apartments on Mary Street."

"Now, how did you organize to carry out the service of the two search warrants?" >> We divided up into two teams. Officer Ron Jones was in charge of my team and Agent Darryl Graves was in charge of the other team."

"And Darryl Graves was an agent with who?" >> Pearl River Basin Narcotics Task Force.

I repeat to myself: Ron Jones, Stephen (No Relation) Jones, Darryl (Task Force) Graves.

"Had you been on any other search warrants with Darryl Graves and Ron Jones before?" >> I had with Officer Ron Jones.

"I'm going to show you what's been marked as Exhibit Number 1. You see the board over here?" >> Yes, sir, that's the apartments.

Exhibit Number 1 is a large photograph of a small, yellow duplex viewed from the front. The duplex has a small, covered porch on both the left and right-hand sides. They are nearly mirror images of one another. If you take the three steps up to the porch for the right-hand unit, there would be an over-under window just to your right. The porch extends to the right just beyond that window, not quite to the corner of the duplex. To your left would be the entryway. It consists of an outward-swinging screen door and an inward-swinging wooden door. The wooden door has a nine-pane window. That window and the one to the right are covered with heavy curtains or drapes or something that thoroughly covers the glass.

Each porch is surrounded by a hip-high railing, except in the center where the steps land. The guard railing would prevent anyone from standing directly in front of the door and opening it. The doors must therefore be opened from the side. To enter the unit on the right-hand side, you would grab the screen door handle, probably with your left hand, and step inside the screen door as you swing it open. You would then grab the front door handle, probably with your right hand, turn it, push the door open, and step inside.

The space between the two porches is taken up by a grassy semi-circle. It's the greenest area of grass in the large front yard. Most of the yard is well-packed dirt, used as parking. Where the cars don't drive or park, there are patches of dried, brown grass.

"And is that the apartments there at 1728 Mary Street?" >> Yes, it is.

"I assume this is one building. Is that correct, structurally?" >> Yes, sir.

"Is it divided into two apartments?" >> Yes, it is.

"All right. Who served the search warrant on the left?" >> That was the team that Agent Darryl Graves took in.

"Who served the other search warrant on the apartment on the right?" >> Myself, Officer Darrell Cooley, and Officer Ron Jones was to go to that apartment.

"And was Terrence Cooley there, also?" >> Yes, he was; he was in the back.

Great. Two more names. That makes two Jones and two Cooleys, and two Darryls (or Darrells) to boot. Ron Jones, Stephen (No Relation) Jones, and Darrell Cooley at the front of the apartment on the right. Terrence Cooley at the back.

"All right. Now, where did y'all leave from?" >> We left the police station in Prentiss.

"Were y'all in uniform?" >> I had a police jacket on, police hat, and jeans.

"Were the others in uniform?" >> Yes, sir, Officer Ron Jones was. He was on duty that night.

"Were the cars marked cars?" >> Yes, sir.

"And when they arrived, where did y'all stop or park?" >> I parked my car right in front of the right apartment facing from the road.

"Did you see where the other cars were parked?" >> They were all parked in front.

"There's a light on in this photograph on the porch of that apartment on the right. Was there a light on at the time y'all went there to execute the search warrant on that apartment?" >> Yes, sir, it was on the outside.

"Where did each of you go initially when you got to the apartment?" >> When we arrived, I went to the right of the door. Officer Darrell Cooley was at the door. Officer Jones was behind him.

Darrell Cooley is at the front door, along with Ron Jones, and Stephen (No Relation) Jones.

"What, if anything, was said or done when y'all arrived on the porch?" >> We announced, "police, search warrant." Checked the door, the door was locked. And we announced it again, and then we tried to open the door.

"How many times did you announce 'police, search warrant?'">> It was announced before every kicking of the door.

I presume it was Darrell (Front Door Kicker) Cooley who tried the door, found it locked, then attempted to kick it open.

"Did you see any movement or any type of activity inside the house?" >> The blinds opened. It appeared that somebody opened the blinds and looked out. When the blinds were opened, I noticed a light inside.

"Were you able to hear anything in the building?" >> No, sir.

"When you couldn't gain entry through the front door, what, if anything, did y'all do then?" >> Officer Ron Jones told Darrell Cooley to stay at the front. Myself and Officer Ron Jones went to the back, come around the south end of the apartment and went to the back to see if we could gain entrance on the back door."

Darrell (Front Door Kicker) Cooley stays at front. Ron Jones and Stephen (No Relation) Jones go around the side of the duplex to the rear.

"I'm going to show you this photograph, which has been marked Exhibit Number 4 in evidence, and I would ask if you can identify that." >> Yes, sir, that's the back of the apartment.

Once again, the two apartments mirror one another when looking from the rear. Jones and Jones would be attempting to enter the southern most apartment. From the front, it's the apartment on the right. From the rear, it's the apartment on the left.

The rear entry has no screen door. The rear door has no window; it swings in to open. There is a large over-under window to the left, possibly for the bedroom, and a small over-under window to the right, possibly for the bathroom. Any apartment unit this small can't have more than one bedroom and one bathroom.

The most noticeable feature, or lack thereof, is the absence of a porch. There are simply four narrow steps leading up to the door. The fourth step is at the same level as the floor of the apartment. The steps are small enough that one would have difficulty standing with both feet on the top step if the rear door was closed.

"All right. Now, when you got to the back of the building, was there anyone else there?" >> Officer Terrence Cooley was in the back, and Officer Phillip Allday was back there.

"Who were they officers with?" >> The town of Bassfield.

"And the Bassfield officers were there at the request of the Prentiss PD to assist them in this?" >> Yes, sir, they was.

Okay. Terrence (Cover the Rear) Cooley and Phillip Allday were in back. Darrell (Front Door Kicker) Cooley remained in front while Ron Jones and Stephen (No Relation) Jones went from the front to the back.

"What happened at the back of the apartment when you and Ron Jones went back there" >> We went to the back. Officer Ron Jones checked the door to see if it was open. It was locked. He announced "search warrant, police, search warrant," and no one came to the back door. He decided that he was not going to kick the door in or try to open it because of the risk of getting hurt. He was a big guy. He was a tall guy.

"Were announcements made once or more than once?" >> More than once.

"What, if anything was decided to be done by Mr. Jones?" >> He told Officer Allday if he wanted to kick the door, he could kick the door in. Myself and Officer Ron Jones come back around the apartment. When we started around the corner, they announced from the rear that they had got the door open. Myself and Officer Ron Jones proceeded back around to the back.

Phillip (Back Door Kicker) Allday managed to kick open the back door, so Ron Jones and Stephen (No Relation) Jones, returned to the back of the apartment.

"So when you heard that, what did you do?" >> We ran back around. Officer Jones went up the steps first.

"Was the door open when you got back around?" >> Yes, sir, it was.

"Had anybody entered the apartment at that time before Ron got up on the apartment door there?" >> No, sir.

"What happened then?" >> When Officer Jones was running up the steps, he announced, "police, search warrant." I proceeded behind him. That's when the shots was fired.

"How far in the building had Officer Jones gotten when the shots rang out?" >> No more than five feet maximum.

"And was he standing up?" >> Yes, sir, he was.

"How many shots did you hear fired?" >> Three shots.

Three shots. Stephen (No Relation) Jones heard three shots.

"What, if anything, did you do after you heard the shots fired?" >> I was on the top step when the shots was fired. I stood to the left of the door because I did not know where the shots was coming from, and I did not know where Officer Jones was at that time. When I looked back, Officer Jones was coming back out, and told me that he had been hit. I grabbed him, we come down the steps together. When he got on the ground, I went to the left of the steps to the door. Officer Terrence Cooley went to the right. We told Mr. Maye to throw the gun out. He had stated that he had already thrown the gun. The gun was on the floor. Officer Terrence Cooley started back in. I followed behind him. Officer Cooley went to Mr. Maye. I went through the apartment looking for any other people in the apartment. I did not go into the rooms, I just did a brief search for any other people in the apartment.

"Now, once you made your initial sweep through the house to see if you could see anyone else there, what did you do at that time?" >> When I turned around, Constable Bullock, Earl Bullock, was in there. Officer Terrence Cooley was with Mr. Maye. I then proceeded back out to check on Officer Jones.

Now someone else has appeared: Earl (Constable) Bullock. Where the hell did he come from?

"Where was Jones at the time you found him after that? >> He was at the south side of the building. He was laying on the ground. I noticed that he was in bad shape, so I then told the other officers that we needed to get him to the hospital. I got my patrol car, pulled it down. Myself, Darrell Cooley, and Darryl Graves put him in my patrol car, and I left and went to the hospital with him.

Ron Jones ends up on ground on the south side of building, the left side if you're looking from the rear. Stephen (No Relation) Jones, Darrell (Front Door Kicker) Cooley, and Darryl (Task Force) Graves get Ron into Stephen Jones' car. Stephen Jones drives Ron Jones to hospital. It's not clear if anyone else went with them.

"When Jones entered the apartment, did he have his service weapon pulled out of his holster?" >> No, sir, he did not.

"When you got back around to the side, to where he was on the ground, did he still have his service weapon holstered?" >> Yes, sir, he did.

"Did any law enforcement officers fire any shots in there that night?" >> Not to my knowledge.

"And Mr. Maye was not shot?" >> No, sir, he was not.

"When you went to the hospital, what, if anything, happened to Officer Jones at the hospital?" >> When I arrived at the hospital, I went in to get some help to get him out of the car. The nurses and the doctor come out to help him out of the car, and then they did their work on him.

"All right. And is that where he passed away?" >> Yes, sir.

"In terms of time frame, do you have any idea how long it took from the first time there was an announcement of 'police, search warrant' at the front door to the time Ron was able to get in the back door?" >> It was several minutes.

"After y'all made entrance into the bedroom area, were you able to see a child?" >> Yes, sir.

"And do you recall whether the child was awake or asleep?" >> I do not recall.

"Okay. And do you know what was done with the child?" >> No, sir, I do not.

"All right. Judge, I believe that's all the questions we have of Officer Jones at this time."

That would be Judge Michael R. Eubanks. I know that because of the really large name plate he has on display at the front of the bench.

<<>>

Rhonda Cooper is Cory Maye's lead attorney. She admits to not being as loud as Claiborne Buddy McDonald. Few people are. "I do not speak as loudly as the prosecutor, but I am going to take my time in speaking to you all."

Also unlike Buddy, she uses two words for "you all."

"Good morning, Officer Jones." >> Good morning.

"I think this may be about our third or fourth time meeting. Isn't that correct?" >> Yes, it is.

"And we met for the very first time February 2002, right?" >> Yes.

That's almost two years ago, just two months after the shooting.

"I want to talk a little bit about the lights. When we met in February 2002, we talked about the lights at that time, and I recall you stating that there were no lights on, correct?" >> There were no lights visible from inside the apartment until the blinds were opened.

"No, I'm going back to what you told me almost two years ago, that there were no lights on. And then I asked you again this past spring, May of 2003, and you said, 'Well, my testimony is the same as it was then in February of 2002, that there were no lights on in either unit.'" >> I can't testify to the apartment on the left.

"Well, I'm only really concerned about the apartment on the right. And either unit for me means neither one of them. And then we can just simply concentrate then on the right, that there were no lights on at the apartment on the right. Do you remember that?" >> Yes.

"Now, we're here today and you're saying that this light was on the outside. Is that what you told the prosecution?" >> Yes.

"But that's not what we said almost two years ago. And you also said this morning that there were some blinds. I want you to be clear, now."

She shows him a picture.

"This window here and this window go to this apartment that Cory Maye and his family lived in. Isn't that right?" >> Yes.

"Do you see any blinds here?" >> I can't on the picture.

"And I submit to you these pictures were taken just after this incident occurred." >> Yes. I can't see any on the picture, but I do remember them.

"You don't see any on the picture that was taken shortly, I mean like within hours of this incident, you don't see any blinds on the picture?" >> Not from here, I do not.

"Well, I'm going to give you the picture, then. Do you see any blinds on that picture?" >> I can't tell.

"I don't want to belabor the point, but you said something about a light on towards the bathroom?" >> Yes.

"Were you able to see from the outside which room was the bathroom?" >> I said in that area.

"How would you know from right here what area the bathroom would've been in?" >> I did not know until I entered the apartment.

"So this was after you entered the apartment?" >> Yes. When the blinds that were there that I remember seeing that night, I was standing to the right of the door, and I told the other officers there, I said, 'There' s a light inside to the left.'

"Where were you standing?" >> I was standing to the right of the door, between the door and the window on the right of the door.

"How could you see inside if you're standing here at this wooden post?" >> When I was standing there, when the blinds were cracked, I noticed a light.

"Are you telling the ladies and gentlemen of this jury that someone stood up and opened the blinds so that you could see inside?" >> I'm not saying that, I'm saying that the blinds were open.

"The blinds that are not here on this picture but, just for the purposes of your testimony, we're saying blinds because you've already testified there are no blinds here?" >> Yes.

"So you stood here, looked inside this window without any blinds and you were able to see what?" >> When we were trying to gain access, the blinds cracked open where I could see a light inside.

When Cooper asked that question, she was pointing at the large photo of the duplex. When she asked about the window, she was pointing at the large over-under window, not the nine-pane window in the door.

"Did you see anyone inside?" >> No, I did not.

"Let's continue on with this just for a minute more. You were standing here. Where was Ron Jones?" >> He was at the bottom of the steps.

"He's here, on the ground. Where was Darrell Cooley?" >> He was at the door trying to gain access.

"This search warrant that you say you had, which of you had it?" >> Officer Ron Jones had one and Agent Darryl Graves had the other.

"Did you see it?" >> I did not read it.

"Did you see it?" >> Yes, I did. Before we left the police station.

"And it didn't have Cory Maye's name on it, did it?" >> Not to my knowledge.

"Let's go from there. At the time you entered the apartment, isn't it true that Cory Maye was lying flat on the floor at the foot of his bed?" >> Yes.

"And his baby daughter lay in that bed?" >> Yes.

"And wasn't that baby crying?" >> I do not know.

"You told the ladies and gentlemen of this jury that there were three shots fired." >> Yes.

"And there was lots of commotion, people yelling?" >> Yes.

"And you don't recall if the baby was crying?" >> There was people hollering.

"Now, you were at the door, between the door and the window, Ron Jones was at the bottom of the steps, Darrell Cooley was at the door?" >> Yes.

"Did you all check the door first or announce your presence first?" >> We announced our presence first.

"Then you proceeded to try to get inside?" >> Yes.

"And then you go on to the back." >> Yes.

"How is it that that the door came to be kicked in?" >> Officer Phillip Allday kicked the door in.

"Was he told to kick it in or did he take it upon himself to kick it in?" >> Officer Ron Jones told him if he wanted to kick it he could kick it.

"Now, did Officer Jones tell him to do that before or after he decided that it was too risky to go in that back door?" >> He told him after he decided it was too risky for him to try to open the door.

"But he'd already decided it was too risky to enter, correct?" >> He decided it was too risky for him to try to open the door.

"So Phillip Allday kicked it in?" >> Yes.

"And Ron Jones came back and ran in?" >> Yes.

"And you are telling these ladies and gentlemen that he went into that apartment unarmed?" >> He had his weapon in his holster, on his gun belt.

"Does your training not suggest that you protect yourselves?" >> Yes.

"Did Cory Maye offer any resistance?" >> He was struggling to be handcuffed.

"Struggling with whom?" >> Officer Terrence Cooley.

"Where did he come in at?" >> He entered the apartment before I did.

"Before you did?" >> Yes.

"You did not enter the apartment immediately after Ron Jones?" >> When I was standing in the doorway, Officer Jones came back to me, told me he was shot, that he had been hit, and I helped him down the steps. Then myself and Officer Terrence Cooley told Mr. Maye to throw the gun out. He told us that he'd thrown the gun already. The gun was laying on the floor.

"You saw it. You saw the gun?" >> After I started in the apartment.

"Then you went on in to see what else was going on?" >> Yes.

"Were you aware of what was still going on in that bedroom?" >> I noticed Officer Cooley trying to get Mr. Maye handcuffed.

"Where were you then?" >> I was walking through the apartment.

"And you used your flashlights, correct?" >> Yes.

"Because there were no lights on, correct?" >> That's correct.

"Now, you said three shots were fired." >> Yes.

"And if Mr. Maye wanted to do more harm, he could have continued to shoot police officers, couldn't he have?" >> Yes, he could have.

"Once you were in his apartment, you were able to see him clearly." >> Yes.

"As he lay on that floor." >> Yes.

"Who else was at the apartment on the left? Do you recall?" >> The team was Mike Brown, Darryl Graves, Earl Bullock, and Allen Allday.

Two more new names, and a second Allday. Team on the left was led by Darryl (Task Force) Graves, followed by Earl (Constable) Bullock, Mike Brown, and Allen Allday. Now that's two Jones, two Cooleys, two Alldays, two Darryls. This is insane.

"Did you provide him with a search warrant?" >> I did not at that time.

"When did you, then?" >> I'm not sure when he was provided with the search warrant.

"Who had it?" >> Officer Ron Jones had it.

"Did you see the search warrant?" >> Not at that time, I did not.

"When did you see it, the search warrant?" >> I saw it before we left the police station, is the only time I saw it.

"But you didn't see it anymore after that?" >> No, I did not.

"And the one that you saw at the police station, did it have Jamie Smith's name on it or persons unknown?" >> I did not read the warrants.

"Thank you."

<<>>

Claiborne Buddy McDonald has some questions on redirect.

"On the search warrants that you've participated in serving before, have there ever been delays with people opening up to allow you in after you announced?" >> Yes.

"In that situation, do you do anything to speed entry into the building?" >> Yes, to try to gain access to keep the evidence from being destroyed.

"When you went through the house there with your flashlight, did you shine your light in the living room?" >> Yes, I did.

"I show you this picture and ask if you can identify that photograph." >> Yes. That's a picture of the front door, the inside of the front door.

"Now, I'd like you to look at the picture showing the front of the duplex again. I believe Ms. Cooper just questioned you about it. She questioned you whether or not you could see the blinds on this door or this window. Is that correct?" >> Yes.

"All right. In the photo showing the inside of the living room, what is this?" >> That's a blind.

"It didn't show up good on that front picture, did it?" >> No, it did not.

"But the blind was there, right?" >> Yes.

"And to be clear in my mind, the blinds you saw cracked were the blinds on the door or the blinds on the window?" >> The blinds on the door.

Now I'm confused. I thought he previously testified blinds on the large window were the ones that were opened. Now he says it was the blinds on the window in the door that were opened.

"On the door or the window?" >> The door.

He confirms he said door. That's not what I recall.

"Is it unusual for search warrants to be issued stating that the person in possession of the premises is not known? Does that happen sometimes?" >> Yes.

Now, the rush to enter was to prevent a flush or other destruction of evidence?" >> Yes.

"And about how long did it take y'all to actually gain entry into the apartment?" >> Couple of minutes. To be exact, I'm not sure.

"Is that a big apartment?" >> No, sir, it's not.

"Let's go back to the bedroom. You say you saw the child. Is that correct?" >> Yes.

"And where was Maye lying by the time you entered?" >> He was laying at the foot of the bed.

"And could you see where the child was on the bed?" >> The child was laying on the end of the bed on the left-hand side, at the foot, closest to Mr. Maye.

"So, if, when he fired he was laying behind the bed, he's firing right around the child?" >> Yes.

"And I believe this diagram shows some shell casings, one shell casing up here, and two shell casings back here." >> Yes.

"Shell casings were ejected from the gun?" >> Yes, sir, it would've had to have been.

"Standing in one place when he fired all the rounds, wouldn't you think that all the shell casings would be close together?" >> Yes.

"I believe that's all the questions we have."

<<>>

Judge Eubanks excuses the witness, and Stephen Jones begins to step down, but Rhonda Cooper wants to ask him some more questions.

"Your Honor, might the defense have just a moment on re-cross?"

Judge Eubanks asks why, she says something about windows, lighting and exigent circumstances. He instructs them all to approach the bench so we can't overhear their discussion.

The bench conference breaks up. Cooper must have scored at least a partial victory, since she begins asking questions of the witness.

"Officer Jones. I understood you to say, and I just want the ladies and gentlemen to be clear, you said when you stood here, you looked into this window because the blinds were cracked so that you could see. Isn't that what you said?" >> Yes.

Now he's back to saying the blinds were on the over-under window, not the nine-pane window in the door. Buddy gave him a chance to confirm the blinds were on the door, and he confirmed that. Now he just tells Cooper what he told her before, that they were on the big window separate from the door.

"You said you couldn't tell if there were any blinds here or not?" >> Not in that picture, no.

"Okay. But it was the blinds here at the window that you were able to look through. Isn't that what you said?" >> Yes.

Now he confirms it was the over-under window where the blinds opened, just as he confirmed for Buddy it was the window in the door where the blinds were opened. I'm confused.

"And then the picture of the living room shows the blinds are at the door, correct?" >> Correct.

"There's no picture of any window shown in this photo, is there?" >> No.

"Now, I really didn't understand what you and Mr. McDonald said about the shell casings because I think he kind of caused you to say something. So let's tell the truth here. When you all came inside this apartment, how many officers came inside this back bedroom?" >> I know of myself and two more: Earl Bullock and Terrence Cooley.

Earl (Constable) Bullock and Terrence (Cover the Rear) Cooley wrestled with Cory Maye while trying to cuff him while Stephen (No Relation) Jones cleared the apartment then went to help Ron Jones.

"Isn't it possible that in rushing in and coming in and moving about, you could've kicked those shell casings about?" >> Yes.

"Okay. Now, you didn't know if anyone was in this apartment or not, did you?" >> No, we did not.

"And you certainly didn't know anything about Cory Maye?" >> Did not.

"So what, if any, were the situations that made you think things, you know, if there was narcotics present, that they were going to be flushed or gotten rid of, such that you had to rush on in there?" >> It's just what we always do, rush in, not knowing.

"Okay. Thank you."

DELIBERATION OF STEPHEN JONES
Friday, January 23, 2004

I guess it was just two days ago. Seems longer.

Angela intends to take control of the situation. She's had her fill of my generous and insightful suggestions. I'm confident she'll now attempt to short-sheet the discussion of Stephen Jones' testimony.

"Okay. If we're going to do this, if we're going to talk about each and every witness, we're going to do it quickly. No foolin' around, no wastin' time. Let's get this done. Here's the way I see Jones' testimony. They had two search warrants, one for each apartment of the duplex. What's his name Graves ..."

"Darryl," Doris adds helpfully.

"... Yes, Darryl Graves led the team to the left-hand apartment. Ron Jones, the officer killed by Cory Mayes ..."

"Maye. Not Mayes. Maye." I add, being generously helpful.

"Whatever. Darryl Graves led the team to the right-side apartment. Stephen Jones, who was no relation to Ron Jones, was part of the three-man team that Ron Jones led to raid the right-side apartment.

"They were in uniform, they yelled repeatedly that they were policemen, the outside light was on, Mayes peeked out the window and saw them, but wouldn't let them in. So they tried to kick open the door, couldn't do it, went to the back, and someone back there kicked the back door open. Ron Jones went in first, three shots rang out, and he stumbled back out of the apartment, shot. Stephen Jones went in while someone else ..."

"Terrence," Doris adds helpfully.

"... Yes, Terrence, Terrence Cooley I think, tried to handcuff Mayes. But Mayes struggled so another officer, a constable of some sort ..."

"Earl," Doris adds helpfully. She remembers everyone by their first names. Interesting.

"... Yes, Earl something or other ..."

"Bullock," I add helpfully.

"... Yes, thank you," she replies icily. "Earl Bullock came in and helped Cooley cuff him. Stephen Jones loaded Ron Jones into a patrol car and took him to the hospital, where Ron Jones died.

"It doesn't look good for Mayes, does it? He knew they were police, that they had a search warrant, and he shot at them anyway as they came in. And he killed one of them. Pretty simple. That's capital murder."

The room grows quiet for a bit as the jurors begin to process what's taking place. I'm hoping one of them will speak up. Anyone.

Make that anyone but Webbie.

"Uhh... yeah."

It's Webbie.

"And did you catch that there was no lights on inside when they got in there. He saw a light inside when Mayes ..."

"It's Maye, singular, not Mayes," I add helpfully.

"Lemme finish, will ya? Jeez. So -- where was I -- oh yeah, so he saw a light on inside when Mayes opened the curtain, but there was no light on inside when they went in. Had to use his flashlight. That means Mayes must of turned off the light so he could lay in waiting. You bet your ass it's capital murder."

This is how we end up with bad verdicts and hung juries. Neither Angela nor Webbie is attempting to engage in impartial discussion of the evidence. They are instead campaigning for a specific vote to correspond with their pre-conceived notions. They think Cory Maye is guilty, they want everyone else to agree with them, and they want to go home. They make bold pronouncements that sound reasonable on the surface, and they all but dare others to disagree with them. The meek and mild-mannered will remain silent, while the assertive will either join the chorus or take a hard stand in opposition. Assuming there is in fact an opposing perspective, the battle lines are quickly drawn and aggressively defended.

This is why I oppose early votes. I don't want people staking out early positions. It makes it too hard to back down later, to lose face, to change one's mind if discussion of the evidence so indicates.

I figure I'll take Webbie on first. He's not particularly well-respected by the group, so he's likely to be easier pickings.

"Webbie, it's Webbie right? Is that, by the way, short for Webster?"

"It's Webbie. Just Webbie. Alright?"

"Sure." I adopt Angela's word. "You argued that Maye turned off the light so he could lay in waiting. That presumes the light was on when the police arrived. When Stephen Jones first testified about the raid, just months after the shooting, he apparently said nothing about a light being on, or curtains being moved. He apparently reiterated that testimony in another pre-trial hearing. So this trial was apparently the first time Rhonda Cooper heard him claim that he saw a light on either inside or outside the apartment."

"Doesn't mean it's not true. He was under oath. You callin' him a liar?"

"I'll hold off on that. He did, however, give conflicting testimony to us, to you and me, to everyone in this room. He initially told Cooper, told us actually, the blinds opened on the window just to the right of the steps, not on the door. Then he twice told Buddy McDonald, told us actually, the blinds opened on the door. Then he switched back to the other window when Rhonda Cooper challenged him on his flip-flop testimony. In one version or the other, he gave us false testimony."

"I don't remember that."

"I guess it's too late now for you to go back and listen carefully."

"Asshole."

Angela intervenes as her two favorite jurors get into a spat.

"There's no need to argue. It's easy to get confused up there, and I think she confused him with her questions, that's all."

Now it's Angela and me.

"So you've been a witness in a murder trial before?"

"What?"

"You said it was easy to get confused up there. Are you speaking from experience?"

"Well, no. I just figure it's easy to get confused up there."

"So which window, if either, had the blinds that got pulled open?"

"I'm not sure it makes much difference which one. The point is someone pulled the blinds back and Officer Jones saw a light on inside."

"How do we know that?"

Doris decides to help out.

"Because he told us. He testified under oath. He's a police officer. He's not on trial."

Now it's Doris and me.

"You're right. Cory Maye is on trial, and the state bears the burden of proving his guilt beyond a reasonable doubt. It's in the jury instructions." I helpfully point to them once again. She declines to look. "If the state wants me to rely on Stephen Jones to convict Cory Maye of murder, then I expect Stephen Jones to at least provide testimony that doesn't argue against itself. I also expect him to give a consistent story over time, not one that grows increasingly damaging to the defendant each time he tells it."

"So what if he got a few minor details wrong? I'm not saying he did, but even if he did, what's the big deal? It doesn't change the fact that ..." She catches herself and changes course. "... it doesn't change the basic facts."

"It might. We weren't there. We didn't see it with our own eyes. We're relying on Stephen Jones and anyone else who testified to tell us what happened. We have to decide how accurate their testimony might be. I intend to look at their testimony very carefully, all of their testimony, not just that of Stephen Jones', before accepting it as true and accurate."

I call in reinforcements. I pick the tie and matching kerchief to my left.

"Kyle, how about you? What do you make of Stephen Jones' ever-changing, self-contradictory testimony about the blinds and the lights?"

I catch him off guard.

"Uhh ... I'm not sure."

"Marion, how about you?"

"Uhh ... well ... I guess it bothers me some."

"Holy crap!"

It's Webbie, of course. Angela is also aghast at the possible defection. She turns on Marion.

"Are you saying Officer Stephen Jones is lying about the death of his fellow officer?"

"Uhh ... I guess not."

"Okay then. Enough of this, really. We're bogged down in the minutiae and losing sight of the big picture. We'll never get out of here if we don't get moving. I suggest we get on with the next witness. That will be Terrence ..."

"Why didn't he have his weapon drawn when he entered the apartment?"

It's me again. I didn't raise my hand this time. I'm nowhere close to moving on.

"What?"

Angela's frustrated. I explain.

"Why didn't Officer Ron Jones have his weapon drawn when he entered the apartment? According to Stephen Jones, Ron Jones did not draw his weapon. He had been trained to have his weapon drawn, at least according to Stephen Jones, and he had his weapon with him, so I have to wonder: Why didn't Ron Jones have his weapon drawn? That seems strange to me. That seem strange to anyone else?"

I pass the question to the man who can weld anything to anything.

"Jerry, what about you? That seem strange to you?"

"What seem strange?"

"That Ron Jones took the trouble to arm himself, and put on a vest, but then went against his training and did not draw his weapon as he led his team into a darkened building?"

"Uhh ... I don't know?"

"Would you have drawn your weapon in that circumstance?"

"Guess so."

Angela intervenes.

"He told the others that there would be no weapons there. He thought there wouldn't be any weapons, so he didn't draw his. I think it was very clear. Why would he lie about something like that?"

"I have no idea. That's why I was asking around, to see if anyone else had any thoughts on the subject. What about you, Angela? You have a theory on why Ron Jones didn't draw his weapon?"

"I just told you. He had information that there would be no weapons in -- Look, I'm not going to waste any time fretting over it. I don't see where it makes any difference one way or the other. So I suggest we move on to the testimony ..."

"He's manipulating us. You realize that, don't you?"

Angela's hands begin to clench once again. She's slow to respond, so I just continue my thought.

"I'm not talking about Stephen Jones right now. I'm talking about the DA, Claiborne Buddy McDonald. And I can prove it."

I probably can't prove any such thing, certainly not to my satisfaction. I have their attention, however, and I push on.

"Think about the questions he asked Stephen Jones about the shell casings. The shell casings were spread around the floor, not all together in a neat grouping. At that point, Buddy knew something we wouldn't learn until later. He knew that Cory Maye would testify he fired all three shots from a prone position, while lying near the foot of the bed. He knew also he would be bringing in forensic evidence to contradict Maye on this point. He knew finally that he would hammer on this point during his closing argument to convince us Cory Maye is a liar, and that we should therefore disbelieve his entire testimony."

I can't believe they're giving me this much floor time.

"Buddy knows all this when he's questioning Stephen Jones, but we don't know it. Not yet. So he asks Jones a question about the spread-out arrangement of the shell casings. His question, it was a small speech actually, suggested that if someone had fired all three rounds from the same place, the shell casings would be close together, not spread apart. And Stephen Jones dutifully agreed with him."

I've actually captured the attention of a few jurors.

"But Buddy knew it was a crock. Jones knew it too. They both knew that the room had been trampled through by any number of cops. Jones conceded that point instantly when Ronda Cooper asked him about it. Anybody familiar with the case knew the shells would have been kicked around. But Buddy wanted to play with our minds. He wanted to plant an early thought inside our heads about Cory Maye shooting from different positions."

Angela wants to get a word in, but I hold up one finger, my index finger, to indicate I need just a minute more. She takes a breath and opens her mouth, but I press on. It takes her a few seconds to close her teeth. I can hear them snap together from my end of the table.

"So he asked the question to plant the thought in our heads, and took a chance that Cooper wouldn't catch it. And he almost got away with it, too. He was clever enough not to ask the question during direct examination. Cooper would certainly rebut the point during cross. Nope. Buddy McDonald is too clever for that. He asked the question during re-direct. Cooper should have objected, but she didn't. You're not supposed to introduce testimony on new subjects during re-direct. You're only supposed to ask questions about issues brought up in cross."

A few jurors are increasingly interested. Most are simply impatient. I'm running out of time.

"So Buddy waits for re-direct and asks his question. No one objects. When he's done with re-direct, the judge dismisses the witness and Cooper was pissed. Remember that? She wanted an opportunity to re-cross, but the judge almost didn't give her that chance. The judge made her come to the bench and argue her point. I presume Buddy tried to prevent the re-cross, but the judge allowed it. That's when Cooper finally had her only chance to ask about cops kicking shells around the apartment, and she almost didn't get that. It's but one of the little mind games Buddy played with us."

I'm rudely interrupted by a knock on the door, and the door swinging open. It's the bailiff, our warden. He has a tray of sandwiches, bottles of water, some soft drinks, and chips. It's our lunch. I lose my audience as they scramble for the sandwich of their choice.

Angela announces we will be taking fifteen minutes for lunch, no more. No more, and she means it. And then, no matter what, we'll be going on to the next witness. No matter what.

Jurors queue for the bathroom. A lone sandwich remains on the tray. It's an egg salad sandwich, with celery and red things in it. It's kinda runny. I settle for the last bag of chips.

They're Funyuns. I feel like Frank on *Everybody Loves Raymond*. Frank was pissed because Ray and Robert spilled his bag of Bugles while fighting. Frank pouted and said "Now I'll have to eat Funyuns." I can feel his pain.

The disappointment is made worse by the lack of Diet Mt. Dew among the beverages. It looks like it will be either water or Mr. Pibb. Lord have mercy.

I feast on a small bag of Funyuns, which is second worst only to a big bag of Funyuns, and a bottle of Dasani water. Dasani is an ancient Sumerian word meaning "filtered water from whichever tap is closest to the Coca Cola bottling company."

It occurs to me that this sequestered jury process is similar to how they elected popes early on. It seems as if back then no one wanted to be Pope. According to tradition, all the early popes were martyred, including thirty of the first sixty-four. Eight succumbed within their first year. Many died exceptionally unnatural deaths. St. Peter was supposedly crucified upside down. Clement I was tied to an anchor and thrown from a boat into the Black Sea. Sixtus II was decapitated. Martin I was arrested, scourged and exiled; he died of starvation and exposure. Steven IX was severely tortured and died of the injuries. Lucius III was stoned.

So people didn't campaign to be Pope as much as resist the honor. Early conclaves lasted months, even years. Gregory X therefore decreed that the electors would be locked up and have their food rationed until they elected one of their own as Pope. It sounds unpleasant, I'll grant you that, but I'm pretty sure they weren't forced to wash Funyuns down with Dasani water.

TESTIMONY OF TERRENCE COOLEY
Two Days Earlier: Wednesday, January 21, 2004

"The state calls Terrence Cooley."

It's Buddy's colleague, the other guy who has been sitting at the prosecution table, who will do the questioning. His last name is Miller. He was introduced briefly at the start of the trial. I can't remember his first name. Miller will have to do.

"Would you state your name for us?" >> It's Officer Terrence Cooley.

Okay. This is the guy that Stephen (No Relation) Jones said went to the back, the guy who went in the apartment after Ron Jones was shot, the guy who cuffed Cory Maye. This is Terrence (Cover the Rear) Cooley.

"On December 26, 2001, where were you employed?" >> Bassfield Police Department.

"Did you go to Prentiss on that day or that night?" >> Yes, sir. Officer Earl Bullock, chief of police at Bassfield, advised that Prentiss was needing some assistance in serving some warrants. I was on duty that evening, and I just met up with Chief Bullock there at the police department, and we rode up to Prentiss together.

That explains where Earl (Constable) Bullock came from. He was the chief of Bassfield PD. Stephen (No Relation) Jones described him as a constable. I guess that's the same thing, or maybe Earl is both chief and constable, if they are different offices.

"When you got to the Prentiss Police Department, what happened?" >> We met with Officer Ron Jones, Darryl Graves, Mike Brown, several other officers, Stephen Jones, and discussed the layout of the houses and everything, or the duplex that they was wanting to do the search warrant on.

Terrance (Cover the Rear) Cooley testifies the following people were at the pre-raid meeting: Himself, of course, Ron Jones, Stephen (No Relation) Jones, Darryl (Task Force) Graves, Mike (Left Side) Brown, and others.

"And y'all said you had two search warrants?" >> Yes, sir.

"Was it for both sides of the duplex?" >> Yes, sir.

"Who was in charge of this operation?" >> Officer Ron Jones.

"When you got to the police department in Prentiss, you said you went over the layout of the duplex. Who did that with you?" >> Officer Darryl Graves and Ron Jones.

Same as Stephen Jones just testified. Ron Jones and Darryl (Task Force) Graves gave the briefing jointly.

"Did y'all divide up into two teams?" >> Yes, sir, because it was a duplex. There was two separate families living at this duplex. At that time, we decided who was going to go where. We went to the vehicles, and we proceeded to the residence.

"Which side of the duplex did you go in initially?" >> Initially, I was supposed to be at the left-side apartment on the back door.

"Who was in charge of that team?" >> Darryl Graves.

"And who was in charge of the team on the right side?" >> Ron Jones.

"When you got there, what did you do?" >> We pulled up. I was riding with Darryl Graves and Mike Brown. When we got out of the car, I made it around to the back of the house before Officer Phillip Allday had made it back there. And he come around the same way I did, so I went on over to the next apartment door and was watching the back door, and stood at the first apartment door.

A lot to process here, quickly. Terrance (Cover the Rear) Cooley rode with Darryl (Task Force) Graves and Mike (Left Side) Brown. Terrence Cooley went round the back to where he was supposed to be, but moved to the other side because Phillip (Back Door Kicker) Cooley showed up just after he did.

"You would have been on which side of the apartments?" >> I'd have been on the right side of the apartment.

"The right side. That's this one that Ron Jones was in charge of?" >> Yes, sir.

Right side from the front, left side from the rear.

"What was the purpose of going to the duplex?" >> We had two search warrants to try and locate some narcotics that was supposed to have been there.

"Where were you at?" >> I was standing just to the right side of the back steps.

"When you were standing at those back steps, who was at the front steps?" >> Officer Darrell Cooley, Officer Stephen Jones, and Officer Ron Jones.

That checks with what Stephen Jones just testified.

"Did you hear anything when you were at the back steps?" >> I could hear them hollering from the front, saying "police, we have a search warrant."

"Do you know who was hollering that?" >> No, sir, I don't know which officer was saying that.

"How many times did you hear that?" >> About three times.

"Did you hear anything else?" >> At that time, it got quiet for a few minutes, and Officer Ron Jones and Stephen Jones come around to the back of the house and said that they couldn't get the front door open and was going to try to do the back door. Officer Ron Jones looked at the stairs, and with his height, he was afraid if he tried to kick the door, it might knock him back down the steps. So Officer Ron Jones and Stephen Jones had started back around to the front and Phillip Allday said, "I'll kick it." And he come up the steps and kicked the door. It broke free, but it didn't come completely open.

"What happened then?" >> I told Officer Ron Jones that we had it broke open, and Ron started back around where we was at. And Phillip kicked the door again, and just as he kicked the door, it came open. And as Officer Ron Jones was going into the house, I heard "police, we", and then the shots started ringing off from inside the house.

"You said Ron was going in the house and he did what?" >> He stated "police, we have a" -- and he never finished it from there. He went to trying to find cover, I guess.

"Then what happened?" >> Officer Stephen Jones come back out the door. Officer Ron Jones turned and he told me, he said "I'm hit!" I told him "Ron, get out of the door." Ron come down the steps, come out in like a circle and come back around to the other side of the house. The door had done come back to, and I was hollering into the house to, "Throw the weapon, throw the weapon." And I was pushing the door open trying to find where the suspect was laying or standing or whatever. And he said, "I ain't got it, I ain't got it." And I pushed the door on open and I got my light to where I could see the suspect laying on the floor close to the wall at the foot of the bed. I told him, "Show me your hands." And he had his hands, brung his hands out in front of him laying on the floor. And I pushed the door on open a little further, keeping my weapon on the suspect, pushing the door open with my light, and I seen where the weapon was laying, approximately eight to ten feet away from him.

So Cory Maye was lying on the floor, arms out-stretched. He had already pushed the gun away by the time Terrance (Cover the Rear) Cooley yelled for him to do so.

"What did you do next?" >> Then I entered the house and I went over there and got between Cory and the bed. And I put my knee on his back, and at that time Officer Stephen Jones had re-entered the house. He did a brief check of the house, and then he come back over there where I was at and then went back towards the door. Officer Earl Bullock come in the house. Officer Bullock did a thorough check of the house, making sure nobody else was in there. I was trying to get Cory to give me his hands, get them behind his back. Officer Bullock come over and put a knee, I want to say it was on Cory's left shoulder, right in the neck area, and helped me get his hands around behind his back and get him handcuffed.

"Now, were you able to handcuff Cory by yourself?" >> No, sir, Officer Bullock had to give me some assistance.

"Why were you not able to handcuff him by yourself? Was he resisting?" >> Yes, sir.

"And when Officer Bullock came, were you able to both of you handcuff him?" >> Yes, sir.

"Do you see Cory Maye in the courtroom?" >> Yes, sir.

"Would you point him out for the Court?"

Terrence (Cover the Rear) Cooley points an accusing finger towards Cory Maye. Everyone in the jury box, I suspect everyone in the courtroom, stares at Cory Maye. He sits there, trying to display no reaction, but the discomfort is obvious.

Miller makes the standard request to the court, just like you would hear on television.

"I'd like the record to reflect he's identified the defendant as Cory Maye."

Judge Eubanks says "All right," the court reporter types away on the funny little court reporter thing, and Miller gets back to his questioning.

"Then what did you do?" >> We took him out to the car, put him in car, took him to the sheriff's department, and we got him secure at the jail. We rode by the hospital, and then we came back to the scene.

"When you were going in there, you said you saw Cory behind the bed?" >> Yes, sir, he was laying on the floor at the foot of the bed."

"Was anything obstructing your view from the door to where Cory was?" >> The bed had him partially obstructed. All I could really see was from about his armpits up to where he had his arms laying out in front of him.

"Okay. So you could see he had his arms laying out here past the bed?" >> Yes, sir.

"Okay. How many shots did you hear?" >> I heard three to four shots.

Three to four shots. Terrance (Cover the Rear) Cooley testifies he heard three to four shots. Stephen (No Relation) Jones testified he heard three shots.

"Before those shots, did anybody announce "police"? >> Yes, sir.

"Was that loud?" >> Well, I was at the back door and heard them at the front door saying, "police." And then, when Ron was going through the back door, he said it again.

"How many times did you hear them announce "police" at that apartment before they went in?" >> At that apartment, about four times, at least.

"And some of those you were on the back of the apartment, and they were at the front of the apartment?" >> Yes, sir.

"Tender the witness, Your Honor."

<<>>

"Tender the witness!" That's cooler than "No further questions." Actually, I think it would be best to save the "No further questions" for when you end the questioning of an opposing witness. "I have no further questions of this witness, Your Honor." Make sure you show your disdain as you spit out the word "this."

Rhonda Cooper is going to cross-examine Terrance (Cover the Rear) Cooley.

"Officer Cooley, I'm Rhonda Cooper. We've not met before, but I do have the benefit of a statement that you gave December 27th, the day after this incident." >> Yes, ma'am.

"And then I have the benefit of your testimony this morning. Who was it that briefed you on the layout of these apartments?" >> It was Officer Ron Jones and Darryl Graves.

"And what did they say about it? I mean, had they been inside the apartments before?" >> I don't recall if they said anything about that. They showed what appeared to be the layout of the apartment.

"You're talking about the exterior, the outside?" >> Yes, ma'am.

Now that's what I call a leading question.

"Not the inside." >> No, ma'am.

"And you'd not ever been to these apartments before, had you?" >> No, ma'am.

"Now, which search warrant did you have to execute?" >> I was with Officer Darryl Graves to begin with. And we proceeded to the houses. Like I say, I was the first one around to the back of the house. I went to the second apartment, which was Cory Maye's apartment.

"Okay. Hold that right there. I want the jury to be clear so that they'll know what you're talking about. Now, is it your testimony, Officer Cooley, that you were going to the back of the apartment? If you were facing the apartments, it would've been the apartment on the left." >> Yes, ma'am. There was another officer coming around in behind me, Officer Phillip Allday, and he was supposed to be on Cory Maye's apartment, but I made it around there first. I went on and took Cory Maye's door, and Officer Phillip Allday took the other apartment door.

I find that just as odd now as I did before. Since when did first-come first-not-served become the standard for drug raids? Why didn't Phillip (Back Door Kicker) Allday just walk over to the apartment to which he was assigned?

"So you took Cory Maye's apartment, and Allday took the other apartment. What was going on over there?" >> They were serving a search warrant on that side too.

"Do you know, had they gotten in? What exactly was going on?" >> Yes, ma'am, I could hear the commotion going on inside that apartment over there.

"Commotion such as?" >> Just them telling them to get down and stuff like that. They had one come back towards the back of the apartment there, and I don't know what they was telling him, but I heard them saying something about, "Get down, get down." And I was standing right there at Cory Maye's door.

"And you didn't hear anything going on inside Cory's apartment, did you?" >> Not on the inside, no, ma' am.

"Have you had any training on executing search warrants?" >> Yes, ma'am.

"Did you see the search warrant?" >> Yes, ma'am, at the police department. And when Ron went through Cory Maye's door, it was in his cargo pocket. It was sticking out of the pocket.

"In your training, what, if anything, are you supposed to do with the search warrant? Do you enter the premises with or without it?" >> You enter the premises with it.

"Do you know what happened to it subsequent to Ron Jones being shot?" >> No, ma'am, I do not.

"Did you have on a vest?" >> Yes, ma'am.

"Now, let's talk a bit about after you were inside the apartment. I understood you to say Cory was lying flat." >> Yes, ma'am.

"The gun was eight to ten feet away from him?" >> Yes, ma'am.

"And at what point in your cuffing him did you then start striking him?" >> I never struck Cory Maye.

"And what about Officer Bullock?" >> Not that I seen.

"Not inside of his apartment after he was handcuffed?" >> No, ma'am.

"You said Officer Jones announced 'police' as he was entering the door once it had been kicked open?" >> Yes, ma'am.

"Now, as you all discussed, as you stood back there, how you were going to do it, you said you kicked it and it only opened a little bit, right?" >> Yes, ma'am.

"And who kicked it at that time?" >> Officer Phillip Allday.

"And then he kicked it again, which caused it to open more fully?" >> Yes, ma'am. There was a chain -- I want to say he had a chain on the door.

"Okay. How long were you all back there discussing, you know, how you were going to enter it?" >> We never really discussed how we was going to enter it.

"Well, who made the decision to kick the door in?" >> Officer Ron Jones said that it was too much for him to do, and Officer Phillip Allday said, "I can do it." And he said, "If you can, do it." And then that's when Officer Ron started around to see if he could go into a window.

"Okay. Thank you."

DELIBERATION OF TERRENCE COOLEY
Friday, January 23, 2004

"Okay. That's fifteen minutes. Let's get this show on the road."

Angela is ready to go. I'm not. I still have a Funyun left, one Funyun, and I won't be rushed. In protest, I rustle the bag in exaggerated fashion as I feel around for the last morsel of Funyuny goodness. I extract it with flair, examine it with feigned adoration, and crunch on it for all the world to hear.

My flamboyance goes completely unnoticed. Angela's already well into her spiel.

"... and just like I said, his testimony simply mirrored the first guy's testimony. Three of them went to the apartment on the left-hand side. Three of them went to the apartment on the right-hand side. Two went to the back. Ron Jones and his team couldn't get in the front door because what's his name couldn't kick the door in."

Doris: "Darrell."

Angela: "That's right, Darrell Coolidge."

Kyle: "Cooley"

Angela: "Thank you, Lyle."

Kyle: "Kyle."

Angela: "Sure. Anyway, this Darrell guy couldn't kick the door in, so Ron Jones and Stephen Jones head around back. Ron doesn't want to kick the door in back there because he's big and the steps I guess are too small. So this other guy ..."

Doris: "Phillip."

Angela: "... yeah, Phillip kicks the door open for him. Ron goes in, says "Police ...," and before he can finish he's shot three times."

Doris, sheepishly: "Uh ... one time. Cory Maye shot three times but, remember, the coroner said he found only one gunshot wound."

Angela: "No, the coroner said he had three gunshot wounds."

Doris: "Actually, the corner said there were four gunshot wounds, but only one entry wound. There were multiple internal wounds, but they were caused by just one bullet."

Angela: "Whatever. The point is, Cory Mayes shot and killed Prentiss Police Officer Ron Jones. No one is denying that. No one. So -- where was I? Oh yeah. So Terrance Coolidge races in and cuffs him. But he can't do it himself because Mayes is putting up a fight. Some Constable ..."

Doris: "Earl."

Angela: "Yes, Earl Bullock has to come in and help. I think that about covers it. Anyone have anything to add? If not, we'll get on with the next witness."

I wait without much hope that someone will chime in. I would be happy if they talked about almost anything. There is one crucial, overarching issue with Terrence Cooley's testimony, however. I don't want to point it out myself. I want one of the others to take an active role.

"Okay then."

I'll stall for time by starting with some smaller issues. Maybe someone else will jump in later. I raise my hand.

"Why am I not surprised?"

"Why do you think Terrence Cooley reassigned himself from the Smith apartment to the Maye apartment simply because he got to his post before first?"

Angela: "What? That made no sense."

Me: "Exactly."

Angela: "I mean you. Your question made no sense."

Me: "Oh. I'll try again. Terrence Cooley was assigned to cover the rear of the Smith apartment. He said that he got there, and got in position just as Phillip Allday came around the corner behind him. Phillip Allday was apparently supposed to cover the back of the Maye apartment. Phillip Allday could have just continued walking to the Maye apartment, it was only twenty feet or so, but Terrence Cooley testified that he then volunteered to take Maye's apartment instead, and he walked the twenty feet. He abandoned his assigned post to another officer for no apparent reason. So, why did Terrence Cooley reassign himself from the Smith apartment to the Maye apartment? Why didn't he simply let Allday finish the short walk to the Maye apartment?"

Webbie: "You're kidding, right?"

Angela: "I'll handle this."

Webbie: "You're fuckin' kidding me, right?"

Angela: "Webbie! Please."

Webbie: "Tell me you're kidding me."

It seems as if I'm unlikely to get any cogent discussion from Webbie, so I try to draw Bonnie, the stay-at-home mom, out of her shell.

"Bonnie. You have any thoughts on the subject?"

Bonnie: "I guess it's a bit odd."

Angela: "But do you think it's a significant issue?"

Bonnie: "I guess not."

Angela: "Do you think we should be wasting our time on such trivia?"

Bonnie: "Probably not. Not unless someone can explain why it matters."

Me: "Maybe Marion has some thoughts. How 'bout it Marion?"

Marion: "Same as Bonnie. Maybe it's odd, but I don't see how it could change things."

I'm not giving up. Not yet. I try Cathy. She's the community college student sitting next to the actuarial suit.

"Cathy. You have any thoughts on the subject?"

"Well .... I do ..... but ...."

"Yes. Go on." I'm good at encouragement.

"Something else bothers me."

"Yes."

"Well..."

She's killing me.

"I remember the lady defense attorney asking him why didn't Cory Maye shoot more cops, or something like that."

Bingo!

Webbie decides to take her on.

Webbie: "So one dead cop isn't enough for you? You'd feel better if we was sitting here talkin' about two or three dead cops?"

Cathy: "Never mind. Sorry I brought it up."

Me: "No, no, no. You've got a point. You see something others haven't seen yet. You just need to explain it."

Cathy: "Well, what I don't understand is why he decided he was going to kill the police, but then stopped shooting before he had used up all his bullets. He didn't wait for the next one to come in, or try to trick them to come in. He shot three times and then laid down his gun and pushed it towards the door. Remember? Terrence Cooley said he yelled at him to throw out the gun, and Cory Maye said 'I already did,' and Cooley confirmed he could see that Cory Maye had done just that, just as he said. And Cory was already laying there on the ground with his arms stretched out above his head."

The room goes quiet as jurors begin processing this thought.

Cathy continues: "I mean, he had to know if he killed a cop they would probably kill him right then, or at the least he would be executed for being a cop killer. They can only kill him once, no matter how many cops he kills. I'm sorry, I'm not making any sense."

Angela helps her out: "It's okay. Remember what Coolidge said as well."

Me: "It's Cooley. Terrence Cooley."

Angela: "Whatever. You can never tell how these people will behave. They change their mind right in the middle. Remember? He said sometimes they surrender then start to fight when you try to cuff 'em, just like Mayes did. They change their minds, right in the middle, for whatever reason. We can't figure out how these people think. Who knows what Mayes was thinking?"

Cathy: "I guess you're right, but ..."

Angela: "Of course I'm right."

Cathy: ".... but, aren't we supposed to figure out what he's thinking? Aren't we supposed to figure out if he knew he was shooting at an intruder or a policeman? Didn't the judge tell us that if he thought he was defending his home we don't have to convict him of anything."

Me: "Excuse me, Cathy. I just want to clarify the instructions. If we decide that Cory Maye thought he was defending his home against an intruder, whether he was right in that belief or not, as long as that belief was reasonable, then we must not convict him. The instruction doesn't tell us we don't have to convict him. The instruction says we must not convict him. But you're doing great. Hang in there."

Cathy: "Yeah. We can't vote guilty unless we figure out what he was thinking, unless we decide he meant to kill a policeman."

Angela: "That's not true. Even he ..."

And she points an accusing finger in my direction.

Angela: "... says Mayes had to have a reasonable belief it was an intruder. I mean seriously. The police were out there several minutes, that's their words, not mine, several minutes yelling 'Police, search warrant', and banging on doors and trying to get in. Their cars, patrol cars with lights and everything were parked in front. They had on their uniforms. Hell, Mayes even opened the blinds and peeked out at them when they were on the porch. It's after that he went and got his gun. It's just not reasonable that he didn't know they were police. Not reasonable at all."

Cathy: "I guess."

Angela: "Good. Now that we have that settled, maybe we ...."

There's a hand up, and it's not mine. It belongs to Marion, the stay-at-home grandmother. This is great.

Angela: "What?"

Marion: "Two things. First, his last name is Maye, not Mayes. You keep gettin' it wrong."

Angela: "Okay. Fine. What's the next thing?"

Marion: "Well, he didn't invite them over than night, so it's not like he decided he was gonna go out and kill a policeman. And it's not like he was facing a long time in jail for just a little bit of marijuana. And don't dare get me wrong, I don't think he shoulda had any, especially with that little girl in the house, and I don't like that at all, not one bit, but still, it doesn't seem like you would suddenly decide to kill a policeman or take on the entire police department just 'cause you didn't want to get caught with that tiny bit of marijuana. I mean, it was so small, I couldn't hardly see it. It's not worth killing someone over."

Webbie: "So you're saying he went crazy?"

Marion: "What?"

Webbie: "I don't get what you're trying to say."

Marion: "It just doesn't seem likely to me that someone would spend their whole life without getting in any trouble, then all of a sudden decide to kill a policeman, just like that, over nothing big. It doesn't make any sense to me."

Angela: "We don't know he didn't have a criminal record, or that he didn't do a lot of bad things before. We don't know that. They wouldn't have been allowed to tell us if he did."

Marion: "Then after deciding to kill the police, to give right up after killing the first one. Just like she said, like Cathy said there, it doesn't make any sense."

Angela: "You're just going on emotion. That's all. We've got to look at the facts. Fact, they arrived in marked police cars, lights flashing. Fact, they yelled 'Police, search warrant," a whole bunch of times, real loud. Fact, they knocked on the door, they kicked at the door, and he didn't open the door. Fact, he looked out the window and saw them. Fact, he went and got his gun and loaded it. Fact, he hid behind his little girl and when Ron Jones came in the back door, he shot him and killed him. Now those are the facts, not emotions, facts."

Joyce, the teacher, joins in for the first time. "I think you got some of your facts wrong. I don't recall anyone saying all the cars were marked, or exactly how many cars were there, or whether their lights were flashing, or their sirens wailing. I do remember hearing Stephen Jones testify he didn't see anyone in the apartment when the blinds came open, assuming they ever came open, so if he couldn't see Maye that might mean that Maye couldn't see them. Also, I'm not sure I remember anyone saying they ever knocked at the door. I remember someone saying they kicked the door, but I don't remember knocked." She pauses, then concludes. "I think that's about it for now."

I'm impressed by her recollection of details, assuming she got them all correct. Angela is less impressed.

"We're not going to go over that whole window blind business again, are we? I thought we settled that. Come on everybody, it shouldn't be this difficult. We're never going to get through this today if we keep arguing over this touchy-feely stuff. We need to focus on facts, on cold hard facts."

Angela, through trying to unify the jury, is polarizing the jury. By quickly dismissing the viewpoints of those who disagree with her, by treating them as if their thoughts are unworthy of consideration, she is only driving them into what she perceives to be the enemy camp.

Cathy: "You want facts? How 'bout these facts? Fact, Cory Maye didn't ask them to raid his house that night. Fact, they showed up late at night when he would be sleeping. Fact, they started screaming and banging and kicking. Fact, he didn't keep shooting until he was out of bullets. Fact, he didn't try to reload. Fact, he laid down and spread his arms out. Fact, he shoved his gun toward them before they ever told him to do so."

Wow. Cathy is pissed. In just a few minutes time, Angela has converted the shy, diminutive Cathy from an uncertain community college student into an in-your-face firebrand.

Angela: "Okay, now we're just going around and around. I think a lot of this will become more obvious to you as we proceed."

Nice condescension, Angela. I'm sure that will fix things up.

Angela: "We need to just move on to the next witness, and that would be, uh, uh, ..."

Doris: "Darryl."

Angela: "Yeah, Darryl Graves."

TESTIMONY OF DARRYL GRAVES
Two Days Earlier: Wednesday, January 21, 2004

"State your name for us." >> Darryl Graves.

Looks like what's his name Miller will be doing the direct examination again.

"Darryl, where are you employed?" >> Pearl River Basin Narcotics Task Force.

"What are your duties there?" >> I'm a narcotics agent.

"On December 26, 2001, did you get a call to go to Prentiss?" >> Yes. Got a call that a possible drug search warrant was going to be executed.

"Who contacted you?" >> Officer Ronald Jones.

"And when he called you, what did he tell you?" >> He asked me if I could come back to Prentiss. He had a search warrant that he wanted to run, and asked if I could assist him.

"And did you do that?" >> Yes.

"When you got to Prentiss, where did you first go?" >> I went to the Prentiss PD. I met with Officer Jones. We went in his office. He briefly briefed me about what he had. And at the time, he was getting ready to go and get a search warrant signed."

Briefly briefed him. Must have been brief.

"Did he go get a search warrant signed?" >> Yes. It was for a duplex apartment, and we was supposed to execute the search warrants on both apartments at the same time. And it was supposed to be for drugs. Actually, marijuana and crack cocaine.

"Do you know who was in the apartments?" >> I knew who was in the left apartment. That was Jamie Smith.

Jamie Smith, left-hand apartment, when looking from the front. Darryl (Task Force) Graves knew him.

"Was the search warrant issued for Jamie Smith?" >> Yes, it was.

"Was there another search warrant issued also?" >> Yes. It had unknown occupant. It was for the right side.

Cory Maye, right-hand apartment, when looking from the front.

"When the other officers got there, did y'all go over what you were going to do?" >> Yes, we did. Ron did the briefing. He broke us down into two teams. He put me in charge of one of the teams that was going to go to the left apartment, and he was going to be the team leader for the apartment on the right.

Darryl (Task Force) Graves says Ron Jones conducted the briefing.

"After you finished the briefing, did you leave and go to the apartments?" >> Yes.

"And when you went to the apartments, did you have a search warrant?" >> Yes, I did. That was for Jamie Smith, the apartment on the left.

"When you got there, what did you do?" >> We were in the second vehicle going in. The first vehicle parked kind of in front of the apartment on the right. We exited out the vehicle and went to the apartment on the left.

"Did you see who went to the apartment on the right?" >> Yes.

"Who was that?" >> That was Ron and his team.

First vehicle driven by Stephen (No Relation) Jones who was accompanied by Ron Jones and Darrell (Front Door Kicker) Cooley. That car parked in front of apartment on the right. Darryl (Task Force) Graves was in the second car. He and his team went to the apartment on the left.

"When you got to the apartment on the left, what did you do?" >> There was another officer that was in front of me. He knocked on the door, said "police, search warrant," and they came to the door. We walked in, we put them all on the ground. We told them we had a search warrant. We secured everybody and began our search.

"Did you find anything at that time?" >> Yes, I did. I found marijuana.

"And then what happened?" >> While we was doing our search, we got information that there was an officer down. And at that time we stopped our search and went over to find out what was going on.

"Did everybody leave apartment one?" >> No. I left one deputy there, to keep the area secure.

"When you went over to the other apartment, what did you find?" >> I never made it inside the apartment. I saw Officer Ron Jones laying on the ground and one of the officers kneeling next to him. I assisted the officer that was with Jones, and we got him into a car and they took off with him to the hospital. We taped off the area with caution tape. We stopped our search on both apartments and we called the Mississippi Bureau of Investigation.

"When the investigators arrived, who came?" >> I believe it was Eric Johnson that was the first one I talked to. The scene was turned over to him when he got there.

"Did you ever go back into the apartment on the left where you initially started your search." >> Once they got there, we did go back in and finished up. We found cocaine, scales with cocaine residue. And I believe there was a tin can that also had cocaine residue in it, also.

"So you found cocaine residue in a tin can, on scales, and marijuana?" >> Correct.

"After that, what did you do?" >> After that, we waited till the state was finished with their investigation. Once they finished theirs, they told us that we could come on in and go ahead and start our search of the apartment on the right.

"Who went in and did the search then?" >> Myself and Deputy Mike Brown.

"That's the apartment where Cory Maye was?" >> Correct.

"Did you find anything in that apartment?" >> Yes, I did. I found marijuana. I put it in a evidence bag and secured it, brought it back to the office, put it in our safe, then transported it to the crime lab.

"I hand you what's been marked Exhibit 20, and ask you if you can tell me what that is." >> It's like cigars. It's part of a cigar that you put marijuana leaves in and smoke it. And it's the butts or the ends of it.

"Did you send that to the crime lab?" >> Yes, I did. The results show that it was marijuana, 1.1 grams.

That's about a tablespoonful. Not exactly the tonnage we'd been led to expect.

"I hand you what's been marked Exhibit 21 and ask if you recognize it." >> Yes, I do. It's marijuana. This was found in the hallway on a shelf in Cory Maye's apartment.

"Did you send that to the crime lab?" >> Yes, I did.

"What was it identified as?" >> Marijuana, 0.1 grams.

One-tenth of a gram. More than a pinch, less than a tad-bit, as my new neighbors would say.

"And you didn't initially start the search on that apartment?" >> No, I didn't.

"Why did you complete the search?" >> Because the officer that was going to do it had been shot and killed.

"Now, when you were at the front door going in the apartment on the left-hand side, could you see anything of what was happening on the apartment on the right-hand side?" >> Yes.

"Did you hear anyone announce 'police'?" >> Yes. I heard him say, "police, search warrant." Because they got to their door before we could. We had parked right in front of that door, and I could see them going up to their door as we was going to ours. And they were already yelling, "police, search warrant."

"Okay. And you heard that at the apartment on the other side?" >> Yes.

"I tender the witness, Your Honor."

<<>>

Rhonda Cooper will conduct the cross-examination.

"Agent Graves, it's not very likely that a suspect that has surrendered himself will then resist arrest, is it?" >> We've had them do it before. You go on search warrants, you never know what's going to happen. And there is times when they resist, sometimes they don't. It all depends. It's just like if I was out on a traffic stop, they turn on you at any time.

"I was talking about a suspect who has surrendered. Is it likely that he's then going to resist?" >> I can't speak for any one person.

"Have you had that in your experiences?" >> Yes, I have. We've had them on the ground, and when we get ready to try to cuff them, they want to fight or want to resist.

"And could these people have had a weapon?" >> I have to think. I don't think any of them has ever had weapons. There's times we've found knives and stuff like that in their pockets.

"But not a gun." >> No.

"I understood you to just say that you got the search warrant from Officer Jones that he had for Cory Maye? Was that your testimony?" >> No, I didn't get it from him. I picked it up off the ground. I secured it. I kept it with me.

"When did you first see Cory Maye?" >> I think when they was bringing him out of the house.

"Why didn't you give him the search warrant then?" >> We hadn't conducted the search warrant. We had secured the area. We hadn't conducted the search warrant at all at that time.

"Is that what you did on the apartment on the left? You withheld the search warrant until you conducted it?" >> Right.

"So you didn't give it to Jamie Smith or anybody in his apartment to let them know why you were there." >> Yes, we did. What we do is, when we do a search warrant, we will show them a copy of the search warrant so they'll know that we are there legally. Once they get through reading it we get it back from them so once I finish my search, I can put down everything that's on there that we're going to take, showing that we're not stealing anything. Everything that we take out of there, that's what we found in the house, we put onto the search warrant.

"So you do make it available to the suspect, so they can see exactly what you're doing and why you're doing it, right?" >> Yes.

"And I'm asking in this instance, as it relates to Cory Maye, why did you not do that?" >> There was an officer had been shot. We had to secure that area. There was a lot of things going on at that time, and all we wanted to do was secure the area and get the state investigators down.

"Okay. And on that search warrant that you claim you left there, it didn't have anybody's name on it, did it?" >> No.

"Now, when you spoke with Ron Jones about executing the search warrant, were you told how much marijuana was in these apartments?" >> He didn't give me an exact amount.

"You all didn't discuss any amounts?" >> He just said there was a possibility there was a large amount of marijuana there. I'm not for sure. I don't know which apartment, but he did say there was drugs in both apartments.

"And you did find marijuana and cocaine in Jamie Smith's apartment?" >> Yes.

"Now, I understand you knew Jamie Smith before December 26, 2001, correct?" >> That's correct.

"And it was you, the narcotics agent, who was given the search warrant for Jamie Smith, who you knew as having dealt drugs before. Is that correct?" >> Yes.

"Could you please tell the ladies and gentlemen of the jury the normal procedure that is followed in executing a search warrant once a suspected dealer has been identified?" >> Normally, what we do is, we try to pull surveillance on the location. We try and get a buy out of the place if we can. We have informants that may know these people real well. The informant may go to the place and see the drugs there. And usually, these informants are reliable sources that we use, that we've used in the past, that are very reliable. And if they say there's drugs there, there's usually drugs there. We put all those together and get a search warrant signed by a judge.

"Do you use the confidential informant for the buy? >> Yes, there's times we do use the CI for buys.

"Okay. We're now at the point where you've obtained the search warrant and you're ready now to serve it on your identified suspect. How do you approach the suspect or suspect's home?" >> Normally, the way we do it is, if we're in a vehicle, everybody exits the vehicle. What we try and do is get a marked unit to go to the house first. Once we pull up to the residence, we all get out. We usually knock and respond with "police, search warrant." And that's the norm. Every time we go to a location we do announce "police, search warrant," and the reason we do that is for our safety and for the safety of the people that are inside the house. We want them to know that we are out there and we are getting ready to execute a search warrant, and hopefully it runs as smoothly as possible.

"As you approach the house to execute the search warrant, do you wait until your team is set up and ready to make the entry or do you shout as you run up to the house?" >> Well, the way we do it is, the entry team is usually in one vehicle. It's usually at least four of us that's going to make the entry. We try and get all four in the vehicle, in one vehicle, and, the team that's going to pull the security outside is usually in another vehicle. Once we get up to the house, once we pull in, soon as we get up to the door is when we say "police, search warrant."

"Now, as you approach the house or the place where the identified suspect is and you're preparing yourself to serve your warrant, do you have your weapons drawn?" >> Our norm is, we have our weapons drawn, yes. Yes, my weapon is drawn.

"And you would continue to have your weapon drawn as you enter the dwelling? "Yes. There is one person that usually don't have his weapon drawn sometimes, and he could be the person with the ram. A ram is a metal bar that we use to open a door sometimes because normally they won't open the door. So we have to break the door down. And we have a ram. And that person won't have his weapon drawn.

"And then that person will not have a gun. Is that correct?" >> He has one, but he doesn't draw it until he puts the ram down. Once he gets the door open, then he drops the ram, and he should usually draw his gun by then.

"Now the officer who obtains the search warrant, isn't that the primary officer to execute the search warrant?" >> Correct. The way our procedure is, the person that's running the search warrant, the officer that has the search warrant, he's the last one that's going to come in, usually. And that's the way the task force does that. The team leader, he's going to be the last one in. And the reason why we started doing that is because of what happened that night in December. Just in case something goes wrong, at least he's there with the search warrant.

"Based on what you've shared with the jury about your normal procedure being followed to execute a search warrant, was that followed by Ron Jones and that team?" >> They said, "police search warrant." Whether their guns or anything like that was drawn, I'm not sure. We did. My team did. We had our guns drawn.

"I mean the things that you shared earlier about the surveillance and the buy and those things, those were not done in this case, were they?" >> I don't know. That was his search warrant.

"You said on your side, the left side, your team did follow the procedures that you shared with the jury?" >> As far as drawing the guns, correct.

"Did you have to announce 'police' or was the door already open?" >> We announced "police."

"And they just opened the door?" >> Correct. We knocked on the door, announced "police," and they came to the door. It was pretty much simultaneous. They opened the door pretty much a few seconds after we got there.

"So they saw you when they opened the door." >> What I'm saying is, one of the guys knocked on the door, and as he was knocking on the door, the door was opening. They heard who we were because we said, "police, search warrant."

"Who said it?" >> The agent in front of me, Mike Brown.

Left-hand apartment, Jamie Smith's apartment. Mike (Left Side) Brown first, Darryl (Task Force) Graves second.

"And you had the search warrant, though?" >> Correct.

"Did you read either of the search warrants?" >> I looked over the search warrants when we was there at the police department.

"Did you have any questions or concerns about the one that said persons unknown?" >> No, I didn't.

"I understood you to say once before, I think when we met last May, that when you execute a search warrant, you know to whom it's going and whether or not they live there. Isn't that correct?" >> Sometimes I do.

"I think you said usually, when I execute a search warrant, we know who lives there." >> I said usually. There are times we don't know who lives there. This was Ronald Jones' search warrant, so I'm not for sure what all he knew about that. All I knew is what he told me.

"You said that Ron Jones told you there was a large amount of marijuana in both apartments?" >> Correct.

"Okay. And you've just testified that this marijuana was -- would you call that a small amount?" >> Yeah, that's a small amount.

"And this small amount of marijuana, that's why Ron Jones got shot or lost his life, because of this small amount of marijuana?" >> Prior to that, to us getting there, I don't know how much marijuana was there. I'm not sure how much marijuana was there other than what I found.

"Was there anything about your investigation to indicate that there had been some marijuana that had been disposed of or gotten rid of?" >> I can't answer that. From the time we first got there to the time I was in my apartment and by the time they got into the other apartment, I don't know what could've happened over there. I wasn't there.

"And you really don't know because you couldn't make out the sounds?" >> No. I was in the other apartment. I heard a commotion. I don't know what was going on when I was in that other apartment. The walls are so close together you can hear something. I could hear a little bit, but not much.

"Did you hear muffled voices?" >> I didn't know what it was. It just sounded like something was banging on the wall or something. I don't know what it was.

"Did you hear a toilet flush?" >> No.

"You said it sounded like a bang in Cory Maye's apartment?" >> Right. It was banging. It was more like something hitting up against the wall. That's what I mean when I say banging.

"But did you hear what might have sounded like a toilet flushing?" >> No.

"Agent Graves, did you say you looked at both warrants or you read both warrants when you first met with Officer Jones, Ron Jones?" >> I briefly looked at the warrants.

"Was the information on the warrant for Jamie Smith's apartment the same as the information on the warrant for the apartment on the right?" >> The only thing I believe was the difference was the apartment number and the names.

"Where is Jamie Smith today?" >> I'm not for sure.

"Do you know if he's in custody?" >> I'm not for sure of that. I know he's been indicted, but I'm not sure where he's at.

"In your experience as a narcotics agent, isn't there usually a drug buy or some surveillance that would come before the execution of a search warrant?" >> At some points, yes. You can do buys or you can do surveillance, as long as you do your homework on it. What Ron had done that day I don't know. I have no idea.

"Did you all discuss whether or not there had been a buy?" >> No. There had been buys at the apartment on the left.

"Jamie Smith's apartment?" >> Correct. And I'd done those. He wasn't the one who done those. What he did that day I'm not for sure, or days prior, I'm not for sure.

"Now, I understood you to tell these ladies and these gentlemen that you couldn't hear what was going on inside the apartment on the right that we now know was Cory Maye's apartment, right?" >> Right. Once I got inside the apartment, I couldn't hear.

"So, if you couldn't hear these men yell 'police,' how could Cory have heard them?" >> I can't speak for him.

"Okay. Well, you're inside an apartment, he's inside an apartment, you didn't hear it. Supposedly, they're trying to get in his apartment. How could he have heard more than what you heard?" >> I'm not for sure, but the people in the other apartment heard us when we said, "police."

"And if you're inside and Cory Maye's inside, how could he have heard more or different than you?" >> I'm not for sure. I can't speak for him.

"At what point did you know which apartment you were going to be going to?" >> I knew while we was there at the PD. When we did the briefing, I knew which one I was going to.

Darryl (Task Force) Graves now says he and Ron Jones did the briefing.

"And he gave you the warrant for the place where marijuana and a small amount of cocaine was found." >> Right, correct.

"Nothing further, Your Honor.

<<>>

What's-his-name Miller will conduct the redirect examination.

"My understanding was that there were at least three agencies operating out there in the service of these search warrants. There was you from the Pearl River Basin Narcotics Task Force. There was the Bassfield Police Department had officers out there. And Prentiss PD had officers out there. That correct?" >> That's correct.

"All right. The individual that was in charge of the operation that night overall was who?" >> That was Officer Ron Jones.

"And the reason for that was because it was his informant that held gotten the information with respect to the issuance of the warrants?" >> That's correct.

"Ms. Cooper has asked you several questions about different ways search warrants can be issued. Isn't it a fact that search warrants can be issued based on reliable informants and that's it?" >> Yes.

"If the judge thinks it's sufficient to issue the warrant?" >> Yes, that's correct.

"And have you done search warrants like that yourself?" >> Yes, I have.

"Matter of fact, isn't it the case that probably the bulk of search warrants are issued like that?" >> Yes.

"And probably fewer issued based on CI buys inside a place?" >> That's correct.

"Now, isn't it true sometimes with the use of nicknames or street names or other things that, when you serve a search warrant on a place, you're not actually certain what the name of the person is that may be in the premises?" >> Yes, that's correct.

"As a matter of fact, many times you issue a search warrant that may be directed to unknown persons in control of the property?" >> That's correct.

"Isn't it also true that a lot of times you go on search warrants and you don't find anything?" >> Yes, that's correct.

"I would assume that's because sometimes it takes a while to get a search warrant, doesn't it?" >> Yes.

"So many times there are periods of hours in between the time the information is obtained and the time the warrant is served, correct?" >> That's correct.

"Sometimes what was there when the informant was there has ceased to be there by time you get there with a warrant?" >> That's correct.

"Matter of fact, isn't it common for you to hear or find out later from your informants when you go to a place and there's no dope or very little dope, you just missed the dope?" >> Yes.

"Did you particularly find anything strange about the fact that there was supposed to be marijuana or cocaine in an apartment and you went out there and there might be just a small amount of marijuana left in the apartment?" >> No, that wasn't strange at all.

"Did you think Officer Ron Jones was incompetent or stupid out there?" >> No, I'd done many warrants with him, a few warrants with him before, and he was prepared.

"Did you think it was unprofessional?" >> No.

"I believe there was a pre-search warrant service meeting. Were you advised at that meeting that Officer Jones did not believe there would be any weapons at the apartments?" >> Yes.

"Do you think that might've been the reason some of his people didn't have their weapons drawn?" >> That could've been the reason.

"Let me ask you this. You went inside both apartments throughout the night. Are they both the same on the inside?" >> I believe they're fairly the same.

"And you were in this apartment over here on the left at first?" >> Yes.

"When you approached the door, you said, I think, Agent Mike Brown knocked on the door?" >> Yes.

"When he knocked on the door, did they open the door?" >> Yes. After he yelled "police," they opened the door as he was knocking.

"Why do you think they opened the door?" >> They heard "police," they saw who we were.

"No further questions, Your Honor.

<<>>

Rhonda Cooper asks to approach the bench. It seems as if she has to ask permission to re-cross each time. I don't get it. I thought the defense had an automatic opportunity to re-cross just as the prosecution has an automatic opportunity to redirect. Whatever the case, it looks like she will ask Graves a few more questions.

"Agent Graves, you just testified that Ron Jones told you that there were large amounts of marijuana in these two apartments?" >> Yes.

"Okay. And when you went back to Cory Maye's apartment, you didn't see anything in your investigation that would have indicated any of these large amounts of marijuana had been disposed of, did you?" >> No.

"Agent Graves, will you tell the ladies and gentlemen what confidential and reliable mean as it relates to a confidential informant." >> Confidential and reliable means that we've used him in the past, he's confident, we're confident enough that the information he gives us is good information. Reliable means that we've used him in the past, that everything he tells us is usually true, and we are confident enough to know that, if he tells us something is there, it's usually going to be there.

"When you all did your investigation, what evidence was there that supported what the CI supposedly had told Ron Jones?" >> We found crack in one apartment, found marijuana in the other apartment.

"You found that small amount of marijuana in Cory Maye's apartment." >> Correct.

"Tell the ladies and gentlemen what your understanding about the marijuana was, the amount, if any?" >> Well, we was told that there was a large amount of marijuana and crack cocaine at both locations.

"And tell the ladies and gentlemen of the jury whether or not that was true." >> No. Once we got there, there wasn't a large amount there.

"Was there a thorough investigation prior to the attempt to execute the search warrant?" >> I'm not for sure. I wasn't there.

"You weren't where?" >> I wasn't there when he was doing his investigation of this.

"What record, if any, do you have, Sergeant Graves, about the confidentiality or reliability of the CI? >> I'm not for sure. I don't know who he was. He wasn't my CI.

"Thank you, Agent Graves."

DELIBERATION OF DARRYL GRAVES
Friday, January 23, 2004

Angela is feeling the clock bearing down on her. Graves will be just the third of eight witnesses we have to discuss. The first two didn't go as quickly or smoothly as she hoped, though I felt we rushed through them. We're about to see how smoothly the deliberation of this witness goes.

"Now we really need to get serious here with Darryl Graves, everyone. We simply can't afford to keep getting bogged down by small, insignificant issues. We need to focus. So I'll try and clarify all the critical points with my summary. Darryl Graves worked for the Pearl River Narcotics Task Force. He ..."

I rise from my chair and walk to the chalkboard. She notices that, suspends her summary and glares at me. When I arrive at the board, I pick up the single, stubby piece of chalk and begin a bulleted list.

> *Darryl Graves:*
> - *Only officer from Pearl River Narcotics Task Force*

"Go ahead," I say. I'm tempted to call her 'Angelica' just to piss her off. "Don't allow me to bother you."

"Umm, he arrived at the Prentiss PD shortly before Ron Jones left to have his warrants signed. He ..."

My scribbling once again gives her pause.

> - *Only officer to meet with Ron Jones prior to having warrants signed*
> - *Only officer to have read both warrants*

"Please," I say. "Continue."

"Uh ... he ... uh ... when the other officers showed up, he helped Ron Jones brief them."

I'm surprised she picked up on that point. Perhaps she didn't notice that Graves initially testified that "Ron Jones gave the briefing." Anyway, I add that to the bulleted list.

> - *Only officer to assist Ron Jones in briefing the team during the pre-raid meeting*

"Do you mind?" she asks. I sense she's irritated.

"No, not all at. Please continue."

"Where was I? Oh yeah, Ron selected him to lead ..."

I don't wait for her to finish before I began writing on the board.

- *Only officer to chosen by Ron Jones to lead a raiding team*

She closes her eyes, tilts her head downward just a bit, and rubs her forehead with one hand. Her eyes are still closed when she continues.

"Darryl Graves led the team that went to the left-hand apartment."

- *Only officer from left-hand apartment to testify*
- *Only officer to know Jamie Smith, occupant of left-hand apartment*
- *Only officer to have previously been in left-hand apartment*
- *Only officer to have conducted a controlled purchase of drugs from Jamie Smith*

"Will you please stop that?"

"I'm just making some notes. Please continue."

She takes a deep breath. "As he was approaching the left-hand apartment ..."

She looks at me, expecting me to write something. I stand there silently.

"... he could see Ron Jones' team approach the right-hand apartment, where Cory Maye was staying. He could hear them yelling 'Police, search warrant.'"

Again she pauses and looks my way. I stand there silently.

"They yelled 'Police, search warrant' as they approached the left-hand apartment."

Doris: "Mike."

Angela: "What?"

Doris: "The one who yelled 'Police, search warrant' as they approached the left-hand apartment. His name was Mike."

Angela: "Mike who?"

Doris: "I'm not sure."

Vera: "Mike Brown. My grandson has a friend named Mike Brown, so I remembered him right off."

Angela: "Okay, fine. Mike Brown. He was in front. He yelled 'Police, search warrant.' And just as he was knocking on the door, they were opening the door over there, because they heard them yelling 'Police, search warrant.' Cory Mayes says he didn't hear, but the people on the left didn't have any trouble hearing, did they?

"So they go on in and they put everyone on the ground and they begin their search. Once they're in the left-hand apartment, Graves can't hear anything that's going on in the right-hand apartment. So he doesn't know whether

Cory Mayes is flushing drugs down the toilet or whatever. Mayes could have been flushing 'em, and maybe that's why he took so long to open the door, and he never did open the door, did he? Anyway, whatever went on over there, Darryl Graves couldn't hear it."

I add my final item to the list.

- *Only officer not to hear gunshots*

This one ignites Webbie.

"Bullshit. You don't know that. How do you know he didn't hear any?"

"Because he said that once he was in Jamie Smith's apartment, the only thing he heard from the other side was a large bang, like someone banging up against the wall. Also, he said he went over to the Cory Maye apartment after he learned that Ron Jones had been shot. He didn't go over because he heard gunshots. He went over because someone informed him that Ron Jones had been shot. Informed him. His words, not mine."

Webbie: "Well, umm, you don't know whether any of the other cops heard shots or not. Some of 'em didn't even testify, and the ones that did, she didn't ask 'em. Maybe Graves wasn't the only one didn't hear any. So you still don't know that's true, that he's the only one not to hear gunshots."

Me: "Good point."

I amend the heading. When I'm done, my list looks like this:

> *Darryl Graves: (As far as we know, based on trial testimony only)*
> - *Only officer from Pearl River Narcotics Task Force.*
> - *Only officer to meet with Ron Jones prior to having warrants signed*
> - *Only officer to have read both warrants*
> - *Only officer to assist Ron Jones in briefing team during the pre-raid meeting*
> - *Only officer chosen by Ron Jones to lead a raiding team*
> - *Only officer from left-hand apartment to testify*
> - *Only officer to know Jamie Smith, occupant of left-hand apartment*
> - *Only officer to have previously been in left-hand apartment*
> - *Only officer to have conducted a controlled purchase of drugs from Jamie Smith*
> - *Only officer not to hear gunshots*

I place the chalk back in the tray along the front of the chalkboard and return to my seat. I wait for Angela to continue.

"So, uh, that's about it. No wait. Graves goes over to the other side, sees Ron Jones laying on the ground. Helps get him in the car, then secures the area. Once the guys from the Bureau of Investigation get there, they let Graves and his team search the left-hand apartment. Not Cory Mayes', but the other one. And Graves finds some marijuana and some crack and a crack scale. Right? Yeah.

"Then after the guys from the Bureau do their investigation in Mayes' apartment, Graves goes in there and searches that place. And he finds some marijuana type cigar butts or some such thing, and some marijuana on the counter. So the confidential informant, it seems, was right. There was marijuana in both places.

"And I guess that's about it for Graves. Anybody got anything to add? Be quick though. We have to move along."

Raymond, the pharmacist sitting along the right side of the table, my right, is staring at what I wrote on the board.

Raymond: "What do you think that means?"

Me: "I think it means Darryl Graves had a bigger role in this raid than he wants to let on for some reason."

Raymond: "Any idea?"

Me: "Couple."

Raymond: "Like?"

Raymond seems to be a man of few words.

Me: "Well I can't prove it, but it occurred to me that perhaps Jamie Smith was the target of the raid, and somehow they ended up in Cory Maye's apartment by mistake."

Webbie: "Bull .... crap. They had two warrants. One for each place. They had a CI tell 'em there was drugs in each place, and there was, just like he said. You and your hair-brain theories. I'm getting' sick of this."

Me: "As I said, I can't explain it all. I figure there's a whole lot going on out there we're not allowed to hear about, for whatever reason. I don't think we'll be able to figure it out in here based only what they've given us, but it doesn't feel right to me."

Angela: "It doesn't really make any difference, does it? If Mayes knew there were cops out there, and he shot anyway, that's it. Guilty. Guilty as sin. And he knew they were cops. He had to know."

Raymond: "I'm not so sure anymore. Good point by Cooper. Graves couldn't hear from inside. Why should Maye?"

Doris: "The people on the right side, I mean left side, they could hear from the inside. They opened the door. If they can hear then Cory Maye can hear."

Raymond: "Then Graves can hear, too. But Graves wouldn't even say he heard gunshots. So he's right." He points casually in my direction. "Something's up."

Webbie: "You're crazy. You callin' Graves a liar?"

Raymond: "Getting' there." He gets up, walks to the board, and adds an item to my list.

- *Only one to discuss police procedures in detail*

As Raymond returns to his seat, Angela attempts to recapture the discussion.

"Now that we have that out of our system, I think we can proceed to ..."

I rise and walk to the board. I pick up the chalk and begin an entirely new list. The other jurors quickly realize the nature of the list and begin pointing out errors and offering suggestions. I add, replace, and erase as necessary. When we're all done, the new list looks like this:

Drug Raid Procedure (as described by Darryl Graves):
- *Find yourself a confidential informant (CI)*
- *Sometimes, but not usually, have CI stage a controlled purchase*
- *Sometimes, but not always, surveil the location*
- *Sometimes, but not always, find out who lives at the residence*
- *Secure search warrant, frequently based solely on word of CI*
- *Do not share name of CI with judge*
- *Round up officers to participate in raid*
- *Brief other officers*
- *Do not share name of CI with them*
- *Do not tell them about any surveillance*
- *Do not tell them about any controlled purchase*
- *Do tell them, however, if CI says no need to worry about guns*
- *Break into two teams: entry team and security team*
- *Entry team consists of at least 4 people; travels in same car*
- *Security team consists of unspecified number of people, at least 2*
- *Security travels in their own car*
- *Draw weapons*
- *Approach door*
- *Yell "Police, search warrant" while knocking on door*
- *If occupants don't answer door, breach door with a battering ram*
- *Person using battering ram drops ram and draws weapon*
- *Charge inside, place everyone on floor, secure residence*
- *Show occupant or occupants the search warrant*
- *Take search warrant back*
- *Search residence*
- *Don't be surprised if little or no drugs are found; happens frequently*
- *If no drugs found, assume occupant disposed of them earlier*
- *Under no circumstance assume CI was lying about presence of drugs*
- *Write on search warrant a list of everything that is to be taken*
- *Leave copy of search warrant with occupant*
- *Don't repair door or other damage, even if drugs not found*

I added that last item on my own. I don't recall Darryl Graves actually making mention of it.

Angela rises to the occasion, literally. She stands, determined to regain control.

"Are you through?"

I detect a hint of sarcasm mixed with a dash of frustration. She really wants to move on.

"I'm through writing, at least for now. I want to talk about this though."

Angela allows her chin to fall to her chest. Her shoulders slump and she plops back into her chair. She slouches and murmurs something under her breath.

I remain standing at the board.

"Good list, everyone. Now, I see four prominent steps not followed by Ron Jones and Darryl Graves. They seemed to be running the operation together. And that makes it even more mysterious. It's one thing if Ron Jones doesn't follow Darryl Graves' procedure. It's another thing if Darryl Graves' doesn't follow his own procedure. He was after all, in charge of one team, responsible for the success and safety of that team.

"Anyway, the first problem is that each entry team should consist of four officers. Ron's team only had three. That would be Ron, Stephen Jones, and Darrell Cooley. Graves' team had four I guess: Graves, Mike Brown, Allen Allday, and Earl Bullock.

I place a big check mark next to the entry team item.

"The second problem is that each security team should have more than one officer, and each security team should arrive in their own car. I'm really confused about the cars, and who rode with whom, but it's clear that each security team had only one person. Terrence Cooley initially was to secure the rear of the Smith apartment. Phillip Allday initially was to secure the rear of the Maye apartment. For some bizarre reason, however, they switched sides because Terrance Cooley got to his position first."

I place a big check mark next to the security team item.

"The third problem is that Ron Jones didn't have his weapon drawn, at least that's what they tell us."

I place a big check mark next to the weapons-not-drawn item.

"The next big step not followed by Ron Jones, as I see it, is this one. Right here. The battering ram."

I put a large check mark next to the battering-ram item.

"At least that's what they tell us. Anybody have any thoughts on that pairing?"

Webbie can no longer restrain himself.

"Here's a thought for you. This is a crock o' crap. He said there was three different agencies involved in the raid, and they each have their own set of rules, and that it was Ron Jones' raid and Ron Jones' rules. And I don't remember him saying half of what you got up there anyway."

"I didn't say these were everyone's rules. In fact, I just said the opposite. I just said that the procedure followed by Ron Jones was different. This list is simply the procedure Darryl Graves would follow, based on his direct testimony, or what we can infer from his testimony. Except for maybe the last item, which I just threw in there. And maybe a few other items which are a bit sarcastic, but you get the point I was trying to make."

Webbie thinks about that for a moment longer than he should have.

"Okay, anybody." I open it to the floor.

They look puzzled.

"The list is telling us something significant."

They stare at the list. I assume they focus on the items with the check marks. I wait a bit, then I underline the weapons-not-drawn and battering-ram items.

I wait quietly, if not patiently.

Marion, the postal worker, sees it first: "Ohhhhhhh!"

The others concentrate harder by squinting.

Community college student Cathy whines: "What?"

Marion simply nods her head and says: "I'll be."

Joyce, the teacher, is the next to see it: "I'll be darn."

Cathy implores her: "Tell us."

And then, finally, we hear from Kyle.

"He's suggesting that Darryl Graves, Stephen Jones, Terrence Cooley, and Darrell Cooley all conspired to falsify the events of that evening, presumably because they have something to hide, something they don't want us to know."

I put the chalk in the holder at the base of the board, and I return to my seat.

Doris asks: "Is that true? Is that what you're saying."

I shrug.

Angela: "I gotta agree with Webbie on this one. You're crazy. There's no way that list tells us anything of the sort."

Webbie: "See. Told ya."

I shrug.

Kyle: "Oh, it's there all right."

Kyle is as animated as I've seen him, which means just barely. He's added a sardonic grin to his appearance, though. It's payback time.

Angela looks at the board again, but can't see it. She adopts Cathy's line: "What?"

Kyle savors the moment. Revenge is a dish best served cold, and all that crap. But revenge is just a part of the reason for Kyle's grin. For the moment, he is in control. Everyone is waiting for him to speak. He savors it, milks it for all it's worth. He lingers until he thinks he's going to lose them, and only then let's them in on the big secret.

"Ron Jones didn't have his weapon drawn because he had a battering ram in his hand. No one kicked any door open. Ron Jones breached the back door with a ram. Cory Maye fired before Ron Jones could drop the ram and draw his weapon."

After a moment of silence, the uproar began. The cackling was like a flock of chickens when the fox arrives. Everyone had an opinion, and Angela's voice rose above us all, trying to get us to settle down.

We lost twenty more precious minutes before she could get us to start considering the next witness. It's settling on her: we might not make it to a verdict tonight.

TESTIMONY OF JIM STONE
Two Days Earlier: Wednesday, January 21, 2004

"State your name, please." >> Jim Stone.

Claiborne "Buddy" McDonald is back for the questioning.

"By whom are you employed?" >> By the Mississippi Bureau of Investigations.

"And were you employed by them on December 26th, 2001?" >> I was.

"And in what capacity were you employed by them at that time?" >> As a special agent.

"On that evening, did you have occasion to be called to an investigation on Mary Street in Prentiss?" >> I was.

"And what was the purpose of being called to that scene?" >> A death investigation where a police officer was fatally shot while serving a search warrant.

"What other officers responded with you?" >> Special Agent Darrell Perkins and Agent Eric Johnson.

Holy nomenclature, Batman! Another Darrell.

"When you arrived at the scene, were you briefed by the officers with respect to what had happened?" >> Agent Johnson, I spoke with him briefly.

"Were you advised that a suspect was in custody?" >> That is correct.

"Were you advised as to who that suspect was?" >> Not by name at that time; only that one was in custody.

"Did you learn where he was in custody, where he was being held?" >> At the Jeff Davis County Sheriff's Department.

"Did you have occasion to proceed to the Jeff Davis County Sheriff's Department?" >> I did.

"When you got there, did you have occasion to determine whether or not the suspect wanted to be interviewed?" >> Myself and Special Agent Perkins escorted Mr. Maye down to an interview room. At that time, he was Mirandized, given the opportunity, he did agree, and he was interviewed.

"Was that interview tape-recorded?" >> Audiotape, yes, sir.

"Do you see Mr. Maye in the courtroom today?

Rhonda Cooper doesn't like it that each prosecution witness is asked to point an accusing finger at Cory Maye. She objects.

"Your Honor, we would object to this continuous reference. I think the witnesses before have already identified Cory Maye as the defendant, he's sitting here at defense table, and we would just object to each witness having to identify Cory Maye for the record."

Judge Eubanks doesn't see it that way.

"Overruled."

"Thank you, Judge. Do you see Mr. Maye in the courtroom today?" >> Yes, he's to my left.

"All right. I'd like the record to reflect that he's identified the defendant. Do you have with you the original Miranda warning statement?" >> I do.

"All right. Could I see that! please?"

It's interesting, to me at least, that the witnesses seem to carry the documentary evidence into the court with them. Stephen (No Relation) Jones brought in one, just one, of the two search warrants. Now Jim Stone brings in the signed Miranda warning.

"Did Mr. Maye sign that in your presence?" >> He did.

"I see you and Agent Perkins signed as witnesses?" >> That is correct.

"At the bottom, under the waiver of rights, that's his signature down there?" >> That is correct.

"Did you or Agent Perkins do anything to threaten him or coerce him or did you promise him anything in order to get him to do the waiver or give you a statement?" >> No, sir.

The audio recording of Cory Maye's interview is played for us. He explained that his daughter was asleep in the back bedroom, and that he was asleep in the living room. He was awakened by a loud noise at the front of the house, and was afraid someone was trying to break in. He rushed to the bedroom, got his gun from the shelf above the bed and inserted the ammo clip, which he kept separate for safety reasons. Just then, there was banging at the back door. As it came open, he dropped to the ground and fired in the direction of the door. He didn't see who was at the door, he just shot at whoever was there coming in.

He heard people yelling at him that they were the police. He pushed his gun towards the door and extended his arms out over his head. They came in and handcuffed him. Then they kicked him. They took him to the police station. It wasn't until he got to the police station that he learned he had shot one of the policemen.

"Okay. I believe that's all the questions I have for Officer Stone."

<<>>

Rhonda Cooper will cross-examine. The other attorney sitting at the defense table never gets to ask questions.

"Good afternoon, Agent Stone. I'm Rhonda Cooper." >> Yes, ma'am.

"Now, the statement that Cory Maye gave to you, was on that Thursday morning, December 27th?" >> That is correct.

"And that was within two or three hours of the incident. Isn't that correct?" >> Yes, ma'am.

"Okay. And the statement was given to you voluntarily, right?" >> That is correct.

"He was very forthcoming about the information?" >> Yes, ma'am.

"Did he appear to be honest in what he shared with you?" >> Yes, ma'am.

"Thank you. Now, I just want to confirm for the jury that when you spoke with Mr. Maye that morning that he did tell you that had the police knocked, he would've opened the door. Is that correct?" >> That's what he stated, yes ma'am.

"And he said that had they knocked and said who they were, that this would not have happened. He would not have shot a police officer?" >> I believe his statement was that if they had knocked on the door and he knew who they were, he would've let them in.

"And he told you that he was scared?" >> That is correct.

"And he did this to protect himself and his daughter." >> He did not say he ran to the back room to protect himself. He only made reference that upon hearing the noise, he left the couch where he was asleep and went to the bedroom.

"Because he was afraid?" >> I'm assuming from the noise, yes, ma'am.

"Okay. Thank you, Agent Stone."

DELIBERATION OF JIM STONE
Friday, January 23, 2004

"Now you've got him doing it."

Angela's looking at me, but pointing at Kyle.

"You mean my main man, Kyle?"

Kyle's grin grows ever so slightly.

"Whatever. And him too."

Now she's pointing at Raymond.

"We're never going to get out of here if you guys make stuff up and refuse to stick to the facts and the evidence, like it says were supposed to do, right here."

She points at the jury instructions, the ones she has yet to read.

Doris tries to reinforce the point: "Do we have to read them to you?"

"Yes, please."

Angela brushes Doris off. "We've been over that. The jury voted. We heard them during the trial. We don't have -- I want to discuss the guy who talked about Cory Mayes' taped confession. What was his name?"

She looks to Doris for the first name, but Doris draws a blank. Doris gives her a shrug instead.

"Anyone?"

No one seems to know. I'm not particularly surprised. With note taking disallowed by the court, I surprised the jury has done as well as it has working from memory. And the tape-recording guy, for lack of a better name, testified the least. Most of the time he was on the stand, we were listening to the tape, not to the witness. That seemed to be his job, get the tape recording into evidence.

Angela: "Well, it doesn't make any difference what he said, anyway. It's what Mayes said. He admitted it. They Mirandized him, and he admitted it. He said he shot him, pure and simple. Case closed. I can't seriously imagine there's all that much to discuss here. So you can go on with your lists, and make up all sorts of hare-brained theories, but Cory Maye admitted it. Pure and simple."

I wait for someone from the recently-energized jury to begin the discussion.

And I wait.

And I ....

"He never said he shot Ron Jones."

It's Kyle. I'd forgotten about him already.

"He said he fired towards the door. He didn't know they were the police. He didn't know he shot anyone until they told him at the station. That's what he said. And the witness, the guy from the Mississippi Bureau of Investigations said even he thought Cory Maye was being truthful when he said that."

Angela's clearly frustrated by her increasingly argumentative jury.

"It doesn't make any difference," she retorts. "He had to know they were cops. They yelled it over and over. The people next door could hear. You can't tell me he couldn't hear. And he peeked out the window. He had to know they were cops, and he shot in their direction when they came in. He admitted that. You had to have heard it. He admitted it. That's capital murder."

Webbie: "Damn straight."

Jerry: "Well there's an original thought."

Webbie: "Piss off."

Angela calls for a truce.

"Look we've been going for a while. Everyone's tired. Let's take a break. A ten minute break."

Several people scramble for the bathroom. Kyle gets up, walks to the evidence box, and thumbs through the paperwork. He pulls out the jury instructions, returns to his seat, and begins flipping through the stapled pages. He finds what he's hunting for and begins reading. He flips another page, and reads. And another.

Angela watches him like a hawk. While he's reading, she gets up and casually strolls towards the exit door, peeking over his shoulder as she walks by. She purses her lips as if she's just swallowed a bee, continues to the door, and knocks on it from the inside.

The bailiff opens the door slightly. Angela speaks to him in hushed tones. I'm reasonably close to the door so I can hear that she's asking for drinks and snacks. The bailiff seems sympathetic. He closes the door behind him as he leaves.

Angela returns to her seat, surreptitiously checking out Kyle's reading material on the way back. As she is sitting down, Kyle is standing up. He walks to the chalkboard, then uses the remaining free space to write his own bulleted list.

The State Must Prove The Following Beyond A Reasonable Doubt:
- *The shooting took place in Jefferson Davis County (undisputed)*
- *The shooting took place on or about Dec 26, 2001 (undisputed)*
- *Cory Maye willfully, not accidentally, killed Ron Jones (undisputed)*
- *Cory Maye did not act in self-defense*

For The Three Different Charges, The State Must Also Prove:
- *For Capital Murder: Cory Maye knew victim was a peace officer*
- *For Murder: Cory Maye acted with a depraved heart*
- *For Manslaughter: Cory Maye acted with negligence*

Depraved Heart:
- *Utter disregard and indifference to human life*

Self defense:
- *Cory Maye must have been in actual, present, and urgent danger OR*
- *Cory Maye must have had reasonable grounds to believe the victim intended to kill or do great bodily harm to himself or his family.*

As Kyle nears the end of his list, the bailiff returns with bottled drinks and packaged snacks. I score a diet Pepsi and a bag of peanuts as he passes. The Pepsi is cold, the peanuts are salty, and life is good for those few moments surrounding the first taste of each. Pop tabs pop, wrappers rip, and morale rebounds, at least a bit, at least for now.

Kyle has the floor, literally, and has no intention of giving it up. He speaks while we munch and crunch.

"Okay, this isn't so hard to understand. I've read through the instructions," which he holds high in one hand, "and I've summarized everything on the board."

He lowers his hand and stands to the side just a bit, making sure everyone can view his handiwork.

"The first three items are the same, regardless of whatever charge we will be voting on. They just specify the where and when of the shooting, and that it wasn't an accident. The defense did not dispute these points, so I think we can presume them to be proven beyond a reasonable doubt."

"Also we must find that Cory Maye did not act in self-defense. There's two ways he could have acted in self-defense: either there was a real and immediate threat to his safety or his daughter's safety, or he had a reasonable belief that there was. The defense argued the second one, it seems like.

"So this seems to be the logic tree. If we conclude that Cory Maye had good reason to believe he or his daughter was threatened of life or limb, we have no choice but to vote Not Guilty on each charge.

"We vote first on the capital murder charge. That charge requires that the prosecution prove beyond a reasonable doubt that Cory Maye was not acting in self-defense and also that Cory Maye knew the people trying to get in were police. I'm not saying he did or didn't know, I'm just describing the instructions that we're supposed to follow.

"If we find him Guilty of capital murder, that's it. We go back into the courtroom for some more testimony I guess, about whether or not he should be executed. If we find him Not Guilty, however, then we move on to the plain murder charge.

"To find Cory Maye guilty of plain murder, we must conclude that he acted not in self-defense, but instead with a depraved heart. I put the definition up there."

He points to the board.

"It just means that he showed an utter disregard and indifference to human life when he shot at whoever was coming through the door. Again, I'm not saying that's what he did, just talking about the rules we're supposed to follow.

"Finally, if we don't find him guilty of plain murder, then we vote on manslaughter. The only difference there is that he acted negligently rather than with a depraved heart. He was simply careless. It's not that he didn't care about human life, it's that he was just careless.

"So the first thing we need to do, no matter what, once we get to voting, is decide whether or not he acted in self-defense. I'm not saying he did or he didn't. I want to listen to what you all have to say before I make up my mind."

And with that performance complete, he walks to the evidence box, suspends the jury instructions above it for just a moment, and drops them in. He returns to his seat and settles into his prim and proper seating position. He looks to the snack tray. Not much left there. Just a Mr. Pibb, three bottles of Dasani water, and a small bag of Funyuns.

I smile at him and pop the last peanut into my mouth.

TESTIMONY OF ERIC JOHNSON
Two Days Earlier: Wednesday, January 21, 2004

Looks like Buddy is going to examine the next witness as well.

"Would you state your name, please." >> Eric Johnson.

"And by whom are you employed?" >> The Mississippi Bureau of Investigation.

"Were you employed by them on December 26, 2001?" >> Yes, sir, I was.

"And during that month or on that date, did you have occasion to be called to Prentiss, Mississippi, to conduct an investigation with respect to the shooting of an officer?" >> I did.

"When you arrived at that location, what was the principal role that you played?" >> Upon my arrival on the date in question, Chief Deputy Ronnie Barnes with the Jefferson Davis County Sheriff's Department informed me that in an execution of a search warrant where several officers were involved, that a particular officer named Ron Jones had sustained a gunshot wound. At that time I was notified that Officer Jones had died as a result of his injuries.

"And were you involved in the collection of evidence?" >> Yes, I was.

"And the investigation of the crime scene?" >> Yes, sir, once we secured the scene, prepared a search warrant to preserve the integrity of the evidence therein, and once the search warrant was signed, that's when we made entrance for the purpose of collection of evidence and photographing inside the residence.

"Now, there'd been a previous search warrant, but this search warrant was because it was a homicide scene. Is that correct?" >> That is correct, sir.

"How did you begin going through the house?" >> As I recall, we made a cursory look through the house. But when we entered the back, we documented the time we entered. I can reflect those times based on my notes. As I reflect in my notes, approximately four a.m. on the 27th, the early morning hours of the 27th, I made entry into the house with Investigator Perkins, who also works in my office, and began to collect evidence.

It seems everybody but the jurors can take notes. The attorneys take copious notes. The judge takes occasional notes. There seem to be reporters in the gallery, and they take notes. Now the witness is referring back to his notes before answering the question. He obviously took notes. We jurors are the only ones expected to rely on our so-called collective memory.

Anyway, Buddy now shows Eric (Notes) Johnson a series of photos and asks if he can identify them.

That is the weapon which was inside the back bedroom of the residence. It is a Lorcin brand .380 caliber handgun.

That is a shell casing that was recovered in the back bedroom of the residence in question.

That is a close-up shot of the two shell casings found separate from the first, also in the back bedroom.

That is a bullet hole in the back door frame, facing on the inside of the bedroom.

"Do your notes reflect how far it was from the bottom of the door to that hole? >> Yes. It was 57.5 inches from the floor up and 4.5 inches to the right to the center of the projectile hole.

"Do you recall anything about the projectile entry point itself? Could you tell if it went in at an angle, straight on, or what?" >> Based on what I recall about that and also looking at the photograph, the entry that the projectile made into the wall appeared to be on more of a level-plane-type trajectory when it hits it. What I have seen in the past in different things is, had it been at an angle, it would have put more of a mark or a groove. Had it went into the wood paneling, or the wood in this particular case, on the bottom side or at a downward angle, it would've caused more disturbance from the top angle. But as you can see in the picture, the paint on this particular wall is kind of flaked off. The hole looks round and smooth.

Rhonda Cooper asks to approach the bench. Judge Eubanks indicates it's fine with him, so Rhonda and Buddy amble on up. The discussion seems amiable enough. They chat for a while, then Buddy returns and changes his line of questioning.

"And what is that?" >> This photograph is Officer Ron Jones' duty weapon, handgun.

"What is that stuck between the frame of the gun and the holster?" >> It's grass.

"And is that the condition the weapon and holster were in at the time that you received it?" >> If I may reflect to my notes once again, I examined the weapon in the wee hours of that morning, around 5:50. The weapon in question is a Beretta model 96. It is a .40 caliber handgun. And when I looked at the weapon, it had 11 rounds in it. As the picture depicts, that is grass from where Officer Jones had fallen outside the residence. The weapon was still secure in the holster.

"Is a .40 caliber weapon a different caliber than a .380?" >> Yes, sir, it is.

Now Buddy hands him an actual handgun, not just a photo.

"What is that?" >> This is the Lorcin model .380 semi-automatic handgun that I recovered from the scene.

"Did you have occasion to have that gun tested?" >> Yes, I did.

"Where did you send it for testing and analysis?" >> I sent the gun and other items of evidence that was collected for examination to the Mississippi State Crime Lab.

"And were you present when a projectile was removed from Ron Jones' body?" >> Yes, I was.

"And was that projectile sent to the crime laboratory?" >> It was.

"I ask if you can identify that?" >> That is the projectile that was recovered from the body of Ron Jones.

"Can you identify that?" >> This is a Mississippi Crime Laboratory report indicating items that were submitted and tested or cross-tested between the two. In this particular one, it is referring in particular to the Lorcin .380 that I have here, and to the testing of the projectiles.

"What was the result that you received back from the crime laboratory?" >> It says the bullet recovered from Officer Jones' body and the bullet recovered from the back door facing were both fired from the Lorcin .380 that I have here in my hands.

"And that is the gun that was recovered at Maye's apartment." >> Yes it is.

"Did you submit the cartridges that have been introduced into evidence to the crime laboratory for comparison with the Lorcin .380 pistol that was recovered at the scene?" >> I did submit the shell casings or the cartridges, yes.

"What were the results of that examination?" >> I'm going to refer to the crime lab report. Two cartridge casings were fired from the Lorcin .380 that I have in my hands. The third cartridge case bears class and some individual characteristics consistent with those produced by this gun, but could not be positively included or excluded as having been fired from this the gun to the exclusion of all other firearms bearing the same class characteristics.

"All right. And did you find that unusual?" >> No, I didn't find it unusual.

"I believe that's all the questions we have."

<<>>

Rhonda Cooper with the cross-examination.

"Agent Johnson?" >> Yes, ma'am.

"You are the official investigator for the State of Mississippi for this case. Is that correct?" >> I happened to be the one on call that particular night.

"Okay. Well, in that you were the one on call, are you not or have you not been considered as the official investigator for this case?" >> Not necessarily. In a case of this magnitude, it is not uncommon for the rest of the guys or some of the guys in my office to come out and assist. A one-man gang in this situation would've been a burden.

"Okay. But you are the individual who filed the charges?" >> That is correct.

"And signed the affidavits?" >> Yes, ma'am.

"And you also obtained from Judge Kruger, as you stated earlier, a warrant to search this apartment occupied by Cory Maye?" >> Yes, ma'am.

"And you've been referring to your notebook there. Do you have the search warrant that you obtained from Judge Kruger?" >> No, I do not. However, I do have a copy of it. In referring to my copy of the affidavit for search warrant, it says 1728 Mary Street, apartment number 1, which is the apartment in question here.

"Okay. And if you'll look at the search warrant that was actually signed by Judge Kruger, does that also say apartment 1?" >> Yes, correct, my copy does say search warrant 1728 Mary Street, apartment number 1. And it does bear Donald Kruger's signature.

"But as we move this up, if you look to the left of the diagram where the areas in the house or the apartment as they're presented, what address does that bear?" >> It appears to be 528 Mary Street, but it says apartment number 2.

"So that's the apartment that's going to be Jamie Smith's apartment, would it not?" >> That's correct.

"But we do know the address is actually 1728." >> I believe there was a discrepancy that night, was it 528 or 1728. And based on the search warrant and the affidavit for search warrant prepared, it was our determination at the time that it was 1728.

"And the apartment 2, now, does not in any way refer to Cory Maye's apartment, does it?" >> No, ma'am. The reason that was printed there depicts that it was a duplex. In other words, this side is where apartment 2 was at.

"I think you testified about the cloth that is beneath the blinds." >> Yes, ma'am, I did.

"And that cloth would have been facing the window or closest to the window, between the window and the blinds, correct?" >> The cloth is actually between the window panes and the pulled down blinds.

"And in your investigation, did that cover the entire pane?" >> Yes. As I recall, it extended from the top down.

"Okay. And with that, no light can be seen from inside this room to the outside." >> I couldn't speculate because I wasn't there when the initial search warrant and entry was gained in the apartment. I was fifty-three minutes later because I live quite a piece away. So I don't know what the condition was at that time.

"Well, when you arrived, did you see the front of the apartment?" >> Yes.

"Were the lights on at that time?" >> The outside porch light was on, which would if I can describe it best, caused some sort of a night blindness because you've got this outside porch light on. It would be hard to see beyond that, what was inside. But do I recall? I don't recall whether the lights were on in there, but I do know the outside porch light was on, based on the photographs we saw earlier.

"When you got inside, were the lights on in this room? Do you recall that?" >> Yeah, the lights were on when I got there.

"You're telling the jury that as you approached this building, because of the outside light, you couldn't see whether or not there was light on inside?" >> I do not know if the lights were on inside when I arrived.

"But this cloth that separates the blinds and the windowpane is dark in color, is it not? >> Yes, it is.

"You read the results of the crime lab report for the firearm. Do you have a copy of that?" >> Yes, ma'am, I do.

"Now, there have been lots of photographs of the door casing with the projectile. Now, there's no bullet in the door, the actual back door to that apartment unit, was there?" >> No, ma'am, there was not.

"Now, are you telling the ladies and gentlemen of this jury that one shell casing could not be positively included or excluded?" >> That is correct.

"There was three shell casings. And you're saying that one could not be included or excluded as having been fired from the gun?" >> That is correct, based on his report.

"Thank you, Your Honor."

<<>>

Buddy McDowell with the redirect.

"Do you know what they mean when they say class characteristics?" >> Yes, sir. The shell casing was a .380. It matched the class, the size, the characteristics. But it's been my understanding through experience in this line of work that it's not uncommon sometimes for the impression of the chamber where the cartridge is to not match because when you fire a weapon, a weapon causes friction, you have heat. You have variances like that that may not match the other two shell casings exactly. And I think that was what I understood to be the problem in this situation. Not necessarily a problem, but just the facts of it.

"And that's why they couldn't include or exclude it?" >> That's correct.

"They'll only include it if they're absolutely certain." >> That's correct.

"In the course of your investigation, was there any evidence found that indicated that any other firearm other than the Lorcin had been found?" >> No, none.

"I believe that's all the questions we have."

Kyle loosens his tie, ever so slightly. In its new state, it would look nicely-knotted on anyone else. On Kyle, it looks downright casual. His unauthorized trip to the chalkboard must have been draining.

It seems though as if Angela intends to let Kyle's hard work go by without comment.

"Okay. The next witness was ..."

But Kyle's not yet done. Something is boiling inside him, and the slightly-loosened tie allows it to escape. He speaks, without being called upon, without having been asked a question. When he starts, his voice is just a bit too high, but his confidence builds with each word.

"I summarized the instructions up there," he says, referring to the chalkboard, "because you," referring to Angela, "said that he," referring to Cory Maye, "confessed to shooting Officer Jones. That's correct as far as it goes, but it is insufficient for us to perform our designated function as jurors. We must weigh all the evidence against all the elements of the crime that the prosecution must prove.

"The primary difference among the four possibilities of capital murder, murder, manslaughter, and self-defense is what Cory Maye knew or believed at the moment he shot towards the doorway. If he knew it was a peace officer coming through the door, then he is guilty of capital murder. That's what the jury instructions say.

"He told the police officer who made the recording that he didn't know it was the police who were trying to get in. The police officer said even he believed Cory Maye was being truthful. The state's own witness said he believed Cory Maye was being truthful when he said that he didn't know it was a police officer out there."

Then Kyle ices the cake.

"You left that part out, Angela."

Angela is clearly caught off guard that Kyle would speak to her so bluntly. She takes a moment to gather her thoughts. She shocks me with her response.

"You're right, Kyle. I gave an incomplete and biased summary. Thank you for correcting me."

She seems absolutely sincere.

"I think that what's-his-name's testimony was pretty much as you stated it. He did say he believed Cory Maye when Maye said he didn't know it was the police. That's true. It doesn't mean, of course, that we have to believe him.

After all, they were yelling police, loudly and repeatedly, and several officers testified that someone peeked out, or a least moved the curtains enough to peek out. And the neighbors apparently had no trouble hearing, but you are right. The witness testified that he believed Cory Maye when Maye said he didn't know they were police."

Angela concedes the battle, if not the war. Kyle is gracious in victory.

"Thank you."

And Angela moves on. I suspect that was her motive for not arguing with Kyle.

"We need to talk about the next witness. Doris, do you remember his name?"

She does.

"Eric."

"Anybody know the last name?"

No one speaks up. Maybe it's because they weren't mentioned by name frequently by the officers who were there when Ron Jones was shot. Maybe that's why we can't remember their names.

"Okay, we were talking about Eric, the other guy from the Bureau of Investigation. He said they recovered two bullets: one from the door frame and one from Ron Jones. He said they both matched the handgun found in Cory Maye's apartment. No one disputed that. Cory Maye did not dispute that he fired the handgun. It seems that even we won't be arguing over who shot Ron Jones."

She looks at me. I shrug my shoulders ever so slightly.

"They found three shell casings. Two matched the gun, one only matched the type of gun or something like that. He said though that there was no evidence anyone else fired a gun."

Jerry the welder helps her out.

"Cory Maye fired a .38 caliber Lorcin. Ron Jones carried a .40 caliber Beretta 96. You could easily tell the difference between a .38 and a .40 caliber casing. If it had been a .40 caliber casing, I'm guessing his attorney would have been making a big deal of it. Instead, this guy says same class and characteristics, so we can figure it's a .38 caliber casing, just like the others. They all match, at least that's what he said."

Raymond the pharmacist picks it up from there.

"And he said the bullet hole in the door was fifty-some inches off the ground. I remember it was just under five feet, less than sixty inches. And he said the bullet went straight in. I think that means Cory Maye was standing up when he fired that one, even though he said he was laying down. I don't see a way around that."

I don't want that one to slip by unchallenged.

"If you were going to measure the angle at which the bullet entered the door frame, how would you do it?"

"What do you mean?"

"Would you just look at a picture? Remember, Eric was right there. He was investigating the shooting. He finds a bullet in the door frame. Put yourself in his spot. What would you do?"

"Well, I guess I would take the bullet out first."

"I assume you would be careful not to damage the bullet any further, and careful as well not to damage the door frame any further. I assume you would take pictures before you removed the bullet, and after."

"Yes. I guess so."

"So now you have the bullet out, and you have a nice clean hole in the door frame. How would you measure the angle the bullet was travelling as it entered the wood? You're right there, remember. Would you just look at the picture, or just look at the hole, or would could you think of a better way of estimating the angle."

"I would put a stick in it, a rod, something like that. That's what I'd do, I guess. It would show which way the bullet came in."

"Then I wish you had been investigating the crime scene, instead of Eric 'I Can Tell From The Hole' What's-His-Name. That way we would know if the bullet came in horizontally or came in from the floor. That way we would know if Cory was standing or lying down. They must have known they could do that. They're crime scene investigators, for God's sake. The very fact that they're giving us the 'hole was kinda round' story tells me that they're hiding something from us. It makes me suspicious as to what else they might be hiding."

Raymond concedes the point graciously.

"So maybe we can't figure out from his testimony the defendant was standing up or laying down."

"I believe you're right about that. Maybe they don't want us to figure it out."

Angela's had enough.

"Enough with the conspiracy theories. Really. He said he could tell from the paint, and he said it went in almost parallel to the floor. That's the evidence. He's the expert. You're just making things up."

"I'm not making anything up, at least not yet. It was Raymond's theory. He made it up. I just agreed with him."

Raymond defends himself.

"He asked me what I thought. I told him. And I stand by it. And don't start telling us how to think now. Just because you're the foreman ..."

He leaves it at that, allowing the gender confusion to hang in the air. Angela seems to have upset another juror.

"Look. We're all tired," she says. "I'm not trying to make anyone angry, really. If you think this is easy up here then -- I'm sorry."

The wrangling is taking a toll. It's going to get worse. Angela is seemingly trying to reform her ways.

"Does anyone else have anything they would like to add about this witness?"

The room is quiet.

"Then the next witness is Darrell Cooley."

Amazing. Angela remembers both the first and last name. Doris is crushed.

TESTIMONY OF DARRELL COOLEY
Yesterday: Thursday, January 21, 2004

"Would you state your name for us." >> Darrell Cooley.

So this is Darrell (Front Door Kicker) Cooley. I've been hoping to hear from him. Mr. Miller will be asking the questions.

"Darrell, where are you employed?" >> I work for Bassfield Police Department and Prentiss Police Department.

"I want to call your attention to December 26, 2001. Do you remember that day?" >> Yes, sir.

"Did you get a call to go to Prentiss that day?" >> The chief got a call.

"And were you contacted?" >> Yes, sir.

"Who contacted you?" >> Earl Bullock. He's the constable and the chief in Bassfield. I got my gear together, and we went to Prentiss.

"When you got to Prentiss, where did you go?" >> I went to the police department in Prentiss. Officer Ron Jones had said that he needed some help serving some search warrants. We all met inside. Officer Jones and Officer Graves went over where we were going and what we were going to do.

"What were y'all going to do?" >> We were going to serve search warrants on Mary Street at a duplex.

"How many?" >> Two.

"Did you see the search warrants?" >> I saw one.

"Which one was that?" >> I saw the one for apartment 1, which is the right apartment looking at the duplex.

"Do you know who was in that apartment?" >> I didn't know the name of the person that was going to be in it, no.

"Did you find out later who was in that apartment?" >> Yes, sir. It was Cory Maye.

"Did y'all divide up in teams?" >> Yes, sir. I was on Ron Jones' team. It was myself, Stephen Jones, and Ron Jones.

"Who was on the other team?" >> Mike Brown, Darryl Graves and Allen Allday, I think.

"Who was in charge of the team you were with?" >> Ron Jones.

"How did you go to the apartment on Mary Street?" >> I rode with Stephen Jones and Ron Jones. It was a Prentiss Police Department car.

"Was it a marked car?" >> Yes, sir. Parked right out front of the house. We exited the vehicle and went to the front porch. Me and Ron went up on the front porch. I believe Stephen stayed down on the ground right by the steps.

I recall Stephen (No Relation) Jones testified that it was he who went on the porch with Cooley, and Ron Jones who stayed at the bottom of the steps.

"I show you what's been marked as Exhibit 1. Can you see that, Officer Cooley?" >> Yes, sir. That's the duplex on Mary Street. Apartment 1 is on the right, apartment 2 is on the left.

"The apartment you went to was which one?" >> The one on the right, apartment 1. We went up on the front porch, right there to where the door is.

"I show you what's been marked as Exhibit 5. Can you identify that for me?" >> Yes, sir. That's the front porch at Mary Street. The one I went to.

"Where did you go?" >> We come up on the front porch. Myself and Ron Jones went to the door. I tried to open the door, and the door was locked. I announced "police," and someone behind me announced "search warrant," and then I kicked the front door.

"Okay. What happened when you kicked the front door?" >> Nothing.

"Door didn't open?" >> Door didn't open.

"Okay. How did you announce 'police'?" >> We were standing right about where the door handle is, kind of by the wall. And I hollered "police," and then I turned away and then just kicked straight into the door.

"You said you hollered. Did you do that loudly?" >> Yes, sir.

"What did you do then?" >> Stepped back again straight away from the door, hollered "police" again straight at the door, and then tried kicking it again.

"Okay. Did anyone besides you holler that time?" >> Yeah, someone behind me.

"Who was it?" >> I can't tell you.

"What did they yell?" >> "Search warrant."

"What happened when you kicked the door a second time?" >> Nothing.

"Did you notice anything after that?" >> Stephen Jones said, "There is a light," and I looked back in towards the window on the door, and I could see a light back to the left side of the door.

"Did you see a light before that time?" >> No, sir.

"Did anyone from the house call out and ask who's there?" >> No sir.

"Did anyone open the door?" >> No, sir.

"What did you do after you saw the light?" >> After we saw the light, I backed up and I hollered "police," and then I shouldered the center of the door just below the window.

"What do you mean when you say shouldered the door?" >> I backed up and, instead of kicking with my foot, I backed up and hit it with my shoulder.

"When you shouldered the door, what happened to the door?" >> Nothing.

"What did you do after that?" >> Ron Jones and Stephen Jones left the front. Ron told me to stay in the front. So I backed down off the steps and got just to the left of the steps.

"Where did Ron and Stephen go?" >> They went to the back of the house. The next thing I heard was, I heard some crash in the back. It sounded like someone kicking the door back there. And then I heard "police" a few seconds later then the gunshots.

"Okay. You heard a crash like someone kicking a door, 'police,' and gunshots?" >> Right.

"How many gunshots did you hear?" >> I thought I heard five.

Darrell (Front Door Kicker) Cooley heard five shots. Terrance (Cover the Rear) Cooley testified he heard three to four shots. Stephen (No Relation) Jones testified he heard three.

"Okay. And what happened after that?" >> I left the front porch, went around the side of the house and went down the side of the house and met Ron Jones coming back around the corner towards the front. Ron was still upright. He started crouching down. He said, "Get me to the hospital, I been hit." And I said, "Where?" He said in his stomach. He went to his knees, stated, "Good Lord, help," and then collapsed on the ground. I grabbed Ron as he was going down, rolled him up towards the house because I didn't know what was going on inside. Got him up close to the house, pulled his vest off and pulled his jacket back and pulled his vest off.

"Okay. Did you notice where Ron's gun was?" >> It was still in his holster.

"And what did you do after that?" >> After that, Stephen Jones pulled the car up. I was calling for an ambulance on the radio. Stephen Jones pulled the car up, and I picked Ron up, his back towards me, drug him over to the back of the car. Darryl Graves grabbed me and pulled me on into the car. I pulled Ron in the car on top of me and Stephen got Ron's feet, and we went to the hospital.

"When you got to the hospital, did you learn the condition of Ron Jones?" >> It was a little bit later. I know they were in there working on him. Chief Jones showed up and then Dr. Lott come out to talk to Chief Jones. And then I found out.

"Okay. And what did you find out about Ron?" >> That Ron didn't make it, that he had died.

"We tender the witness, Your Honor.

<<>>

Rhonda Cooper, as is always the case, cross-examines the State's witness.

"Good morning, Officer Cooley." >> Good morning.

"Do you recall our meeting about two years ago in Prentiss for the preliminary hearing?" >> Yes, sir. Yes, ma'am.

He seems a bit nervous.

"I recall your testimony at that time is that there were no lights on inside, that it was dark inside. Do you recall that?" >> When we went up on the porch, yes, ma'am.

"Now, you just told the ladies and gentlemen of this jury that was it Stephen Jones who told you there was a light on inside?" >> Stephen told me after I had kicked the door, Stephen stated, "There's a light." And I turned and looked back towards the door and could see a light back to the left side of the door.

"So let's just kind of break it down this morning. Where were you standing when Stephen Jones told you that?" >> I was standing right by the doorknob, and I turned back over my shoulder and looked back into the windows on the door.

"You were able to see through the windows on the door?" >> I was able to see a light back to the left side of the door.

"How was it that Stephen Jones was able tell you that there was a light on inside?" >> I don't know. He stated, "There's a light on." I looked back over my shoulder because I was standing almost in front of the door. I looked back over my shoulder. I could see a light shining through the window. And then I stepped between the window and the door.

"To the right between the window and the door?" >> Right.

"And where was Stephen when he told you?" >> I can't tell you where he was standing.

"Was he on the front porch?" >> I can't tell you. I don't remember.

"Are you able to tell the ladies and gentlemen of this jury how it was that he was able to tell you there was a light on inside?" >> No ma'am. I can't tell you. I have no idea how he knew there was a light come on inside.

"What, if any, was the discussion about this search warrant?" >> We talked. They drew a diagram of the duplex on a board at Prentiss Police Department, and we talked about who would go into what side, what was supposed to be in there and what wasn't supposed to be in there.

"Who drew the diagram?" >> Darryl Graves, I believe, is the one that drew the diagram on the board.

Darrell (Front Door Kicker) Cooley testifies that Darryl (Task Force) Graves drew the diagram.

"And the diagram, what did it consist of?" >> What the inside -- what the house looked like. Just kind of a basic layout of the house.

"His diagram included the inside of the house?" >> It included a basic layout of the house. This is the front door …

"Inside or outside?" >> I don't remember whether it showed all the inside rooms or not.

"But you do recall what?" >> It showed the front door and the back door.

"Of the entire property?" >> I don't remember.

"Well, when you saw the layout, you were aware that it was two front doors and two back doors?" >> Correct.

"You never went inside either of these apartments, did you?" >> No, ma'am.

"Had you ever executed search warrants with Ron Jones before?" >> Yes, ma'am.

"And in executing this search warrant, did he tell you that he'd done surveillance on this property?" >> He said that he had been working on this property for a while and that he had a CI that said that the drugs were supposed to be there and that there weren't supposed to be any weapons in the house.

"Did he tell you whether or not he had done any surveillance on the property at 1728 Mary Street?" >> No, ma'am.

"Did he tell you whether or not there had been a controlled buy involving the CI?" >> No, ma'am.

"And basically, you all participated in the execution of this search warrant based on what Ron Jones said someone else had told him. Isn't that correct?" >> We participated in the search warrant.

"Based on what Ron Jones said someone had told him. Isn't that correct?" >> He told me that he had been investigating.

"Did he tell you what that investigation included?" >> No, ma'am.

"You stayed at the front while Ron Jones and Stephen Jones went to the back?" >> Yes, ma'am.

"What were you doing while you were posted at the front?" >> I was just standing there in case anyone come out the front door.

"Did you hear anything going on inside?" >> I heard what was going on towards the back of the house.

"On the outside?" >> And then the gunshots.

"No, before that, as you stood on the front, as Ron Jones and Stephen Jones went to the back, did you hear anything going on within the house?" >> No, ma'am.

"Did you hear anything that was going on to the left of you?" >> Well, they had already entered the house to the left of us. The apartment to the left.

"Were you able to hear what was going on over there?" >> No, ma'am.

"You couldn't hear anything." >> No, ma'am.

"Did you announce 'police'?" >> Yes, ma'am.

"When?" >> Before I hit the front door the first time, the second time, and the third time.

"Okay. Before you hit the front door the first time, where were you?" >> I was standing just about where the door handle is. I checked the door handle. I checked the door handle and then, whenever I hollered "police," then I stepped back straight away from the door, and I kicked the front door.

"Well, how much time passed between your pulling on it and kicking it?" >> I couldn't tell you. I don't know.

"Seconds?" >> I don't know.

"Enough time for somebody to respond? Or was it simultaneous, snatching on the door and kicking at the door?" >> No, ma'am.

"How much time passed?" >> We usually wait a few minutes -- a few seconds, not minutes, wait a few seconds and then kick the door.

"Why are you usually kicking the door?" >> Well, I've made many entries on search warrants.

"By kicking the door in?" >> Yes, ma'am.

"And in doing that, did you have your gun drawn?" >> I don't recollect whether I had it drawn at that time or not.

"No, no, no, no, no. I'm not -- just stay with me here. On these occasions where you said you usually kicked the door in so that you can gain entry, have you had your gun drawn?" >> Yes, ma'am.

"Now, let's come to Wednesday, December 26. Did you have your gun drawn as you stood at this front door?" >> I don't remember whether I had it drawn or not.

"Come on, now. Come on. You lost your friend, didn't you? You've been able to come in here and tell the jury particulars about that. You tell this jury whether or not you had your gun drawn." >> I don't remember whether I had it drawn or not.

"Did Stephen Jones have his gun drawn?" >> I don't know.

"Did Ron Jones have his gun drawn?" >> I don't know.

"Why would you have not had your gun drawn and you're executing a search warrant?" >> Don't know.

"What does your protocol tell you to do? What does your training tell you to do when you're executing a search warrant?" >> Enter the house with your gun drawn.

"And you do that why?" >> For safety reasons. If they fire at you, you fire back.

"Let's talk about officer safety since you brought that up. What's more important in executing a search warrant, officer safety or going to get whatever it is you've stated in your search warrant that you're going to get?" >> Everybody's safety.

"So officer safety is more important than obtaining whatever is stated in that search warrant. Am I correct?" >> Everybody's safety is more important than that search warrant.

"Who's the everybody that you're referring to?" >> Everybody. Where you're serving the search warrant, the officers' safety, and everybody around the area where you're serving the search warrant.

"So that's more important than effecting the object of the search warrant, correct?" >> Yes, ma'am.

"Did you ever go to the back?" >> I went to the side of the house; never went to the back.

"Okay. What happened at the side of the house that kept you from going on to the back of the house?" >> Officer Jones was shot. I started around the back of the house, and he came around the side of the house where I was at.

"So you were not present when Ron Jones made the decision to forget about trying to get into that apartment from the back. You weren't present when that conversation took place." >> No, ma'am.

"And you said Ron Jones had the search warrant?" >> Yes, ma'am.

"Where was it?" >> When we were on the front porch, he had it in his hand.

"Okay. And then, when you saw him on the side of the house?" >> I couldn't tell you where it was at.

"Was it still in his hand?" >> I couldn't tell you whether it was in his hand or not.

"You told the ladies and gentlemen this morning that you assisted him in removing his vest?" No, I didn't assist him, he was already out. He was already unconscious. I pulled his vest and his jacket off.

"Did you think this apartment was empty?" >> I couldn't say whether it was empty or not.

"What did you think? As you stood there trying to get in it without your gun drawn, what did you think?" >> I don' t know.

"Were you thinking?" >> Yes, ma'am.

"What were you thinking?" >> The whole time, who was in it and how to get in there.

"But was there any indication that there was anybody inside?" >> When the light come on.

"Did you draw your gun when the light came on? Because then you are telling these people that that indicated to you someone was in there." >> I don't remember whether I drew my gun then or I already had it drawn.

"I understood you to say that you only saw one warrant." >> I only looked at one warrant.

"You just looked at it. You didn't know any of the particulars about it?" >> No, ma'am.

"And when you looked at it at that time, who had it?" >> Ron Jones.

"You didn't see anybody inside apartment, did you?" >> No, ma'am.

"And that door that you were snatching on and kicking, it was secured, wasn't it?" >> Yes, ma'am.

"Were you able to get that screen door open?" >> I didn't mess with the screen door.

"What door did you mess with?" >> The main door.

"This door that's shown here? The main door. Were you able to get it open?" >> No, ma' am.

"Were you aware of the screen door or anything about the screen door?" >> Not the screen door, no, ma'am.

"Do you know how the screen door got opened?" >> No, ma'am.

"Now, you said that you heard what you thought were five shots?" >> That's what I thought I heard.

"But you know now that the evidence says there were only three shots. Correct?" >> Yes, ma'am.

"Did any officers fire two shots?" >> Not to my knowledge.

"Thank you, Officer Cooley."

<<>>

Mr. Miller has some redirect.

"When you arrived at the Prentiss Police Department, were you briefed on what y'all were going to do?" >> Yes, ma'am. Yes, sir."

Cooley still seems a little rattled.

"And who did that?" >> Ron Jones and Darryl Graves went over what we were going to do.

"Did anyone mention anything about weapons?" >> Ron Jones stated that there was not supposed to be any weapons in the residence.

"What was supposed to be in the residence?" >> It was supposed to be crack cocaine and marijuana.

"No further questions, Your Honor."

DELIBERATION OF DARRELL COOLEY
Friday, January 23, 2004

Cathy is bugged about the curtains. She doesn't wait for Angela's summary. She takes a deep breath and jumps right in.

"This guy's testimony about the curtains didn't do a whole lot to make things clearer. We already have confusing testimony by the first witness about the curtains. He never mentioned anything about seeing lights before he sprang it on the defense on ...uh...Wednesday? Yeah, Wednesday. Seems longer. Anyway, then he says he remembers the blinds on the wall window, then the door window, then the wall window. And I don't see how he could see through the door window anyway, because he was standing in front of the wall window. And he said the light was at the left rear. If he was in front of the wall window, and saw a small bit of light through the door window, there's no way he would tell if it came from the left rear of the house. But that's what he said.

"Now this guy gets up and does almost the same thing as the first guy. He didn't say anything about a light or blinds moving until the trial, until yesterday. At least he didn't say anything to the defense. And he confused me just as much as the first guy did, 'cause he kept saying 'I looked over my shoulder and I could see the light.' What's he mean he looked over his shoulder? Wasn't he facing the door?" He said he kicked the door then someone said there's a light on, and he looked over his shoulder. Wouldn't he be looking at the street? It just doesn't make any sense, and it makes me suspicious. Sorry. I'm really nervous."

Webbie asks his standard question.

"Are you calling all of 'em liars?"

"I don't want to call 'em liars, 'cause they're cops and they protect us and all, and they watched one of their own get shot and killed, and it's really sad, but it doesn't make sense what they're saying, so I kinda wonder. And it makes me wonder about everything they say."

She lobs the question right back to him.

"Does it make sense to you? Can you explain it to me so I don't feel this way?"

She catches him off guard.

"Well, uh, I guess I figure they were confused a little bit. Maybe they got some of the details wrong, but it doesn't mean they're lying about seeing a light, seeing someone pull back the curtains, or blinds, or blanket, whatever. I figure they saw it all right, but just don't remember each and every little detail."

"Let me ask you this. If you had been there, one of the cops at the front door, when they asked you early, like soon after the shooting, if they asked you about seeing a light, would you have said something about seeing a light through the window?"

"Depends."

"On what?"

"On if they asked me the right question. If they asked if I seen a porch light, I would've said no. If they asked if I seen a light on inside the house, I would've said yes."

"What if they asked if you had seen any lights?"

"I would've said yes. But we don't know what questions they asked."

"If you were the guy kicking the door, and someone behind you said 'I see a light,' would you have looked over your shoulder to see the light?"

"I'd have looked over my shoulder maybe to see who said it."

"But he didn't look over his shoulder to see who said it, remember? He testified he doesn't know who said it. He said he looked over his shoulder to see the light? Would you have said that?"

"I don't know what I'd say. That's what I meant when I said they were just a little confused. That's all. You're pickin' on all the small stuff."

"Maybe, but that doesn't make me feel any better."

The room goes quiet, but not for long. It never stays quiet for long. This time, it's Joyce, the elementary school teacher, who breaks the silence.

"There was something else kinda bothered me about his testimony. This guy ..."

"Darrell," adds Doris helpfully. She's back in the game.

"... Yeah, Darrell Cooley, I think, he said that when he was helping Ron Jones, Stephen Jones pulled up with the car. Then he picked Ron up. He said Ron's back was toward him, and he drug Ron over to the back seat of the car and he pulled Ron in the car right on top of him. Do you remember that?"

The question was directed at Angela.

"Yes."

"Okay. Now do you remember him saying that Darryl Graves grabbed him and pulled him into the car."

"Yes."

"So where was Graves?"

"I don't see your point."

"Was this some sort of Prentiss pyramid? This guy Darrell Cooley says Darryl Graves was pulling him as he was dragging Ron Jones, and he ends up in the back seat of the car with Ron Jones on top of him. So where was Darryl Graves?"

That's a good catch. Very good. I'm interested in seeing how Angela will handle it.

"I don't see that it makes any difference at all about whether Cory Maye murdered Ron Jones or not."

"Then why did they talk about it."

"I don't know why they talked about it. I can't understand why we're talking about it here."

Angela seems determined to alienate another juror.

"Well if they're going to offer it as evidence in a murder trial, then they should explain it so it makes some sense, don't you think?"

"What I think is that we're making mountains out of mole hills."

"Well maybe that's what you think, but I think we're supposed to discuss the evidence, and each of us is supposed to listen to the others. So maybe it's a mole hill to you, but it matters to me."

Oops.

Vera smoothes things over.

"You did lovely, dear."

I have no idea what's going on inside Vera's grandmotherly head. However, despite the outward simplicity, I suspect there's some complex gearing up there just whirring away.

"And another thing, ..."

Joyce isn't done yet.

"... how could he shoulder that door? The top half of that door is window. He slams his shoulder against that window and he might end up in the living room with the door still locked. He said he shouldered the door below the window, but the window goes down to his waist. He's lying."

That's the first time some one has come right out and accused a prosecution witness of perjury.

"And while I'm on the subject, ..."

She's still not done.

"... why didn't he just break one of the window panes, reach in and unlock the door from the inside? It's not like they were afraid of breaking things. Why not break a little window pane? Too easy? Not enough damage?"

A melee ensues at the other end of the table. Kyle, Jerry and I are content to let them duke it out. Jerry grabs for a Dasani. Kyle sits there as proper as can be. I lose myself in thought.

I have my own issue with Darrell Cooley's testimony. I think he slipped up and gave away the game for the prosecution. I had grown increasingly suspicious of the official story with each passing witness. Darrell Cooley was simply the straw that broke the camel's back.

He was the most nervous, the least well-prepared. His answers were the most nonsensical. Cathy and Joyce noticed several of his strange claims, that he looked over his shoulder to see the window directly in front of him, that Darryl Graves dragged him into the police car as he was dragging Ron Jones into the police car, that he shouldered a door at a point well below his waist. Those oddities are not his only problem, though. Not by a long shot.

No one has yet mentioned his inability to remember whether or not he drew his weapon, or his inability to recall that his own police chief was part of the team that entered the left-hand apartment. He couldn't keep straight whether it was Stephen Jones or Ron Jones beside him on the porch, or who told him there was a light on, or how that person would see the light even though he himself was the person right in front of the door.

Darrell Cooley made it clear that it was Darryl Graves, and not Ron Jones, who really gave the briefing. Cooley testified, if you recall, that it was Darryl Graves who drew the layout of the duplex. Cooley caught himself mid-sentence when he said the sketch was of the inside of the house, then claimed immediately thereafter that he didn't know if the sketch was of the inside or outside. Even then, he equivocated, saying he wasn't sure if it showed *all* of the inside rooms, suggesting it showed at least some. I can't figure out, however, what it was that he wasn't supposed to give away.

It is another issue though, something mundane, that causes me to see the entire case in a whole new light; something trivial that makes me suspect the official story might indeed be fabricated. It's time to bring it up.

"What about the screen door?"

They're still squabbling over Joyce's charge of perjury. I ask again, this time raising my voice considerably.

"What about the screen door?"

The room goes quiet. Go figure. I turn to my main man.

"Kyle?"

"Yes."

"As an actuary, what do you think the chance is that Darrell Cooley never kicked the front door, never shouldered it, to use his words, nor even tried the door handle to see if it was locked?

Others in the room are taken aback. Some mutter, some confer, and Webbie informs me I'm unbalanced. Kyle though begins to process the most recent conversation. It doesn't take long at all. A slight grin, a very slight grin, reveals he has it figured.

"I'd say it is likely that Darrell Cooley never kicked the front door, or shouldered it, or even tried to open it."

I rise to my feet, put my fists to my chest as if hooking my thumbs beneath imaginary suspenders, and I begin a mock interrogation.

"And why would you say that, Kyle, if that indeed is your real name?"

He picks up on the idea quickly.

"Because there is a screen door that would have to be opened before Darrell Cooley, or anyone else for that matter, could reach the door handle."

"And why shouldn't these jurors," I sweep my arm in a panoramic arc across the jury room, "simply believe that Darrell Cooley opened the screen door but simply forgot, in all the excitement?"

"Because the screen door was secured shut, from the inside, by a coat hanger."

"Why on earth would the screen door be secured shut, from the inside?"

"Because Cory Maye's young daughter had a tendency to get out, so Cory Maye, or perhaps her mother, secured the screen door from the inside with a coat hanger."

I move around behind him.

"Well, I didn't hear Darrell Cooley or anybody who testified before him say anything about a coat hanger. How do you explain that?"

"Because neither Darrell Cooley nor anyone who testified before him said anything about a coat hanger."

"Explain then, if you would, how you know the door was secured with a coat hanger."

"Because the defendant, Cory Maye, so testified. We simply have yet to discuss his testimony."

"Ahh! But as you point out, Cory Maye is the defendant. Why should we believe him? Surely he doesn't want to be convicted of murder. Surely he has a strong motive for lying."

I've stumped him with this one.

"Well ..."

"Okay, let me ask you this. If we were to automatically disbelieve Cory Maye's testimony simply because he's the defendant, wouldn't we be depriving him of the presumption of innocence?"

"I guess so."

"Wouldn't we be saying 'we don't believe you because we assume you're guilty?'"

"I suppose."

"Shouldn't we instead hold him to the same standard as any other witness? Shouldn't we consider his evidence without bias? Shouldn't we judge his testimony on its merit rather than on whether the witness is or is not the defendant?"

"Certainly we should."

"All right then. Let me ask you this."

I walk behind my chair so he can see me again from his front right quarter.

"After Mr. Maye made his claim about using a coat hanger to secure the screen door, did the prosecution, the State of Mississippi, have a chance to challenge his testimony?"

"They certainly did."

"And did they take the opportunity to challenge him?"

"No, they did not."

"Did they ask him any questions about the wire coat hanger?"

"No sir."

"Did they ask any questions about the screen door?"

"No sir."

"Not a one? Not a single question?"

"No sir."

"Did they present any picture of the screen door handle from the inside of the house that would have informed us whether or not that handle was secured with a coat hanger?"

"They certainly did not."

"But they could have, if they had so chosen to do so?"

"Indeed they could."

"So is it your testimony today that Cory Maye's claim the screen door was secured from the inside by a wire coat hanger went completely uncontested by the State?"

"Completely uncontested. That is correct."

"Well that is certainly interesting. Now, if the screen door was in fact secured from within by a wire coat hanger, as Cory Maye testified, and as the State declined to refute ..."

I lean forward and place both palms on the table.

"... how is it possible that Officer Darrell Cooley stood on the front porch and tried the door handle ..."

I allow my voice to rise.

"... when the screen door was secured in the closed position, when the screen door the state refused to discuss, stood between Darrell Cooley ..."

I pause and allow my voice to fall off.

"... and the very door he attempted to open?"

"I have no idea."

"You have no idea?"

"No sir."

"None whatsoever?"

"None sir."

"Just a few more questions. Given all that we now know, do you feel it is reasonable that Officer Darrell Cooley could have kicked the door without realizing a screen door was between his boot and the wooden door?"

"That doesn't seem reasonable to me."

"What if I were to tell you he claimed to have kicked the door twice, all the while never realizing there was a screen door there?"

"That seems even less likely."

"What if I were to tell you that between those two kicks, he testified he looked over his shoulder to see the light through the window, that someone behind him said had just appeared?'

"I'd say that seems odd."

"And what if I were to tell you he claimed to have shouldered that door after having kicked it twice, shouldered that door though the top half is covered with glass, and still he claims to know nothing of a screen door between his shoulder and the wooden door? What if I were to tell you that?"

"It would border on the impossible."

"Interesting. Now what if I were to tell you that in addition to kicking the door twice and shouldering the door once, and not breaking the glass nor noticing the screen door, that Darrell Cooley testified he could seen a light though a small opening in the curtain, as he looked directly through the screen door, but he could not see the screen door itself?

"I would be at a loss for words."

"Interesting. Interesting indeed. Just two more questions, if I may. Did you see the large picture displayed before us showing the front porch and front door?"

"I did indeed."

"And did you see with your very own eyes that there was a screen door protecting the front door of the Cory Maye apartment?"

"With my own eyes, as I live and breathe."

"So there is no question in your mind, no question whatsoever, that there was a screen door there, though Office Darrell Cooley maintains he cannot recall one being there?"

"No question, sir. None at all."

I preempt Angela. I preempt them all.

"I have no more questions for this witness. The jury is free to take a quick break. Please be ready to resume deliberations in ten minutes."

I reach my hand out to Kyle. He smiles, grasps it and shakes it. As I take my seat, I see Angela walking my way. As she walks past, she bends over slightly and whispers something in my direction.

"Next witness, big shot."

TESTIMONY OF STEVEN TIMOTHY HAYNE
Yesterday: Thursday, January 21, 2004

"Would you state your name for the jury, please." >> Steven Timothy Hayne.

Mr. Miller will be examining the next witness.

"Dr. Hayne, do you hold a position with respect to the State of Mississippi?" >> I do, sir. State pathologist with the Department of Public Safety, Medical Examiner's Office, for the State of Mississippi.

"In your capacity of physician, as state medical examiner, did you have occasion to have delivered to you or brought in to the place where you do your autopsies the body of an individual by the name of Ron Jones?" >> Yes, I did, sir. It was delivered to the Rankin County morgue under the direction of Greg Blackwell, who is the county coroner, medical examiner, and investigator of Jefferson Davis County, the county of jurisdiction, sir.

"And I believe there were officers, investigators present at the autopsy. Is that correct?" >> Yes, sir, there were two representatives of the coroner's office and two representatives of the Mississippi Bureau of Investigation.

"And those individuals identified the body to you?" >> The county coroner, medical examiner, and investigator identified the body, sir.

"Please tell the jury what actions you performed in the conduct of your examination of the body and what your findings were." >> The first step was discussing the case with the officers, especially the Bureau investigators as well as the representatives from the coroner's office, familiarize myself with the circumstances of the death itself. That was followed by an external examination, looking for evidence of disease or injury, collecting evidence appropriate to that step of the investigation, and followed by an internal examination, opening the body cavities, collecting evidence appropriate to that step, and collecting evidence as necessary. And then it was followed by review of the findings with the officers and the representatives of the coroner's office as to the findings of the autopsy and also the findings at the scene investigation. Ultimately, a report was generated after microscopic review of the tissues and other studies being completed. And this autopsy protocol was in compliance with the attorney general's ruling of this state as well as the national standards for the performance of an autopsy. It addressed the cause of death, the manner of death, and it also lists pertinent steps and findings during the course of the examination.

"All right, sir. I believe we have a copy of that autopsy report which we furnished a copy also to the defense. Based on your examination and your autopsy, what findings did you make with respect to any wounds that may have appeared on the body of Officer Jones?" >> There were three traumatic injuries identified on the external surface of the body. There are two small scrapes of the skin, scratches, called abrasions medically, small in size, measuring approximately one-quarter inch. They were found on the back of the second and third digits of the left hand. In addition to that, there was an entrance gunshot wound located over the lower left abdominal wall at a point thirty inches below the top of the head, four inches to the left of the abdomen on the centerline. The entrance gunshot wound was slightly ovoid, measuring approximately three-eighths of an inch in diameter.

"Were you able to determine the track of that wound?" >> I was, sir. On the internal examination, when the body was opened, the track was found to be traveling, that is the bullet trajectory was found to be traveling from left to right. It was going downward at approximately twenty degrees, and it was going towards the back at approximately thirty to thirty-five degrees.

"Dr. Hayne, I'm going to show you what appears to be a frontal and rear diagram of a male body. Can you identify that diagram?" >> This is an illustration diagram taken at the time of the autopsy, and written on this diagram are the two small abrasions, scratches, located on the fingers of the left hand. And it indicates that it was on the decedent, Ron Jones.

"Could you indicate on therewith a pen approximately where the entrance wound was?" >> These were the two abrasions. Did you also want the entrance wound?

"Right. On the frontal part."

Dr. Timothy Steven Hayne seems to make a small mark on the diagram we can't see.

"We'd offer that into evidence, Your Honor."

Judge Eubanks says fine. "All right. No objection, let it be entered and marked."

"And if I could show it to the jury by means of the projector."

Okay. Now we can see it.

"Now, is that what you refer to as an entrance wound?" >> Yes, sir. It was almost circular, located on the left lower abdominal wall thirty inches below the top of the head, slightly lower than the level of the umbilicus or the belly button.

Buddy removes the diagram and replaces it with another.

"I show you this diagram and ask what that diagram represents." >> This is a lateral view illustration sheet. And this was used during the course of the autopsy to demonstrate the downward trajectory of the bullet, entering the abdominal wall, traveling downward at approximately twenty degrees. And also indicating that a large caliber copper-jacketed bullet I felt was consistent with a .380 caliber projectile was located towards to back of the abdominal wall as well as lower than the entrance gunshot wound.

"Thank you. We'd offer this into evidence."

Again, no problem from the defense table or the bench. "All right. Let it be entered and marked."

"All right. Did you note any abrasions or bruising to the deceased's knees?" >> I did not, sir. The only acute non-gunshot wound injuries were the two small abrasions to the back of the second and third digits of the left hand, sir.

"With respect to the internal injuries suffered as a result of the projectile, what did you find?" >> There were a total of four gunshot wounds to the small bowel, but of much greater significance was a go-through gunshot wound of the abdominal aorta, allowing for massive internal bleeding to a volume of approximately three and one-half quarts of blood, which would produce death from exsanguination or blood loss, sir.

"Based on the autopsy, your education, training, and experience, and within the bounds of reasonable medical certainty, have you formed an opinion, expert opinion, concerning the cause of death of Ronald Jones, or Ron Jones?" >> I did, sir.

"And what was that opinion?" >> I described the cause of death as a gunshot of the abdomen consistent with distance and consistent with re-entry and penetrating, sir.

"And do you have an opinion as to the manner of death?" >> I do, sir.

"And what is that?" >> Homicide, sir.

"Were you able to determine the height of Ron Jones from the autopsy?" >> Yes, sir, from direct measurement. He measured six foot two inches in height.

"And the wound was how far from the top of his head?" >> Thirty inches below the top of his head. It was four inches to the left of the mid-abdominal wall.

"Judge, I believe that's all the questions we have for Dr. Hayne."

<<>>

Rhonda Cooper with the cross.

"Good morning, Dr. Hayne." >> Good morning, counselor.

"I'm Rhonda Cooper, as you know, and I just want to clear up some things for the jury. Now, you started off and you indicated that there were some small scratches on the back of Ron Jones' left hand." >> On the back of two fingers, small, measuring approximately a quarter of an inch.

"Did you attribute that in any way to the gunshot wound?" >> I did not, not directly to the gunshot wound. It could have been inflicted as a fall. It was suffered at or about the time of death.

"I just want to establish some things that went into your opinion, Dr. Hayne. Do you know the distance between Ron Jones as he entered the apartment and Cory Maye as he lay on the floor of his apartment?" >> I do not know that distance.

"Do you know how far Ron Jones was from Cory Maye at the time he was shot?" >> I do not know that.

"And do you know whether or not Ron Jones stood erect or was any way crouched or bent down at the time he was shot?" >> I do not know that, counselor.

"Do you know how high the gun was above Cory's head as he lay on the ground?" >> I do not know that, counselor.

"Do you know whether or not the gun was at an angle?" >> It was only at an angle in relationship to the decedent. If the decedent were in a standing position, the weapon would have been held above at approximately twenty degrees and also forward at approximately thirty to thirty-five degrees facing from the left side. I can only give the relative positions. All the trajectories are measured from the anatomically correct position.

"So the trajectories don't take into at account that the decedent may have scaled three stairs and then entered in a crouched position. Are you saying your trajectory does not take that into consideration?" >> The hypothesis that one might ask about that, one could address. The issues of how many stairs a person climbed would be indecipherable.

"We can strike the stairs. I guess I was just trying to recreate Mr. Jones entering that unit. But, again, my question is, does your opinion take into consideration that Ron Jones may have been crouched at the time he was shot?" >> I do not know the position that Mr. Jones was in when the shot was delivered. Only the trajectory of the bullet in the body as the body is placed in an anatomically correct position.

"Which is standing?" >> Standing position, arms to the side, palms forward, feet together.

"And those are the trajectories that are measured from that. They don't indicate the exact position he was in when the shot was fired?" >> All I'm saying is that those are the trajectories of the projectile as it courses into the body in the anatomically correct position.

"So we cannot exclude or rule out that Ron Jones was not standing erect, but could have been crouched?" >> I don't know that. It could be either.

"So there are many factors that could alter this trajectory, or that you have to consider?" >> It would not alter the trajectory. I'm only placing him in the anatomically correct position. It is a relative trajectory. It is the trajectory in the body with him in that position. I don't know the position of the decedent in relationship to the ground.

"I thought you said initially there were three bullet entries or the three wounds caused by the bullet. Then I understood you to go on and say there were four gunshot wounds. I just want to clear that up for the ladies and gentlemen of the jury." >> I think I said that there were three traumatic injuries. Two injuries to the finger, one gunshot wound. The four injuries, I think I was describing the four bullet hole injuries to the small bowel. The small bowel was struck four times, and the aorta was struck one time by the bullet coursing through those organs.

"Dr. Hayne, in your experiences, had the flow of the bleeding been stopped at the scene initially would that have prolonged or even saved his life?" >> If that could have been performed. Of course, this is a deep abdominal wound, and getting access to that would require surgical intervention. A gunshot wound to the aorta is going to cause massive acute blood loss. The blood's going to be pumped out under high pressure from a vessel approximately the diameter of one's thumb. So death would intervene in a very, very short period of time. Irreversible shock would occur slightly before that. I would not expect a person to survive that type of an injury more than a few minutes.

"You shared with the jury all the people that were present at the time of your autopsy?" >> Yes, ma'am.

"Does your opinion in any way take into consideration any of the conversations or statements that you obtained during your investigation?" >> Only in general terms.

"What would be those general terms, other than the fact that you knew he had been shot?" >> That he was a police officer entering a building. That there was an occupant in the building and that there was a shot discharged. Shot struck the police officer, and the gunshot wound was ultimately lethal.

"Dr. Hayne, thank you."

<<>>

Buddy is back up for redirect.

"Of course, you have not heard the rest of the testimony in this case, you don't know the testimony in the case, and I understand what you say about the relative positions of the body of the deceased at the time the wound was inflicted. But the trajectory of the bullet through the body is the trajectory of the bullet through the body. Is that correct?" >> That is correct. The trajectory does not change as the bullet went through the body in relationship to the hypothesis.

"And you would know that certainly the deceased could not have been bent over so much that he would have crossed the plane of the trajectory of the bullet?"

Rhonda objects.

"Objection, Your Honor. Dr. Hayne cannot speak to that. He's already testified he doesn't know the position of the decedent, he knows anatomically the measurements and the trajectory.

Buddy starts to defend his question ...

"Ms. Cooper, I think what I'm getting to ..."

... but doesn't need to finish before the Judge overrules the objection.

"I'm going to overrule the objection.

Rhonda Cooper actually thanks him for the perfunctory adverse ruling.

"Thank you, Your Honor."

And Buddy gets on with his questioning.

"Do you understand my question, Doctor? " >> You're talking about the horizontal plane of ground?

"Well, what I'm talking about is that if the trajectory is like this, and I'm bent over very far, I wouldn't have been hit there, I would've been hit somewhere in the upper part of the body because my body would've crossed the plane of how the trajectory went."

Rhonda gives the objection another shot. She really doesn't like this question.

"Same objection, Your Honor."

And gets the same response from the judge.

"Overruled, if he understands."

Dr. Timothy Stephen Hayne answers without further questioning.

I would expect it to strike higher given that scenario.

"That's my point. And at whatever position the shooter was in, you would have expected the barrel of the gun to have been higher than that entrance wound. Is that correct?"

Rhonda really, really doesn't like this line of questioning. She objects again, is overruled again, and the good doctor proceeds with his answer.

With the decedent in an upright position or even leaning slightly forward, I would expect the weapon to be in a relatively higher position than the entrance gunshot wound.

"Thank you. And your testimony and findings with respect to the actual cause of death and trajectory and all that were not based on what any officers told you, but based on the autopsy." >> Based on the autopsy solely, sir.

"Thank you. I believe that's all we have."

<<>>

Rhonda Cooper claims to have just one question for re-direct. Judge Eubanks will allow it.

"Dr. Hayne, as the prosecution just illustrated with your stick, in order for that gunshot entry to have been higher, wouldn't the decedent have to have been extremely bent over? Because your opinion is based on the decedent standing erect. But in order for that entry to have been higher than as you've just testified, would not the decedent have to have been extremely crouched over?" >> He would have to be flexed markedly. Of course, I don't know the position of the shooter. I know the position relative in your hypothesis of the decedent. And if he were in a standing position and the shooter in some other position, I would expect either the shooter to be firing from over or, if the officer were in a marked flex position, which would be difficult since the flex point of the body would be slightly above the entrance gunshot wound. So he would have to be markedly flexed over, almost on one's knees, to achieve that trajectory.

"Okay. Thank you, Dr. Hayne."

<<>>

Now Buddy wants one more question.

"Let's assume the shooter was laying down flat on the floor and the officer came in and the officer was standing upright. Would you expect the trajectory of the bullet to be like that?" >> No, it would be in an upward trajectory, not in a downward trajectory.

"If the officer was slightly bent over, would you expect the trajectory to be like that?" >> No, it would be an upward trajectory, not in a downward trajectory.

"That's all."

DELIBERATION OF STEVEN TIMOTHY HAYNE
Friday, January 23, 2004

This isn't going to be good.

For those of us who have reservations about the State's case, this isn't going to be good.

Angela has been waiting for this. She has two pieces of paper in her hand, two exhibits taken from the evidence box.

"Okay. It's time to talk about the testimony of Doctor Steven Timothy Hayne."

She didn't need any help with that name. She remembered the title, first name, middle name, and last name. She even recalled that his last name did not end in "s." She really liked this guy. Given that she seems ready to vote guilty on the capital charge, it's pretty clear why that is.

"Dr. Hayne is a vital witness. His testimony is telling. He is the person who conducted the autopsy on Officer Ron Jones. He explained that Officer Jones was killed by a single bullet, entering slightly below and four inches to the left of his navel. He sketched the location of the entrance wound on this page from the autopsy report. You can see it right there, the dark circle shape"

She takes the first of two papers she is holding and places it on the table in front of her. It is one of the diagrams from the autopsy, the one that showed the abrasions on the fingers, the one to which Dr. Hayne added the location of the entry wound during his testimony. She orients it with the feet towards me, so that it looks right-side-up to me and most the other jurors. She slides it towards the center of the table, so that all might get a good view.

BODY DIAGRAM

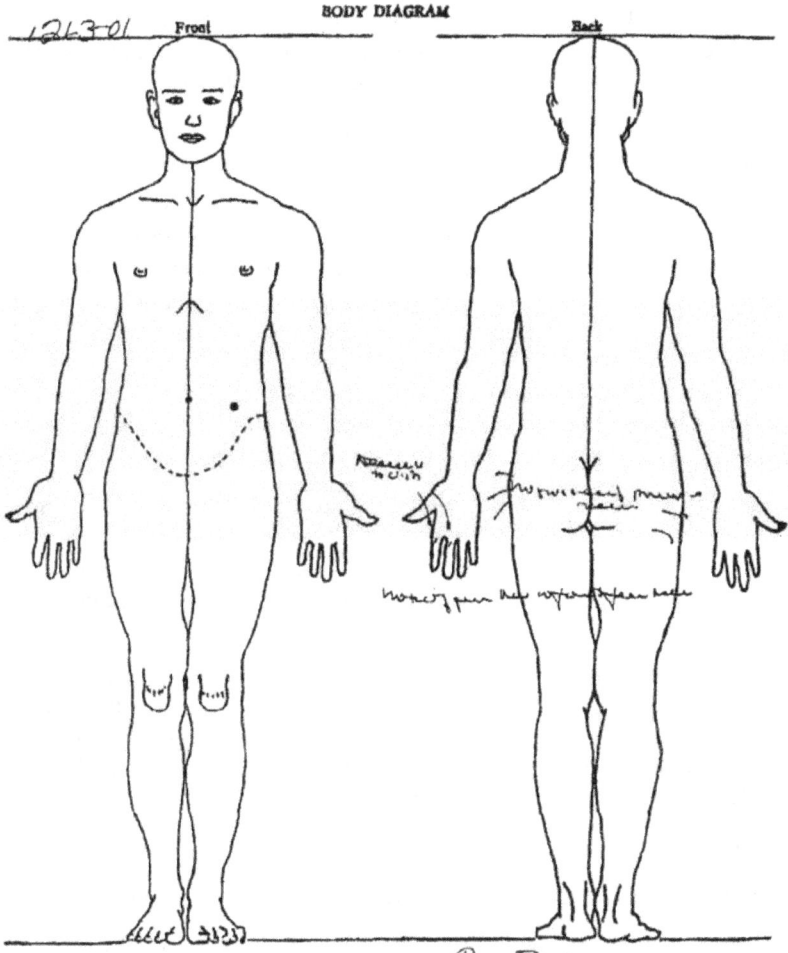

121301   Front   Back

Decedent's
Height _____ inches   Name _Bm Jones_
                                        27 Dec 07

"That single bullet, which Dr. Hayne described to be consistent with a .38 caliber weapon, punctured the intestine in three places, then punctured the aorta. Officer Jones was doomed to bleed to death within minutes. No one could save him.

"We know Ron Jones spoke to several of the witnesses who testified before us. He said 'I've been hit,' and 'Get me to the hospital,' and 'Good Lord, help me!' We know he managed to walk a short distance to the side of the building before he collapsed. He was aware he was seriously injured. He probably suspected he was dying. He could feel his life slipping away. It must have been horrible."

She pauses for effect. Everyone is silent. Everyone can sense it. It must have been horrible.

I recall how it surprised me when Dr. Hayne mentioned the bullet had punctured the aorta. I didn't realize the aorta descended that far into the body. I remember images of the aorta from high school. It was the extra-large artery coming out the top of the heart, always shown in bright red. Smaller arteries branched off to the arms and the brain. As I think about it now, the aorta did curve over and head downward. It must have, in order to carry oxygenated blood to the torso and legs. I just don't recall a picture showing it all the way down inside the abdomen.

I'm not doubting or challenging Dr. Hayne on this point. I'm simply admitting to my poor recollection of my human anatomy lessons. Still, it was shocking to hear that the aorta was as large as your thumb down there. Before, it always seemed to me as if getting shot in the stomach was survivable. Now it seems so serious. You get hit in the aorta and it's all over.

"Dr. Hayne told us the path the bullet took once it entered Officer Jones. If he was standing up, or nearly so, as he probably was, looking from the top, the bullet traveled at a thirty degree angle from front to back, left to right. That means Ron Jones was to Maye's left, assuming Maye was facing the back wall of the house when he fired.

That's bad enough. The worst is yet to come.

"The next sketch, though, tells me pretty much all I need to know."

She places the second diagram just above the first. People lean towards the center of the table to see it.

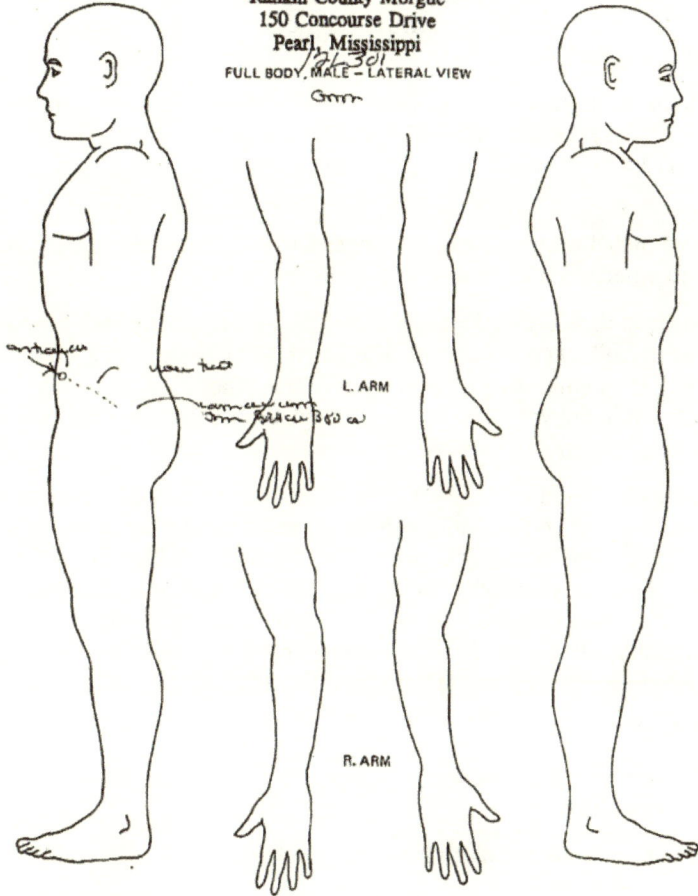

Rankin County Morgue
150 Concourse Drive
Pearl, Mississippi
FULL BODY, MALE – LATERAL VIEW

L. ARM

R. ARM

Name _____   Case No. _121-301_

Date _____

"When you look from the side, you can see that the bullet was traveling down as it moved from front to back. It wasn't moving just from left to right, it was moving down. Dr. Hayne said that was a 20 degree angle. He marked the path on that sketch right there.

"That's powerful evidence that Cory Maye was standing up when he shot at and killed Officer Ron Jones. That's not what he said in his recorded conversation though, and that's not what he testified. He said he was laying down when he fired. Behind the bed where his daughter lay exposed. He hid behind the bed, exposed as little of himself as possible, pointed the gun around the foot of the bed and towards the door, and fired without really looking. That's what he said.

"But that's not what the evidence says, does it? It says he was standing up when he fired the shot that killed Officer Ron Jones. Standing up, not laying down. I don't know why he chose to lie about it, but it's pretty clear he lied about it.

"Now, we've heard that we're not supposed to disbelieve what Cory Maye has to say just because he doesn't want to be executed."

I think that was directed at me. She didn't state it correctly, but perhaps I didn't make myself clear. No matter. She has their attention, and she's going to make her point come hell or high water. The other jurors already know where she's going anyway. She's just putting into words the suspicion that they all harbor, that we all harbor. I'm bothered by it too.

"We've heard that. He doesn't want to be executed but that doesn't mean he will lie. We're supposed to believe him, I guess, unless he gives us good reason not to believe him. Well, here it is, folks. Here's the reason not to believe him. I don't know why he is lying about not standing up, but he's lying about that. And if he'll lie about that, he'll certainly lie about knowing there were police out there. You can believe anything you want, but I'm not ready to believe anything Cory Maye says after this."

She points to the diagram.

"He can tell me he didn't know it was the police out there, but after this, I just don't believe him."

Her words are the sound of a death warrant being printed.

She sits down and gives me a look. The look dares me to refute her. She's telling me I had my fun with Darrell Cooley and the screen door, and I had my fun with Ron Jones and the battering ram, but she'll have the last laugh.

The other jurors turn and look at me. I've got nothing to offer. I'm hoping someone will be coming to my rescue. I know, however, it's a false hope.

It makes no sense Cory Maye would lie about such a mundane matter, but I have no other explanation. I can't rationalize the ballistics. Rhonda Cooper's efforts to convince me that Ron Jones was crouching don't help. Nothing I can think of explains the downward trajectory of the bullet, other than Cory Maye is lying about his position when he fired.

I'm supposed to go where the evidence leads me. I'm supposed to be skeptical. And I am, perhaps to a fault. But even my skepticism fails to provide a reasonable alternative to the evidence that Cory Maye is lying.

TESTIMONY OF CORY MAYE
Yesterday: Thursday, January 21, 2004

"Cory, will you please state your full name for the ladies and gentlemen of this jury." >> Cory Jermaine Maye.

Rhonda Cooper will examine her client.

"And how old are you, Cory?" >> Twenty-three.

"Well, Cory, let's just talk a little bit about your life before this incident. Where did you grow up?" >> Monticello.

"And in Monticello where did you live?" >> I lived with my mom.

"Do you have brothers and sisters, Cory?" >> Yes, ma'am. Three brothers and two sisters by my mom. I'm the last child, the baby.

"Have you lived all of your life in Monticello except for these last two years?" >> Yes, ma'am.

"What school did you attend?" >> Lawrence County High School.

"What year did you stop going to school?" >> '98.

"What grade were you in at that time?" >> Eleventh.

"Tell the ladies and gentlemen why you chose to stop going to school." >> Due to the knowledge and skills that I was given by my father and being a young adult, I felt my education wouldn't affect me in the long run.

"Now, skills that you got from your father, what does your father do for a living?" >> Brick mason, carpentry, remodel houses, painting, etc.

"Are you able to do those things?" >> Yes, ma'am.

"And did you do those things when you stopped going to school?" >> Yes, ma'am.

"And that was in 1998?" >> Yes, ma'am.

"Of course, the incident that we're here about occurred the very end of 2001." >> Right.

"Can you tell the ladies and gentlemen whether or not you worked every day those three years." >> Yes, ma'am.

"What were your hobbies?" >> Hunting, fishing, working and cooking.

"So you enjoyed cooking?" >> Yes, ma'am.

"Did you cook for your family?" >> Yes, ma'am.

"Now, how did you come to be living in Prentiss, Mississippi?" >> I wanted to be a father for my child, so I moved in with my baby's mom.

"Let's talk about your children. How many children do you have, Cory?" >> Two.

"Please tell the ladies and gentlemen their names and their ages." >> Cory Jermaine Maye, Jr. He's three right now. And Ta'Corianna Jamyia Longino. She's three.

"You were living with Ta'Corianna and her mother in December of 2001?" >> Yes, ma'am.

"How long had you all been living together as a family?" >> One month.

"Had you lived at any other place in Prentiss other than 1728 Mary Street?" >> No, ma'am.

"Had you celebrated Christmas in Prentiss with your family?" >> Yes, ma'am.

"What were your plans for your life in Prentiss with your family?" >> Be a father of my child and do the right thing.

"Were you doing any of the things, the brick mason work, the carpentry work in Prentiss?" >> No, ma'am.

"What were you doing there?" >> I was tending to my child because at Prentiss, I did not have any transportation.

"Did Ms. Longino, your daughter's mother, did she work?" >> Yes, ma'am. She worked at Marshall Durbin in Hattiesburg.

"And you were to care for your daughter while Ms. Longino worked?" >> Yes, ma'am.

"And Ms. Longino worked what hours?" >> Between ten to eight that morning.

"So ten at night to eight in the morning?" >> She left like eight o'clock every evening.

"Now, Cory, because of where we are, we cannot get around having to talk about that Wednesday night. Can you share with the ladies and gentlemen what you were doing that evening after Ms. Longino left for work?" >> Just sitting around, watching TV, watching my child.

"How old was your daughter at that time?" >> I think she was fourteen months old.

"What time did you all decide to go to bed? " >> I put her to sleep about eight o'clock.

"And then you continued to watch television?" >> Yes, ma'am.

"And did you fall asleep that night?" >> Yes, ma'am.

"About what time, if you remember?" >> About nine thirty, ten o'clock.

"And what caused you to wake up from your sleep?" >> I heard a loud crash at the front door.

"And where were you sleeping?" >> In the chair right beside the front door.

"And where was your daughter sleeping?" >> In the bedroom, in the bed.

"Continue telling the ladies and gentlemen of this jury about your being awakened from your sleep." >> I was awakened by the loud crash at the door. Upon the loud crash, I woke up frightened and ran to the room where my daughter was.

"Is that the only bedroom in that apartment?" >> Yes, ma'am.

"What did you do when you got into that bedroom with your daughter?" >> Once I got in the bedroom, I retrieved the pistol. I inserted the magazine, chambered a round, and laid it on the floor.

"Let's just go back so that the ladies and gentlemen will know why you had a gun in your home." >> I used the gun when I went hunting, for my protection, safety of snakes, wild animals, etc.

"And you kept that gun in your bedroom?" >> Yes, ma'am.

"Prior to this Wednesday night, when had you last used that gun?" >> Two weeks.

"I'm certain that they want to know how long had you had that gun, Cory." >> Five months at the most.

"And from where had you gotten it?" >> From a friend.

"Now, let's go back to your bedroom. You said inserted a magazine?" >> Yes, ma'am.

"And why did you have to do that?" >> Because I kept the gun unloaded so no kids or nothing, in case they stumbled across it, they wouldn't be able to shoot nobody or hurt their self.

"And you were lying on the floor of your bedroom?" >> Yes, ma'am.

"What happened as you lay on the floor of your bedroom?" >> At the back door, I began to hear kicks.

"What were your thoughts?" >> Thought someone was breaking in on me and my child.

"How were you feeling?" >> I was frightened. Very frightened.

"What caused you to fire your gun?" >> I heard the intruders make their way inside the house.

"What did you do once they made way into your house?" >> I fired shots.

"What happened after firing those shots?" >> After I fired the shots, they started hollering "police, police, you just shot a officer."

"Cory, when you heard those who entered your home yell 'police,' what did you do?" >> I immediately put the weapon down. I slid it away.

"Were you asked to slide it away?" >> No, ma'am.

"Why did you slide it away?" >> Because I had no reason to fire at a officer.

"And what happened after that?" >> After that, they came in and handcuffed me and started kicking me repeatedly.

"And how many officers handcuffed you?" >> It took only one officer to handcuff me.

"You were completely handcuffed with one?" >> Yes, ma'am.

"Well, Cory, you have heard testimony that you resisted the officers' attempt to arrest you." >> No, ma'am, I did not resist.

"Can you tell the ladies and gentlemen what's represented in those photographs?" >> It's a picture of me upon arriving at Forrest County, December 27th, that morning.

"Do they accurately reflect your appearance at that time?" >> Yes, ma'am.

"Were the doors to your home locked?" >> Yes, ma'am.

"Now, the front door, how was it secured?" >> The screen door was secured with a coat hanger because my daughter could open the door. The screen door would not lock by itself, so we kept it secured with a coat hanger tied from the inside.

"How was the back door secured?" >> It was locked, chained.

"And, Cory, were there any window dressings? Anything on the front windows of your apartments, like blinds or curtains?" >> Yes, ma'am.

"Now, the blinds, the jury has seen pictures of there being a cloth between the blind and the windowpane." >> Yes, ma'am.

"Why was that there?" >> It was a pulled down blind. It was there to keep my daughter from standing up in the window because she had it bad about standing up in the window.

"Cory, as you and your daughter were asleep, were there any lights on inside your home?" >> No, ma'am.

"Was the television on?" >> No, ma'am.

"Cory, can you tell the ladies and gentlemen of this jury whether or not there were any announcements or any statements by any of the people that were around your apartment that night?" >> There was no announcement.

"Cory, why did you not look out of your window or open the door to find what was going on?" >> Because they did not knock and they did not announce.

"So why didn't you go to see what was going on?" >> I was afraid.

"Cory, as you lay on that floor, did you see anyone?" >> No, ma'am.

"Did you ever stand to your feet before shooting your gun?" >> No, ma'am.

"Can you tell the ladies and gentlemen of the jury whether you stood to your feet to shoot your gun?" >> No, ma'am.

"Cory, please tell these ladies and these gentlemen whether it was your intent to draw the people on the outside into your home for the purpose of shooting them." >> By no means.

"Cory, did you receive a search warrant at any time that night?" >> No, ma'am.

"Two years has passed since this incident. Have you received a search warrant?" >> Not with my name on it.

"At what point did you receive the supposed search warrant?" >> At the preliminary hearing.

"That was when?" >> A month after the incident, a month and a half after this incident.

"Since this incident until that time, you've been in custody?" >> Yes, ma'am.

"And you've been in custody since December 26, 2001?" >> Yes, ma'am.

"Cory, had there been some announcement or some statement that those individuals around your apartment were police officers, what would you have done?" >> I would not have fired, I would have opened the door.

"What was in your home that you valued?" >> My child.

"Now, Cory, these ladies and these gentlemen know that there was a small amount of marijuana in your home. Had you smoked any marijuana on that day?" >> No, ma'am.

"Why not?" >> Because my child was present that day.

"Had you been with your daughter the entire day?" >> Yes, ma'am.

"How long had that marijuana been inside your home?" >> Approximately a week, maybe.

"Cory, in the twenty-one years before this incident, did you sell marijuana?" >> No, ma'am.

"Now, you know there's been discussion about the people who lived next door. Did you know those individuals?" >> I knew their names.

"And when did you first come to know them?" >> Upon arriving there.

"When you moved to Prentiss?" >> Yes, ma'am.

"Do you know whether or not your neighbors engaged in any illegal activities?" >> No, ma'am.

"Cory, will you tell the ladies and gentlemen of this jury whether or not you've ever been arrested?" >> No, ma'am.

"Have you been involved in any problems or any altercations with any law enforcement officials?" >> No, ma'am.

"Of any city, of any county?" >> No, ma'am.

"Had you had any occasion while you lived in Prentiss to meet any of the police officers from Prentiss, Mississippi?" >> No, ma'am.

"Any police officers from Bassfield, Mississippi?" >> No, ma'am.

"Did you know Ron Jones?" >> No, ma'am.

"When did you first hear his name?" >> The day after the incident.

"I tender the witness, Your Honor."

<<>>

Buddy won't be letting Mr. Miller cross-examine the defendant in a capital murder case. He'll be doing that himself.

"Mr. Maye, you didn't know Officer Jones at all. Is that correct?" >> Correct.

"So you don't know anything about his life or his family or his hopes or his plans or what he had done or what he had accomplished or what his family lost as a result of his death. Is that correct?" >> Correct.

"And it wouldn't be fair for the jury to base its verdict on sympathy for Mr. Jones, would it?"

Cooper objects.

"Objection! Your Honor. I don't think this is proper at this time in this trial."

Buddy argues.

"Well, you're going to give an instruction that says the verdict is not to be based on sympathy."

Judge Eubanks agrees with Buddy.

"That's correct."

But the judge is wrong on this point, as Cooper makes clear.

"This is cross-examination, not closing."

The judge acknowledges his "duh" moment.

"Right, yeah."

So Buddy restates the obvious.

"It is cross examination."

As does Cooper.

"This is not closing."

Judge Eubanks needs to take charge, but he doesn't. That allows Buddy to keep on keepin' on.

"I'm not closing. I'm getting ready to ask him a question."

So Cooper asks for a ruling.

"May I have a ruling on my objection, please?"

And actually wins one.

"I'm going to sustain the objection. He can ask the next question."

So Buddy does, in his own inimitable fashion.

"You don't think it would be right for the jury to base its verdict on sympathy for you, either, do you?"

Which of course causes Cooper to object.

"Objection. The same question, Your Honor."

And then learns to her distress that she only thought she had won one.

"Overruled."

I'm no Perry Mason, but that sure seems like a horrible judicial ruling to me. Witnesses are supposed to answer questions about evidence. Judges are supposed to instruct juries on how they are to weigh the evidence against the law. It seems to me as if Judge Eubanks is having this witness give us his opinion on how we should weigh the evidence. But what do I know? Cory Maye answers Buddy's question.

I believe they should base their decision upon the facts and circumstances.

"That's right. Not backgrounds or families or anything of that sort." >> Correct.

"Now, on the evening in question, you say your daughter was there with you. Is that correct?" >> Correct.

"I was a little confused with respect to the issue about you say you left school in the eleventh grade to work full-time with your father. But am I to understand that you weren't working full-time when this happened? Is that right?" >> Correct.

"And your girlfriend worked full-time?"

Cory Maye nods his head in the affirmative.

"She went to work and you just stayed home?" >> Correct.

Notice the "just" in the question. Now that Buddy has managed to get Cory Maye to say that we should not base our decision on any sympathy for him, Buddy immediately launches into questions intended to demean him in our eyes.

"Okay. And how long has that been going on?" >> Prior to moving to Prentiss.

"How far prior to moving to Prentiss?" >> That month. November.

"Now, I think you said you had that curtain over the window 'cause your daughter would get up in the window. Is that correct?" >> Correct.

"So your daughter could stand?" >> Yes, sir.

"Pull herself up?" >> Yes, sir.

"Sit up? Is that correct?" >> She could walk.

"Now, you said that you were asleep on the couch in the living room?" >> The chair. The chair by the front door.

"And that's the door that has Venetian blinds on the back of it?" >> Correct.

"On the window. And there's not a cloth between the Venetian blinds and the window, is there?" >> Right.

"Okay. And as in all Venetian blinds, there are gaps in the Venetian blinds, aren't there?" >> Sometimes.

"And as I understand it, you initially heard a noise, a crashing of glass. Is that correct?" >> I heard a loud crash.

"So when you heard that, something had happened to your house. Your apartment?" >> Right.

"Well, was it your apartment or was it in your girlfriend's name?" >> My girlfriend.

"It was in your girlfriend's name, not in your name. Is that correct?" >> Correct.

"And she paid the rent on it?" >> Correct.

"And how long had she had it?" >> November. The first of November.

"First of November. So, when you heard that, you woke up, you got off the chair, you walked over and you looked out the blinds to see who was there?" >> No, I did not.

"You heard that, you jumped up, and you yelled, 'Who is that?'" >> No, I did not.

"Okay. Somebody knocks or whams on your door and you don't ask who it is or look to see who it is?" >> They did not knock.

"You heard a noise at that door, didn't you?" >> A crash.

"And you were sitting right there by the door, weren't you?" >> I heard a crash.

"And you didn't get up to check and see what was going on?" >> I did not.

"You didn't call out and ask who was there?" >> I did not.

"Now, after that happened, my understanding is that you went back into the bedroom. Is that correct?" >> Correct.

"And how did you get to the bedroom?" >> I ran.

"In which direction did you go?" >> It's only one direction.

"From the living room, over into the bedroom. Is that correct?" >> Correct.

"Okay. And there's the bathroom there. And is this a little hall area or something there?" >> Correct.

"All right. Now, you heard the officers testify, and there was a crash according to you and to them at the front door. You go in the back and there's some time before one of them is traveling around and there's some crashing on back. Is that right?" >> Correct.

"Before the crashing, you get your pistol, right?" >> Correct.

"And you say you were scared when you heard the crash, right?" >> Correct.

"Well, did you run over here and beat on this wall and holler for help from Mr. Smith?" >> No, sir.

"You didn't call out for help to them or beat on the walls to attract their attention?" >> No, sir.

"But you thought somebody might be trying to break in on you." >> Correct.

"All right. Well, let me ask you this question. When did you form the idea that somebody was trying to break in on you, when you heard the crash at the front door?" >> Correct.

"So were you really terrified at that point?" >> Yes, sir.

"Okay. So you run in here, and where did you get the gun from?" >> From the headboard of the bed.

"So you didn't get it from the table, huh?" >> No, sir.

"You got it from the headboard of the bed?" >> Yes, sir.

"Shelf laying there?" >> It was a high headboard.

"And where was your daughter asleep?" >> In the bed.

"Was she at the bottom of the bed?" >> In the middle.

"Okay. Now, when you ran in there and got the gun, then you grabbed your daughter up and you went back out this way and locked yourself in the bathroom to protect yourself?" >> No, sir.

"You went in here to protect yourself with your daughter. You carried her out of harm's way." >> She was in the bed asleep.

"But you thought people were breaking in there, and you were going to defend your daughter. Isn't that why you said you shot, to defend your daughter's life? Is that what you said?" >> Correct.

"That's the real reason you shot." >> Correct.

"Okay. So you got down here and you got the gun. That took a little while, didn't it? Got the gun, you got the gun loaded, you chambered a round in the gun. Is that right?" >> Correct.

"And then you hid at the bottom of the bed?" >> Correct.

"I'm sorry, what?" >> Correct.

"And that was to protect you, right?" >> Correct.

"You had armed yourself, and you were hiding yourself at the bottom of the bed, right?" >> Correct.

"So there would be a barrier there between you and whatever I think you called them invaders or intruders, or something. Is that right?" >> Correct.

"And before you got down there at the bottom of the bed to protect yourself, you grab your child in your arms and you laid down over your child on the floor at the end of the bed to make sure your child wasn't going to be injured. Is that right?" >> No, sir.

"Now, you took the position at the end of the bed, correct?" >> Correct.

"So who were you really protecting? Were you protecting your baby?" >> Yes, sir.

"You were protecting your baby by leaving her exposed to people you felt might be criminals?" >> By no means. I didn't hear you. By no means.

"Well, you were scared enough where you hid. You were scared enough where you armed yourself. You're scared enough where you protected yourself. But she was left on the bed?" >> Yes, sir.

"Now, there was beating on that back door before anybody got in the door or got the door open, wasn't there?" >> Correct.

"Okay. And you've heard the officers, and I don't want to belabor this point, but there's direct conflict in the testimony between you and all the officers. They say people yelled 'police' and 'search warrant' at the front door and the back door. And I assume your position is, nobody ever yelled anything." >> Correct.

"Okay. They were just going to bust in and take a chance on them getting shot, huh?" >> Right.

"Okay. As you lay down at the end of that bed, at some point after kicking on the door, they gain entry to the bedroom, correct?" >> Correct.

"And your daughter's here. Did you fear those people had guns?" >> Yes, sir.

"And how did you base that fear?" >> Just out of fear.

"You didn't see who was out there, did you?" >> No, sir.

"You didn't hear anybody out there, did you?" >> I heard the rattling from the door, the noise at the door.

"But you say you didn't hear anybody say 'police' or 'search warrant' or anything like that?" >> Correct.

"So you had absolutely no idea who it was out there?" >> Correct.

"You didn't know if it was your girlfriend who forgot her key and was trying to get your attention to open up. You didn't know if it was friends trying to get in to see you, did you?" >> Friends knock.

"These people apparently knocked at the front door." >> They did not.

"Apparently, they tried to get your attention. Well, I guess that depends on whether you believe them or whether you believe you. But you didn't have any idea who it was, did you?" >> I did not.

"Now, when you were laying on the end of the bed with a gun, is that when you called out, "Who's there?'" >> No, sir.

"You never did that, did you?" >> No, sir.

"Is that when you called out, 'I've got a gun, get away'?" >> No, sir.

"You never did that, either, did you?" >> No, sir.

"But you were afraid of them, you wanted them out of there, I guess. Away from your place?" >> Correct.

"Now, the door gets kicked open or knocked open or pushed open or whatever. And the next thing that happens is what?" >> The intruder made their way in, and I opened fire.

"The intruder. You're talking about Prentiss police officer Ron Jones. Is that who you're talking about?" >> Correct.

"That intruder, that's who you're talking about?" >> Correct.

"Guy that had the search warrant? And you recognized it was a human being?" >> No, sir.

"You didn't recognize it was a human being?" >> I never saw the person.

"The person was at the door and in the room and you never saw them?" >> No, sir.

"You never saw that person silhouetted, standing in the doorway?" >> No, sir.

"You never saw any of the people behind him?" >> No, sir.

"You just started shooting?" >> Correct.

"You didn't see him with a gun?" >> No, sir.

"You didn't hear any threat from him. Did you?" >> No, sir.

"You just started shooting?" >> Correct.

"You just started shooting regardless who was there?" >> If they had said something, I wouldn't have shot.

"Well, if you had said something, or if you had gone to the front door, or if you had gone to the back door or if you had called out at the front door, or if you had called out at the back door, even if they don't believe what the police all say, if any of those things had been done by you, the man would be alive today, and you wouldn't be here. That's correct, isn't it?"

I figure this question has to draw an objection and it does.

"Objection, Your Honor."

I figure the judge will overrule.

"He may answer if he knows. Repeat the question."

"If they don't believe anything any of the police said, if they just believe, if you had gone to the front door when you heard that noise and looked out, or called out and asked, 'Who's there?', Ron Jones would be alive today, and you wouldn't be on trial. Isn't that true?" >> Correct.

Cory should have said "I don't know," since he really doesn't know. Cooper objects, too late this time.

"Objection."

And everybody simply ignores her. Judge Eubanks says nothing, and Buddy just keeps on going.

"And on the back door, when noise was made at the back door, if you had called out, 'Who's there?' or if you gone to the door to see who was there, he'd be alive today, and you wouldn't be on trial. Isn't that correct?"

Copper tries again, but in vain.

"Same objection."

"All right. Overruled."

"Isn't that correct?" >> Correct.

"Your daughter could sit up, walk?" >> Right.

"Didn't you think it might be a tad dangerous for you to start opening fire at random up there while she was laying on that bed and you were at the end of the bed? Did you think that was helping in taking care of your daughter?" >> The gun never was raised over the bed.

"Did you think it was good for you to open fire in that bedroom?" >> To protect myself and my daughter.

"Well, but your daughter wasn't down there as protected as you were, was she?" >> She was protected.

"Well, she wasn't as protected as you were because you took care of yourself first. Didn't you get yourself further away from the door than her?" >> Correct.

"And didn't you have a blocking thing there to keep the person from coming through the door seeing you right away? You were hid, weren't you?" >> Correct.

"She wasn't hid, was she?" >> No, sir.

She wasn't blocked, was she?" >> No, sir.

Nothing to protect her from any flying bullets. Were you protecting your daughter?" >> I was.

"Now, as I understand your testimony, you didn't see people even when they came through the door and you didn't see any weapons. Is that correct?" >> I seen no one.

"And you saw no weapons." >> Correct.

"And you weren't afraid your daughter was going to sit up or stand up or crawl to the edge of the bed when you opened fire?" >> She wasn't in the way of the fire. She wasn't.

"You were asleep in that chair in the living room. I believe your testimony was that what woke you up was that crashing or clashing or hitting on the door." >> Correct.

"Okay. And you, instead of asking who was there or looking out to see who was there, you ran in the back room and got a gun because you were scared, right?" >> Correct.

"And you weren't concerned about your daughter being on the bed and getting scared with all this going on and sitting up and you opening fire and maybe hitting her? Or, if somebody else was armed and hitting her, her being exposed up there on the bed like that? You weren't concerned about that?" >> I was concerned.

"Well, you weren't as concerned about her as you were about you, were you?" >> I was.

"You weren't hiding her. You weren't protecting her. You weren't shielding her. True?" >> Correct.

"You opened fire?" >> Correct.

"Now, no question about the marijuana being there, right?" >> Correct.

"No question. You just didn't smoke the marijuana that day because she was there, right?" >> Correct.

"We all know any amount of marijuana is against the law, right?" >> Correct.

"So when we heard earlier there was absolutely no reason for the police to be over at your apartment, there was nothing going on there that was illegal or improper, that's really not true, is it?"

That brings another objection from Rhonda Cooper. This one results in a bench conference.

This one also seems to end in disappointment for Cooper.

"It was there, the marijuana, wasn't it?" >> Correct.

"And they had a search warrant for marijuana, didn't they?" >> I never seen the search warrant.

"Well, we heard testimony about how a copy of the search warrant was left at the house. You say you got a copy of the search warrant at your preliminary hearing?" >> Yes, sir.

"But they were a little busy at that time, after you'd just shot Ron Jones. Now, I guess they could've taken time out and said, well, since we're going to have to carry Ron to the hospital to see if he's going to die, while the others of us formally read the search warrant to Mr. Maye. But that wouldn't have been practical, would it?" >> I'm not sure.

Clearly objectionable. No objection coming, however.

"Really, the way they treated you, I know what you said and I know what they said about what happened when they arrested you, when they took you into custody. But as a practical matter, if they'd really wanted to do something to you, they could've killed you in that room and no one would've ever known there was anything other than you shot an officer and they returned fire. Isn't that correct?" >> Correct.

Where's Rhonda when her client needs her? Perhaps she is simply giving up.

"And they got you out of there, they got you over to Forrest County, and they protected you, didn't they?" >> No, they did not.

"They took you to Jeff Davis County jail and to Forrest County, didn't they?" >> The investigator had me transferred due to them beating me.

"They took you over there. You weren't killed, were you?" >> No, I was not.

"Mr. Maye, you told Ms. Cooper that a friend gave you the gun?" >> Correct.

"That was a good friend, wasn't it?" >> Correct.

"That was a good gun. And you can't remember the name of the friend?" >> Correct.

"Now, you remembered how much you paid for the bullets when Mr. Stone asked you, didn't you?" >> Correct.

"And you remembered where you bought the ammunition when Mr. Stone asked you?" >> Correct.

"And you remembered how much ammunition you bought?" >> Correct.

"And you remembered the last time you fired the gun before you fired at Officer Jones. Is that correct?" >> Correct.

"But you can't remember the name of this friend that gave you the valuable gun. Is that correct?" >> Correct.

"Now, these two pictures, this place under your eye, is that what you're talking about?" >> That's correct.

"This place under your right eye, that's what you're talking about, correct?" >> One of them. I had knots in the top of my head. They kicked me repeatedly.

"They put you on the ground to handcuff you, didn't they? And one of them put his knee on your shoulder. Is that correct? And you're saying none of that happened when they were cuffing you, you're saying they beat you up." >> They beat me after they cuffed me.

"Okay. Just so I understand, your position is that when you opened fire, you weren't aiming at anything, you were just shooting up amongst them, right?" >> Towards the noise, correct.

"Just shooting towards the noise." >> Correct.

"And you didn't look out the window and see it was the police?" >> No, sir.

"And you weren't afraid that they were going to come there about that marijuana?" >> No, sir.

"And that's not why you armed yourself?" >> No, sir.

"And you didn't call out at the rear door?" >> No, sir.

"And you didn't have to call out because you knew they were outside, didn't you?" >> No, sir.

"You actually heard them call out and announce they had a search warrant." >> I did not.

"And what did you do in the interim time between the time that they knocked on the front door, kicked and announced at the front door, and the time they kicked and announced at the rear door?" >> That's when I ran to the bedroom.

"Well, it took a few minutes in there. You had time." >> Only seconds.

"I don't believe we have any more questions."

<<>>

Rhoda Cooper has some redirect.

"Cory, tell me where your daughter was." >> In the middle of the bed.

"And she was fourteen months old?" >> Correct.

"And she was asleep when you entered the bedroom?" >> Yes, ma'am.

"Well, why didn't you grab her up and go somewhere else?" >> I'm not sure.

"How much time passed? The way the prosecution presented this, there was just lots and lots of time passing where you had time to think about each and every thing you were doing. Was this planned?" >> No, ma'am.

"Was this your intent and your design?" >> No, ma'am.

"How much time passed from that crashing sound or that noise at your front door until the time you actually went into your bedroom?" >> It was only seconds.

"Tell the ladies and gentlemen how many if you can." >> No more than ten to fifteen seconds.

"From your lying on the floor of your bedroom to your actually shooting in the direction of that noise, how much time passed from there?" >> Maybe three to four seconds.

"So in say fifteen seconds, your entire life has been changed?" >> Yes, ma'am.

"Now, how was that back door opened? Just gently opened?" >> It was forced open.

"How so?" >> I suppose kicking.

"Now, before these people around your apartment said that they were police officers, who were they to you?" >> Intruders.

"How long had you been asleep?" >> I went to sleep maybe nine thirty, ten o'clock. I'm not sure what time they actually got there.

"Okay. So were you in a deep sleep? Would you say that you were in a deep sleep?" >> No, ma'am.

"Okay. And being awakened, were you able to gather all your thoughts and come up with how you were going to accomplish the defense of you and your daughter?" >> No, ma'am.

"Tell the ladies and gentlemen of the jury whether you were reacting to the noise and all that was going on." >> Correct.

"Cory, the statement that you gave to Agent Stone at about two o'clock on the morning of December 27th, is that what happened?" >> Yes, ma'am.

"And that you are sharing with the ladies and gentlemen of this jury two years after this incident, is that what happened?" >> Yes, ma'am.

"Nothing further, Your Honor."

<<>>

No surprise here. Buddy has some re-cross.

"Mr. Maye, I believe you said you knew where your daughter was in the bed because you saw her when you came back in the bedroom?" >> She was in the middle of the bed.

"And you saw her when you came back in the bedroom. I believe that's what you just told Ms. Cooper, you saw her?" >> I didn't see her.

"You didn't see her?" >> Correct.

"Because based on your previous testimony, it was dark, no lights. Is that what you said?" >> Correct.

"There wasn't a light shining through from the left-hand side over here, huh? Right over here, where you had to come through to get in the bedroom?" >> No lights.

"No lights from the left-hand side." >> No lights.

"No lights from the restroom. Now, the other thing, the other issue that I want to talk about is the issue about time. I believe you told Ms. Cooper from the time you heard the first noise to the time the entry was made in the back of the house was fifteen seconds." >> At the most.

"At the most. They tried and tried and tried to get in the front. They tried and tried to get in the back. You heard Jones and them say they came part of the way back around the building, then went back in when they had kicked the door in. Then Jones went in. And you say that only took at most fifteen seconds?" >> Correct.

"My question is, you really want the jury to believe it only took fifteen seconds for all this to happen from first to end?" >> Yes, sir.

"That's all the questions we've got."

DELIBERATION OF CORY MAYE
Friday, January 23, 2004

Angela figures I have nothing to add regarding the testimony of Dr. Steven Timothy Hayne, and she's right. Just as she's preparing to discuss Cory Maye's testimony, however, a thought hits me. I realize there's something up with the two autopsy diagrams Dr. Hayne showed us. I don't know that it's a big deal, but it's all I have. I'm not sure it's going to change anyone's mind, but it's worth a shot. I'll get it out there before Angela gets too far into summarizing Cory Maye's testimony.

"Excuse me, Angela."

It's my turn to be interrupted though. There's an untimely knock on the door. It's the bailiff, our guard. It's dinner time. We won't be eating in the jury room. They're going to bus us back to the motel, and we will be eating in the dining room under the careful gaze of our handlers. Then we're to come back here and continue deliberating into the evening.

<<>>

The food is dreadful. My mood is sour.

Mostly, I keep to myself and work through the testimony of Dr. Stephen Timothy Hayne, over and over again. It just doesn't feel right, but I can't find anything substantially wrong. Only that one issue about the diagram. I have that one issue, that one small issue. As far as this jury goes, it may be inconsequential.

I pick at my food. It doesn't taste any better disassembled and scattered. It certainly looks worse.

I'm not sure I can convince even myself that Maye wasn't standing when he shot Ron Jones. And if I can't believe him on that, if he's blatantly lying about that issue, how can I believe him on anything?

I push my plate away. Someone delivers a small bowl of vanilla ice cream. I take a spoonful.

If I can't believe Maye, all that is left is the State's case of one police officer after another providing a slightly different perspective of the same story. They knocked, they hollered, they spent time trying to get in. They arrived in marked cars, they were in uniform, they had warrants. The people next door heard them without problem.

The ice cream melts before I can finish it. I push the bowl away.

But the State's case isn't without its flaws. The State, after all, bears the burden of proof. If I can't believe them, then I can't vote Guilty. It's that simple.

They herd us back to the bus. I bring up the rear.

It would be much easier for me to vote Not Guilty if I could believe Cory Maye's testimony. I still think I'm missing something. There's simply no good reason I can think of for Cory to lie about that one aspect of the shooting. Could he possibly believe we would find him guilty if he shot from a standing position but find him innocent if he shot from a prone position? If he's going to lie, why lie about that? It makes no sense. I just don't get it.

The bus is decrepit. I think they started using it as a juror bus once the prisoners complained too much. The holes in the floor where they removed the bolts for shackles seem to confirm my theory.

The State's case bothers me more than the defense case though. They're the ones with the burden of proof. If I can't believe them, if I think they're trying to deceive me about crucial issues, I won't vote Guilty.

I may never figure out what actually happened, and Cory Maye may in fact be factually guilty, but I won't vote Guilty if I believe the State is playing fast and loose with the evidence they present us.

We queue up outside the elevators. We can't all fit in one, so they escort us up in two groups of six. The bailiff goes with the other group. We're guarded by a deputy I haven't seen before.

The State has the burden of proof. They must satisfy each of us, me included, beyond a reasonable doubt, whatever that is, that Cory Maye was not acting in self-defense; that he knew it was the police coming through the door or that he acted callously or carelessly. If I judge their case to be dishonest or not forthcoming, I'll doubt them. They'll have given me good reason to do so.

The elevator is old, slow, and crowded. It lurches when it starts, and jerks when it stops. It takes a few moments to level its floor with the floor beyond, and doesn't get it quite right. The deputy looks out for our safety.

"Watch your step, everyone."

When it comes time, I'll make my best case for the defense. I figure a few of my fellow jurors are uncomfortable with the thought of voting Guilty. I figure a few of them are hoping I can give them good enough reason not to do so. Others feel strongly and passionately that Cory Maye should die for shooting and killing Ron Jones. They are immovable in their intent to find Cory Maye guilty of capital murder.

We're the second group escorted back into the jury room. I bring up the rear of that trailing group.

So I can probably convince some of my fellow jurors to vote Not Guilty. And I can probably convince a couple to vote Guilty only for one of the lesser charges. At least I think I can.

But I know I won't convince all of them to vote Not Guilty on the capital murder charge. That's the problem. That's why I'm struggling. That's why my heart pounds. That's why I feel sick.

Everyone settles into the usual seats.

If we end up without a unanimous vote on the capital murder charge, and it sure seems like that's where we're headed, then that will be it. We won't vote on the other charges. We will be a hung jury. The judge will declare a mistrial. The State of Mississippi will try Cory Maye once again.

I pull my chair back, sit, and scooch forward. I put my right elbow on the table and rest my chin and right cheek in my right hand. I close my eyes and take a deep breath.

It is my conceited belief that the next jury will leave unnoticed the telltale hints that the State is not telling them the truth, the whole truth, and nothing but the truth. It is my self-aggrandizing fear that if I cannot compel a unanimous Not Guilty vote for capital murder with this jury, Cory Maye will die at the hands of the next.

I have no idea how I will live with that.

<<>>

Angela has had some rough sledding today, but she's actually acquitted herself reasonably well. She hit her stride with the last witness, and she's carrying that momentum through with her summary of the Cory Maye testimony. Perhaps she forgot I was going to speak to the testimony of Dr. Steven Timothy Hayne. Perhaps she remembers, but is in a hurry to wrap this up. Perhaps she senses I've got nothing, and she's taking pity on me. Whatever the case, I don't make an issue of it. The bullet traveled at a twenty degree downward angle. I can't see my way around that.

There was no surprise in Cory's testimony, she points out. He claimed he was awakened by a crashing sound, that he rushed to the bedroom, loaded his gun, fell to the floor, and fired as someone came through the back door. It all happened really fast, in less than fifteen seconds, and no one ever yelled 'police' or 'search warrant' or any such thing.

Angela doesn't believe it could happen in as little as fifteen seconds. After all, the police tried to enter the front of the house, kicked the door twice, shouldered it once. Cory heard at least one of those events as a loud crash at the front of his apartment. Unable to get in the front door, two of the officers went around the back, thought about entering through the rear door, but decided otherwise. They went to the side to see if they could enter through a window, only to be called back to the rear because someone had kicked the back door open. Another kick was required, and only then did Ron Jones enter the house.

That had to take more than fifteen seconds. One of the officers testified it took as long as four minutes. Angela graciously grants that four minutes sounds long to her, but makes her case that fifteen seconds is way too short. She adds that if it took much longer than fifteen seconds, and she believed it must have, then Cory Maye must certainly have been aware of what was going on outside.

She promotes the logic Buddy introduced during the State's closing argument. Though the closing arguments are not evidence, and though it's improper to treat them as such, there's no stopping her. She repeats Buddy's closing arguments as if they were fact, as if they were evidence.

Cory Maye thought there was only a single policeman out there, or so Buddy claimed. Cory Maye had no intention of being caught and arrested for the marijuana in his apartment, so he decided to shoot it out. He got his gun, loaded it, chambered a round, and stood by the back door waiting for the single policeman to enter. When Ron Jones came through the rear door, Cory Maye shot him knowing full well he was a peace officer. When the others continued yelling 'Police,' Maye suddenly realized there were more police officers out there. He surrendered at that point to save his own life. He laid on the floor, hiding behind the bed that his own daughter was sleeping in, and he pushed the gun towards the rear door. He struggled while he was being cuffed, and that accounted for the minor injuries shown in the photographs. He should consider himself lucky the police didn't kill him. They could have killed him, claimed it was self-defense, and no one would be the wiser. Only their discipline and training spared Maye such a fate.

Rhonda Cooper's closing argument, on the other hand, was almost insulting. She talked about how the trial affected her personally. She talked about how Ron Jones was partially responsible for his own death because he took the word of a CI, entered a building without knowing if someone was in there, and didn't have his gun drawn. None of this evokes any sympathy from the jury. None of it compels the jury to believe Cory Maye didn't know it was a police officer coming through the door.

Angela completes her overview of Cory Maye's testimony emphasizing that Cory Maye took cover behind the bed on which his own daughter laid. The expression on the faces of Vera, Marion, Bonnie, and the other women is telling. They are appalled.

As Angela finishes, Cory Maye is in serious danger of his life. Literally.

Angela is gracious in victory. She asks if anyone has something to offer in Cory Maye's behalf. No one says anything. No one raises a hand. A few squirm slightly in their seat, but that's about it.

Angela looks straight down the table at me. She challenges me with her words and her demeanor to put forth my best case that Cory Maye is not guilty of capital murder. She only wants to be fair.

<<>>

It's at this point I decide I'm tired of Mississippi. I think I'll try to wrap up my business in Columbia and move on. Yes, it's time I move on. I need to put this trial behind me.

Maybe I won't think too frequently about the sad ending to Ron Jones' life, or the way the witnesses and attorneys bent the truth here during trial.

Maybe I won't lie awake at night wondering if I fulfilled my oath, if I did my duty. Maybe I won't have dreams of Cory Maye being executed because I was unable to get a Not Guilty verdict right here, right now.

Hopefully, the terrible feelings I'm experiencing right now will turn out to be transient. Hopefully I'll feel better tomorrow, and better still the day after. Hopefully the feelings will fade to nothingness with time. Maybe I'm just kidding myself.

I just don't know.

<<>>

I ask for a minute to compose my thoughts. Angela grants me that. She can spare a minute. What's another minute or two, anyway? She grants me two minutes, assuming I want them.

She glances at the clock on the wall above me. She checks the time against her watch. She does some mental math. Her fingers and her lips move slightly as she does so.

And in doing so, she perhaps gives away all her hard work. That small action on her part, that seemingly inconsequential action on her part, crystallizes my thinking. I know what I must do, and I now have an idea on how I might accomplish it.

<<>>

Jack Nicholson: "Ever put your life in another man's hands, and his in yours? We follow orders, son. Otherwise people die. It's that simple. Are we clear?"

Tom Cruise: "Crystal."

<<>>

I look over my shoulder at the clock. I do some mental math of my own. I'm a recovering engineer, so I have no trouble doing it without moving my lips or counting on my fingers.

I need to time this carefully. I need to stretch things out a bit. I need first to take the edge off Dr. Hayne's testimony.

I rise from my chair, move around to the side of the table, and excuse myself as I take hold of the two autopsy diagrams. I study them, seemingly with care, but in reality for effect only. I know what I'm going to say. I'm merely trying capture their attention while running out the clock. I hold one of the diagrams in the air, the one showing the bullet trajectory.

"This diagram, this one right here, this one showing the downward trajectory of the bullet, this is the diagram that the State of Mississippi and Claiborne Buddy McDonald want us to see. They don't want us to see the entire autopsy report, or they would have given it to us, but they want us to see this page.

"And with good reason. This page is bedrock for those of us who want to disbelieve Cory Maye's testimony. Despite his tape-recorded statement that he did not know there were police outside his apartment, and despite the state's own witness testifying that he believed Cory Maye, this diagram ..."

I raise it higher over my head.

"... grants anyone in this room the right, perhaps the duty, to dismiss Cory Maye as a liar."

I toss the diagram back onto the table.

"That is if we trust the State is telling us the truth, if we believe they are not hiding something."

I raise the second diagram into the air.

"This is the only other page from the autopsy report that Buddy and Mississippi and Timothy want us to look at. It must be pretty significant if it is one of only two pages from an entire autopsy report that they want us to see."

I stroll back and forth along the side of the table, holding the diagram so that they can see it more clearly.

"And what is this diagram supposed to show us? This diagram shows the slight abrasions on Ron Jones' fingers. There's one scratch there ..."

I point to the small mark on the back of Ron Jones' left index finger.

"... and a second scratch there."

I point to the small mark on the back of the adjacent middle finger. I've captured their attention.

"Can everyone see them? Here, please pass it around. I'd like everyone to take a good look at the abrasions. It's important."

And I want to kill some more time.

I hand the diagram to Bonnie, the stay-at-home mom. She looks at it and passes it to her left, to Vera, the reassuring grandmother. It makes its way around the table. Community College Cathy is the last to look at it. When she's done, she hands it back to me.

They're clearly confused, but they act as if they're not.

"The State made the world of the first diagram, the one showing the bullet trajectory. They want us to use that diagram to dismiss Cory Maye's claims of innocence. They want us to use that diagram to give them permission to execute Cory Maye. It means everything to them."

I again raise the second diagram above my head.

"The State, on the other hand, made nothing of this diagram. It shows the location of two minor abrasions. Other than mentioning those abrasions when introducing this diagram, they never mentioned them again. So the question is why. Why did Buddy, and Timothy, and Mississippi introduce this diagram? We all know it has nothing to do with showing us the minor abrasions on the back of Ron Jones left index and middle fingers. They don't care about that, and they don't care if we care about that."

I toss the diagram onto the table.

"This is the dog that didn't bark."

It's a Sherlock Holmes reference, from *Silver Blaze*. No one shows any sign of being familiar with it, or of figuring out why this finger-abrasion diagram is in evidence before us.

Webbie is the first to try an explanation.

"You're forgetting that the coroner used this to show us where the entry wound is."

He reaches across the table, snags the diagram, pulls it back towards him, lifts it with his left hand, and points to the small mark Dr. Steven Timothy Hayne added during trial. He swings the diagram back and forth so that everyone can get a good view.

No one responds.

"See?"

No one responds.

"It shows the entry wound. Right there."

No one responds.

"What is with all you people?"

I respond.

"You're right, Webbie. They wanted us to see where the entry wound was. I agree with you on that."

"Okay, then."

"But there must have been a diagram in the autopsy showing the entry wound. Absolutely must have been. They made a separate, dedicated diagram just to show some minor abrasions. Surely there is going to be a diagram showing the entry wound."

Webbie agrees with me.

"I assume there is."

"Then why not just show us that one? Why not show us the diagram of the entry wound if they wanted us to know where the entry wound was? Why go to all the trouble to enter a diagram into evidence showing a few minor abrasions, and then have Dr. Steven Timothy Hayne draw the entry wound on that diagram? Why do that?"

Webbie is not particularly curious.

"I don't know, and I don't care."

But I'm curious.

"Because, ladies and gentlemen, there was something on the entry-wound diagram they didn't want us to see."

I pause for effect.

"We don't know what it is. They know, but they don't want us to know. They're at home popping corn and watching Beavis and Butthead. We're here, under guard, arguing with one another. Tonight, they'll sleep in their nice beds confident we'll not see their revealing entry-wound diagram. We'll be bussed back to some dingy hotel to toss and turn in ignorance."

The suggestion that we might not be going home tonight hits home. That's good. That's very good.

"I cautioned early on that Buddy and his crew hope to manipulate us. They tried first with Stephen Jones' ever-moving light, the one he previously forgot to mention, the one that hopped from window to window, the one that appeared behind moving blinds that couldn't be seen from where Stephen Jones stood.

"Then there was Terrence Cooley's story of how he moved to where he wasn't supposed to be from where he was supposed to be because he arrived at where he was supposed to be before Phillip Allday arrived at where he was supposed to be. If you can make any sense of that reasoning, good for you. To me, it makes no sense whatsoever.

"They followed that with Darryl Graves and his story of how he was simply an innocent follower asked by Ron Jones to lead one team into hostile territory. But Graves conceded he had been in town earlier that day, and volunteered that he knew the person who lived in the left-hand apartment. He had even managed a controlled purchase from that apartment.

"He was the first to arrive at the Prentiss PD, arriving even before Ron left to have the warrants signed. He knows the warrants differ only by the name of the occupants, or the lack thereof, but claims to have only glanced at them. He was one of the people who gave the briefing. He was the person who drew the sketch of the duplex, both interior and exterior. Yet he denies knowing the CI, or whether Ron Jones surveilled the duplex, or whether there was any controlled purchase at either apartment.

"He's conveniently stupid when there's something we're not supposed to know."

"Each of the officers goes out of his way to tell us Ron Jones did not have his weapon drawn. I suppose in the hope it would make Ron Jones seem defenseless, and Cory Maye therefore more ruthless. It occurred to them their story might make Ron Jones seem careless, however, so they each told us a story about how Ron claimed his CI told him there were no weapons in the duplex.

"Ask yourself whether you honestly and sincerely believe such rigmarole. Ask yourself whether it's more likely that Ron Jones didn't have his weapon drawn because he put himself at the front of his team. He protected those behind him with his own body and his own life. He breached the back door with a battering ram, and he took the bullet before he could draw his pistol."

Another pause, but not just to buy time. I'm moved thinking of Ron Jones dying in such fashion. I find also that I'm coming to believe his fellow officers are tainting his memory by the story they are telling. It makes him seem clumsy and unprofessional.

"If you believe Ron Jones was not so foolish that he would enter a darkened apartment unarmed, based solely on the assurance of a CI, if you believe Ron Jones was better trained and more prudent than that, then you have to ask yourself why Buddy and his crew want us to believe otherwise.

"I suggest it's because the battering ram version would add considerable weight to Cory Maye's claim that everything happened quickly. Someone banged at the front of the duplex, to draw the occupant's attention away from the rear, or for some reason I can't fathom. Then Ron Jones attempted to breach the rear door, battering ram in hand, weapon holstered. But the breach was imperfect; a second blow was required. That modest delay, unfortunately, gave a frightened and rattled Cory Maye just barely enough time to insert a clip, chamber a round, fall to the ground, and fire as someone came through the rear door.

"This battering ram theory presumes, of course, that several people are flat-out lying to us about trying first to breach the front door by kicking at it, by shouldering it. It was Darrell Cooley who gave this one away. He gave it away when Rhonda Cooper asked a penetrating question, then failed to follow up on the significance of the answer. She asked Darrell Cooley about the screen door. Darrell Cooley, to my utter amazement, did not remember a screen door. Cooley is unlikely to have kicked the door twice, and shouldered it once, and not have remembered the screen door.

"It's not only that Cooley doesn't remember the screen door, it's that the screen door could not be opened from the outside, even if Cooley remembered it. The screen door was wired shut with a coat hanger to keep the young daughter from sneaking out through the front door. That means Darrell Cooley could not have tried the door handle, as he claimed. It would have been necessary to open the screen door, and the screen door was wired closed.

"We know that is so because Cory Maye told us, and because Mississippi declined to challenge the point. They certainly spent plenty of time challenging his claim that it all happened very quickly. They absolutely spent plenty of time challenging his claim he did not know there were police outside trying to serve a lawfully issued search warrant. And they went out of their way to challenge his claim that he was lying down when he fired his gun. They challenged all that. But they never once asked any question or made any argument to rebut Cory Maye's claim that the screen door was wired shut.

"Then they put icing on the cake. They had Dr. Steven Timothy Hayne come up to the stand and present the most damaging evidence of all, the bullet trajectory diagram. They also conspired with Dr. Hayne to keep from us the entry-wound diagram, because that diagram would show us something they don't want us to see.

"And then, after all that, they ask us to come in here and vote unanimously to allow them to execute Cory Maye. They ask us to trust them beyond a reasonable doubt."

I take a pause from my grand soliloquy, but I don't remain in place. I pace back and forth, as if in thought, but really to maintain control of the moment. I'm not ready to yield the floor. I've merely finished the first part of my carrot-and-stick plan. I've given them the carrot; given them good and noble reasons for voting Not Guilty.

I glance at the clock. It's 8:45 PM. It's now time to focus on the wrong reason for voting Not Guilty. It's time to threaten them with the stick Angela handed me when I saw her performing the mental math.

"I want to thank everyone for humoring me, for being willing to deliberate the testimony of each witness, for giving me this opportunity to summarize my thoughts openly before you. I won't delay a vote any further."

And the entire crowd erupts.

"But I cannot in good conscience, having in hand only that which is currently before us, cast a vote that will expose Cory Maye to a death sentence."

And some of them grumble.

"In fact, because I distrust the case presented by the State of Mississippi for the reasons you so graciously allowed me to just now summarize, I feel duty-bound to vote Not Guilty on each and every charge."

I need to be very careful here.

"I'm not saying I refuse to vote Guilty to any charge under any condition. That would be an improper stance on my part."

I need to remove any grounds for someone trying to have me removed for juror misconduct.

"If after further deliberation, any one of you, or all of you combined can convince me why my concerns about the State's case are unwarranted, then I will vote guilty. I expect, however, that would require us to continue our deliberation well into next week."

Shock.

"I've been involved in a similar jury deliberation previously. On the eighth day, the court finally declared a mistrial."

And awe.

"Because as long as a one juror keeps telling the judge there is a chance for a verdict, and as long as that juror is deliberating in good faith, then the judge is extremely reluctant to declare a mistrial."

Silence, though there are a few jaws hanging open.

"I sincerely believe this jury is capable of reaching a unanimous verdict, as long as we're willing to put in the time. If we are going to deprive Cory Maye of his liberty, and perhaps even his life, then it's not at all unreasonable that we should be willing to spend a week of our time ensuring that we have made the correct decision.

"If we can't reach a verdict tonight, and soon, on this first round of voting, then I suggest we will have to start over, that we will have to work through the testimony of each witness once again. I'm going to suggest that next time we don't rush through each witness as we did this time. I'm going to suggest that each juror be asked to participate, that we work around the table as we deliberate each witness. I sincerely believe that if we go over all the evidence very carefully, if we all participate in the deliberation, we will finally achieve a unanimous verdict.

"I'm not predicting what my vote would be after a more careful deliberation. That would be improper. I would wait until the deliberation is complete before making up my mind. That is the oath I took. But as of now, as of this moment, based on the deliberations we have had so far, I must vote Not Guilty to each count."

It's now 8:50 PM. It's time for my thinly-veiled attempt to pressure everyone to vote as I see fit.

"If each and every one of us is persuaded by force of argument that the State's case is suspect, and if each and every one of us believes we must each vote Not Guilty, then I suggest we are but ten minutes from concluding our business here.

"If, on the other hand, any one of us feels compelled to vote Not Guilty, then we must all be willing to continue these deliberations indefinitely until we can all be of the same mind."

"Madam Foreperson, we haven't much time before we will be instructed to suspend our deliberations for the evening. I suggest we vote without further delay."

VERDICT
Friday, January 23, 2004

The actual jury does not take long to deliberate. They are given the case at 10:39 in the morning. They return one hour and ten minutes later.

<<>>

Judge: "All right. Has the jury reached a verdict?"

Foreperson: "We have, Your Honor."

Judge: "All twelve of you agree on that as the verdict of the jury?"

Each of them responds in the affirmative.

Judge: "All right. Hand it to the bailiff."

The bailiff takes the verdict from the foreperson and delivers it to the court clerk.

Judge: "All right. I'll ask the clerk to read the verdict."

Clerk: "We, the jury, find the defendant, Cory Jermaine Maye, guilty of capital murder."

<<>>

The entire process takes three minutes, after which Judge Eubanks excuses the jury for lunch.

Court reconvenes at 2:20 PM to hold the penalty phase of the trial. Buddy McDonald argues that Cory Maye should be put to death. Rhonda Cooper argues that Cory Maye should be spared. The actual jury retires to deliberate the death penalty at 4:35 PM.

They return after one hour and twenty-five minutes.

<<>>

Judge: "All right. Have you reached a verdict?"

Foreperson: "We have, Your Honor."

Judge: "And all of you agree on that as the verdict of the jury?"

Each of them responds in the affirmative.

Judge: "Hand it to the bailiff."

The bailiff takes the verdict from the foreperson and delivers it to the court clerk.

Judge: "All right. And the clerk will read the verdict."

Clerk: "We, the jury, unanimously find from the evidence beyond a reasonable doubt that the following facts existed at the time of the commission of a capital murder. That the defendant actually killed Ronald W. Jones. That the defendant intended that killing of Ronald W. Jones take place. That he contemplated that lethal force would be employed.

"Next, we, the jury, unanimously find that the aggravating circumstances of the capital offense was committed to disrupt or hinder the lawful exercise of any government function or the enforcement of laws and is sufficient to impose the death penalty and that there are insufficient mitigating circumstances to outweigh the aggravating circumstances.

"And we further find unanimously that the defendant should suffer death."

Judge: "That's signed by the foreman?"

Clerk: "Signed by the foreman."

Judge Eubanks addresses the jury.

Judge: "All right. That will conclude your service at this time. We will finally excuse you. We do thank you for your service. Hate we kept you this time, but there are the difficult cases that have to be resolved, and we do appreciate you doing your service.

"All right. The jury may be discharged. Everybody else remain seated. And if anybody about the press wants to talk to you, just tell them that you can't talk to them at my instructions."

The jury is allowed to leave. Judge Eubanks addresses the defendant.

Judge: "All right. I do need to impose sentence. Stand here in front of this microphone with your counsel. All right. You're Cory Jermaine Maye?"

Cory: "Yes, sir."

Judge: "And a jury of your peers has convicted you of the charge of capital murder. The case then went to the sentencing phase, and they ordered that you be sentenced to suffer death. Is there anything you want to say before sentencing?"

Cory: "No, sir."

Judge: "All right. Then based upon the jury's verdict, I will sentence you to suffer death by lethal injection. All right. That will be the sentence of the Court.

Cooper: "Judge, will we get a copy of that order now?"

Judge: "Yes. Is there anything further for our record?"

Cooper: "No, sir."

Judge: "All right. You all may be excused. We'll stand adjourned."

INTERLUDE

"The badge and the gun don't mean anything. It doesn't mean they found what they say they found." -- Law Enforcement Officer, Jefferson Davis County, Mississippi.

Darryl Graves, I suspect, would be bad at poker. During the capital murder trial of Cory Jermaine Maye, he gave everything away. Things we were not supposed to know, or to figure out, he gave them away.

The jurors didn't pick up on the telltale signs of Darryl Graves' testimony. Those jurors were not so disposed, so they missed, or dismissed, each of the giveaways. History, however, is unlikely to be as kind or as credulous. Truth, noted Francis Bacon, is the daughter of time, not of authority.

<<>>

A gunshot is much louder than most people realize. People wear bulbous headphones at shooting ranges for reasons other than fashion. The gunshots you hear on television have been softened considerably so they don't scare the cat or inflict coronaries among the elderly.

An actual gunshot measures around 140 decibels (dB), at least to the person firing the weapon. By comparison, the noise level of a jackhammer measures around 130 dB. In the strange logarithmic world of decibels, every 10 dB increase in noise level represents an apparent doubling of volume. A gunshot at 140 dB would seem twice as loud as a jackhammer at 130. The gunshot doesn't last as long, and in that sense it may be less noticeable, but it is temporarily twice as loud.

Noises above 120 dB can cause physical pain. Prolonged exposure to noises above 115 dB results in permanent hearing loss.

Sandblasting measures 115 dB, yelling 110, a chainsaw 100. The backup bell on a refuse collection truck comes in at 90, a garbage disposal at 80, and a vacuum cleaner at 70. Normal conversation takes place at 60 decibels.

Keep those numbers in mind as you reconsider the trial testimony of the four officers involved in the raid.

> Stephen Jones: "I proceeded behind him. That's when the shots was fired. ... Three shots."
>
> Terrence Cooley: "I heard three to four shots."
>
> Darrell Cooley: "And then I heard 'police' a few seconds later, then the gunshots. ... I thought I heard five."
>
> Darryl Graves: "While we was doing our search, we got information that there was an officer down. And at that time we stopped our search and went over to find out what was going on."

There it is. Darryl Graves told the jury he did not hear the gunshots. He didn't come straight out and say "I did not hear the gunshots." Instead, he talked around the subject. "We got information there was an officer down."

Later in the trial, he obfuscated in similar fashion.

> Darryl Graves: "I came out when I found out that someone, one of the officers had been shot."

Cory Maye's jury failed to notice or failed to care that Darryl Graves did not hear the gunshots, even though the other three officers who testified had no difficulty hearing them. There is little doubt, however, that Darryl Graves claims to have not heard the gunshots. From a preliminary hearing, we have the following testimony from Agent, now Sergeant Graves:

> Darryl Graves: "Right. We had started the search warrant prior to knowing that Ron had been shot. We had started searching already. And once we heard the call, we stopped our search."

> Darryl Graves: "No, we started the search until we heard that Ron had been shot. We had started our search, and we stopped our search, secured that area also, and went over to see what was going on."

When asked explicitly during the trial "did you hear any of the things that were going on in the apartment on the right?" Darryl Graves provided an unambiguous answer: "No, I didn't hear anything."

Graves provided his testimony with such confidence, and selected his words with such skill, that no one to my knowledge has openly questioned his story. Our common experience, however, should cause us to question whether it is possible that Darryl Graves could be in one unit of a small duplex and fail to hear three, or four, or five gunshots in the adjacent unit.

If for example, someone was sandblasting the outside of your house or apartment building, you would expect to hear it even if you were inside.

If someone was operating a jackhammer at the far end of your house, you would expect that noise to be audible and alarming, even if there were intervening walls.

If the police stand outside your home and yell "Police, search warrant," they expect you to hear it. Darryl Graves expected the jury to believe Cory Maye heard people yelling, but expected that same jury to believe he himself did not hear any gunshots, though he was in the same building and the doors were open. Note that at 110 decibels, yelling is perceived to be only one-eighth as loud as a gunshot at 140 decibels.

There are at least three possible explanations for the difference between my simple acoustic analysis and Darryl Graves' sworn testimony. I claim none of them to be true. I offer each only for your consideration.

First, it's possible my crude acoustic analysis is good on paper only. It's possible a person with normal hearing, standing in the Jamie Smith apartment of the Mary Street duplex would not be able to hear three shots fired from within the other apartment of the Mary Street duplex. This possibility could be proved or disproved by controlled testing at the Mary Street duplex or an equivalent structure. To my knowledge, no such testing has been conducted in this case.

Second, it's possible that Darryl Graves perjured himself when he claimed not to have heard the gunshots from within the Jamie Smith living room.

Third, it's possible that Darryl Graves perjured himself when he claimed he was at the Mary Street duplex when the shots were fired.

<<>>

There were three other officers who claimed to be inside the Jamie Smith apartment when Cory Maye fired at Ron Jones: Bassfield Police Chief Earl Bullock and Jefferson County Sheriff Deputies Mike Brown and Allen Allday. Those three officers would, I presume, argue the first possibility is the only possibility, that my acoustic analysis is simply wrong. Though none of the three officers testified at Cory Maye's trial, each of them signed a report claiming that they were unable to hear any gunshots from the adjacent apartment. We learn of that from Cory Maye's written appeal.

> Officers Mike Brown, Allen Allday, and Chief Earl Bullock, who could have confirmed that from within the same Smith home, they did not hear announcements directed toward the Maye home, and did not know that Officer Ron Jones was shot until hearing an announcement on their police radios.

If Darryl Graves perjured himself on this issue, if he was not in fact at the small yellow duplex that evening when Ron Jones was shot and killed, then it is likely that the other three officers at least mis-reported what they heard or did not hear. If Darryl Graves perjured himself and the others mis-reported the events, that would constitute a conspiracy to cover up the tragic events of that night, and perhaps a conspiracy to frame Cory Maye for capital murder.

<<>>

Equally as surprising as Darryl Graves' claim he did not hear the gunshots is his claim that Ron Jones did not have his weapon drawn because the confidential informant explained there would be no weapons in the duplex. We first learn of that claim from Graves' trial testimony.

> Darryl Graves: "Ron Jones stated that there was not supposed to be any weapons in the residence."

This seems to be the first time Darryl Graves or anyone else swore under oath that Ron Jones' confidential informant claimed there would be no weapons at the Mary Street duplex. Graves gave the response when asked about the issue by the prosecution. It was the prosecution that introduced that new testimonial evidence within the midst of *Mississippi v. Cory Maye*. Later, Graves would be specifically asked, once again by the prosecution, if the informant's assurances might have been the reason that Ron Jones did not have his weapon drawn. Graves allowed that it might have been.

Buddy McDonald: "Were you advised at that meeting that Officer Jones did not believe there would be any weapons at the apartments?"

Darryl Graves: "Yes."

Buddy McDonald: "Do you think that might've been the reason he didn't have his -- some of his people didn't have their weapons drawn?

Darryl Graves: "That could've been the reason."

Clearly, the prosecution desired that the jury to accept as true this new claim. Later in the trial, however, Darryl Graves let slip an alternative explanation why Ron Jones may not have had his weapon drawn. He was asked by Rhonda Cooper about the procedures normally applied by the Pearl River Basin Drug Task Force while executing search warrants. He volunteered the following insight:

Darryl Graves: "There is one person that usually don't have his weapon drawn sometimes, and he could be the person with, if we're using a ram -- and the ram is a -- it's used like -- it's like a metal bar that we use to open a door sometimes because normally they won't open the door. So we have to break the door down. And we have a ram. And that person won't have his weapon drawn. ... He has one, but he doesn't draw it until he puts the ram down. Once he gets the door open, then he drops the ram, and he should usually draw his gun by then."

As time passed, Buddy McDonald seemed to have forgotten his questioning of Darryl Graves regarding this subject. In December of 2005, McDonald responded to thirteen written questions presented to him by Radley Balko, the award-winning writer who brought the Cory Maye case to national attention.

Radley Balko: "If Cory Maye was a suspected drug dealer, and if he was named in the warrant as a suspected drug dealer, and if Officer Jones knew there were two separate residences at the duplex, why was the unarmed Officer Jones the first to enter Maye's home? Do police typically raid the homes of suspected drug dealers unarmed?"

Buddy McDonald: "There were several officers there and they were armed. Jones was armed and his gun was still in his holster after he was shot as I recall. His hands were free so he could force entry on the back door as I recall. He had backup officers with him at the back door."

"His hands were free so he could force entry on the back door as I recall."

<<>>

Darryl Graves' possible slip-up in revealing the battering ram as a breaching option helps highlight and possibly resolve another suspicious aspect of the State's case, this one from the mouth of Darrell Cooley. It's perhaps coincidence that Darrell Cooley was the only other person to testify about Ron Jones having no need to worry about weapons.

> Darrell Cooley: "He said that he had been working on this property for a while and that he had a CI that said that the drugs were supposed to be there and that there weren't supposed to be any weapons in the house."

Coincidence or not, if Ron Jones used a battering ram to easily breach the rear door, there would have been no reason for Darrell Cooley to have kicked futilely and shouldered the front door. It would explain why Darrell Cooley was unaware that the screen door had been wired shut.

> Cory Maye: "The screen door was secured with a coat hanger because my daughter could open the door. And the screen door would not lock by itself, so we kept it secured with a coat hanger from the inside."

Though the prosecution must have feared an attentive juror would notice the incongruity of attempting to open an entry door without first opening its attendant screen door, they made no effort to dispute Cory Maye's claim. They apparently chose instead to assume the jurors would not notice. Rhonda Cooper assisted them by failing to highlight, during he closing argument for example, the conflict between Cory Maye's testimony and that provided earlier by Darrell Cooley.

> Darrell Cooley: "I didn't mess with the screen door."
>
> Rhonda Cooper: "What door did you mess with?"
>
> Darrell Cooley: "The main door."
>
> And later:
>
> Rhonda Cooper: "Were you aware of the screen door or anything about the screen door?"
>
> Darrell Cooley: "Not the screen door, no, ma'am."
>
> Rhonda Cooper: "Do you know how the screen door got opened?"
>
> Darrell Cooley: "No, ma'am."

If Darrell Cooley perjured himself on this issue, if Ron Jones did not have his weapon drawn because he used a battering ram to force entry into the Maye residence, then it is likely that Darryl Graves perjured himself as well on the issue. That too would constitute a conspiracy to convict Cory Maye based on false testimony.

<<>>

In the following section, I present an alternative scenario for the events surrounding the fatal shooting of Prentiss Police Officer Ron Jones. While I argue that the alternate scenario better explains the circumstances surrounding the shooting and prosecution, I do not claim the scenario to be unassailable truth. In fact, I suspect the scenario I am about to reveal is almost certainly wrong in many of its details. I do not know, for example, the exact words each person may have spoken that evening. Nor do I know how each person made their way from the Prentiss police station to the Mary Street duplex. There is sufficient evidence, however, from the trial testimony and the case documents to allow a reasonable recreation of the events surrounding the shooting death of Ron Jones.

It is possible that the testimony provided by the prosecution witnesses at trial was one-hundred percent correct. I cannot prove otherwise, and I do not claim to have done so. It is not for me to judge. It is for you, the reader, to compare the trial testimony with the alternative scenario, and to decide for yourself what may have actually happened at that small yellow duplex in Prentiss, Mississippi.

ALTERNATE SCENARIO: THE INVESTIGATION
Wednesday, December 26, 2001

Ron Jones was on duty the day after Christmas in 2001. He met with Agent Darryl Graves of the Pearl River Basin Narcotics Task Force. The two of them discussed executing a search warrant on the residence of Jamie Smith.

As a member of the Drug Task Force, Graves was familiar with Jamie Smith. He had previously purchased drugs from Smith in an undercover operation. Even as Jones and Graves spoke, Smith had drug charges pending against him in Jefferson Davis County, and had been under investigation by the Drug Task Force for several months.

Usually Ron Jones informed the Drug Task Force of suspicious drug activity within Prentiss, and the Task Force took charge from there. According to Marvin Cooper, commander of the Task Force, Ron Jones did his job well.

> "Most of the cases we made there were by his assistance. He was a diligent officer. He made a lot of cases for us."

For reasons still unclear, this raid was different. It was not to be associated with the Drug Task Force in general, or Darryl Graves in particular. Perhaps Graves was proscribed by the agency or the court from further contacting Smith while charges were pending. Perhaps Graves wished to use the search as an opportunity to train local law enforcement on the proper conduct of a drug search. Ron Jones, after all, was a junior member of the Prentiss Police force and was just then completing another round of drug enforcement training.

Whatever the reason, Graves was going to remain behind while Ron Jones and a medley of officers from Prentiss, Bassfield, and Jefferson Davis County served the warrant and searched the premises.

<<>>

Jamie Smith lived in the left-hand unit of the small yellow duplex located at 1728 Mary Street in Prentiss. He lived there with his girlfriend Audrey Davis, her children, and a fifteen-year-old boy known as Jimmy. Though the building bore no address, it would not be difficult to find. It was within a mile of the Prentiss Police Department. Mary Street itself is short, and there was no other yellow duplex on the street.

The two apartments, however, would not be easily distinguished. Each was the mirror image of the other. Neither bore any letter or number to differentiate it from its neighbor. Neither had the name of its owner displayed in a prominent location, such as on a mailbox. The span of the duplex was aligned northeast to southwest, making compass designations non-intuitive. Terms such as left-hand and right-hand were conditional depending on whether one was looking from the front or rear of the building.

Ron Jones and Darryl Graves together surveilled Jamie Smith's apartment, briefly, by driving past it. They presumably used an unmarked police car or one of their personal vehicles. They presumably were not in uniform.

Graves provided Jones with the phone number of a drug user who would be willing, for a modest price, to purchase drugs from Jamie Smith. That person was acquainted with Smith. The Drug Task Force had used him previously to purchase drugs from Smith. There would be no impediment to a successful purchase this time. The so-called "controlled buy" would then form the basis for obtaining a search warrant for the Smith residence.

Ron Jones wrote the phone number of the CI in black ink on the palm of his left hand. The number was discovered and noted during the autopsy, memorialized in both text and diagram.

A 7-digit number is identified in the palmar surface of the hand consisting of the numbers "8473043" written in black ink.

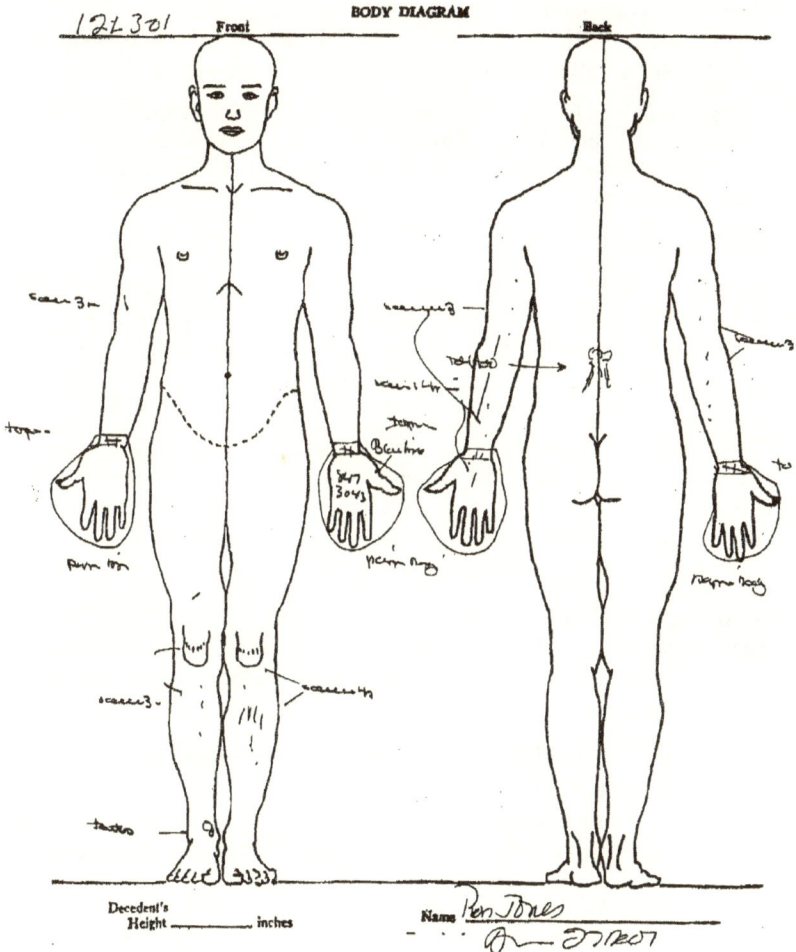

BODY DIAGRAM

The phone number belonged to Randy Gentry.

Randy Gentry, poor and uneducated, was well-known around Prentiss as an unabashed racist. To gain an appreciation of Gentry's feelings towards blacks, consider the following message Gentry would later leave on the answering machine of Cory Maye's appellate attorney, Bob Evans:

> Yeah, this is Mr. Randy Gentry.
>
> Hey, I got to thinkin' about my friend. I got yo' message this morning, Bob. Y'all, y'all threaten me all you want to and everything. I don't like fuckin' niggers from jump street, but call me or whatever and I'll --
>
> But the day I burn five cents on gas to help that fuckin' cocksucker Cory Maye get out of jail is going to be a hell of a damn day.
>
> But, uh, if you want to talk to me like a fuckin' white man, you talk. But don't threaten me on bullshit. Get your NAACP motherfuckers --
>
> I don't give a fuck 'bout niggers, bro. Fuck niggers.
>
> But I'll tell you what. That's a good friend of mine they killed, buddy. I'll, I'll tell you anything. I'll, I'll be honest with you as fuckin' gum street. But I don't like no motherfucker talkin' shit to me or about my friends.
>
> Alright, well look here. Call me today and look here. Y'all buy my fuckin' gas, the NAACP buy my fuckin' gas I'll come talk to y'all or whatever. But look here. I'm, I'm a poor-ass motherfucker too, bro. Call me. You got my fuckin' number.
>
> Don't piss me fuckin' off.

Given Gentry's racial attitudes and contagious charm, it is unlikely that Ron Jones and Randy Gentry were good friends, as Gentry claimed in the phone message. Given Gentry's phone number was found on Ron Jones' palm, it's unlikely that Jones and Gentry were well-acquainted.

<<>>

Darryl Graves and Ron Jones separated. Jones returned to his house, perhaps to change into uniform. From there, he called Randy Gentry. Gentry agreed to purchase the drugs in exchange for cash and perhaps for retention of whatever drugs he purchased.

Gentry dropped by Jones' house, arriving as a passenger in the pickup of his brother, Carroll Dean Gentry. Randy received his instructions and $40 cash to be used for the controlled purchase. The two Gentrys then departed for the Mary Street duplex.

Upon arriving at the duplex, Carroll remained in his truck as Randy went to Jamie Smith's apartment. Randy knocked and was admitted. Randy purchased $40 worth of crack cocaine using the cash provided by Ron Jones. He left the apartment and returned directly to his brother's truck.

Carroll drove the two of them to the Prentiss-Jefferson Davis County Airport to meet with Ron Jones, as per his instructions. It was a ten minute drive from the duplex on Mary Street.

Randy Gentry told Jones that he had been admitted to Jamie Smith's residence, and that he had purchased crack cocaine from Smith. Jones told Randy to drop by Prentiss Town Hall the next day and collect his $25 fee. Jones and the Gentrys then went their separate ways.

<<>>

Ron Jones returned to police headquarters. Having surveilled the duplex on Mary Street, and having orchestrated a controlled buy, he called the chief of police for permission to secure a search warrant. The chief of police happened to be his father.

We learn of the last call between father and son from a New York Times article written by Fox Butterfield. The article was entitled "As Drug Use Drops in Big Cities, Small Towns Confront Upsurge." It was dated February 11, 2002, just seven weeks after the shooting. It reads in part:

> On Dec. 26, in Prentiss, Officer Ron Jones, 29, called his father, Ronald N. Jones, the police chief, for permission to get a search warrant for an apartment where an informer had told him there was crack. An hour later, as Officer Jones led a team into the apartment, he was shot in the abdomen. The suspect in the shooting, Cory Maye, has been charged with capital murder.
>
> "The hardest thing for me is that I'm the one who gave him the approval," Chief Jones said.
>
> His son had been taking classes in drug enforcement and was the town's K-9 officer.
>
> "He thought he could clean Prentiss up," Chief Jones said. "He honestly gave his life trying to make a difference."

<<>>

Ron Jones contacted Darryl Graves by radio, mobile phone, or cell phone. He informed Graves that the controlled buy had been made, and that he had permission to get a search warrant. Graves, as he testified during trial, returned to Prentiss and met with Jones at police headquarters.

ALTERNATE SCENARIO: THE AFFIDAVITS
8:00 PM, Wednesday, December 26, 2001

Rather than prepare paperwork for a single search warrant, Darryl Graves advised Ron Jones that it would be prudent, when dealing with a duplex, to prepare two search warrants, one for each unit. One warrant, the primary warrant, would be for Jamie Smith's apartment. If drugs were found in Smith's apartment, the second warrant, the one for the other unit, would not be served.

If, on the other hand, no drugs were found within Jamie Smith's apartment, the search could be extended to the perimeter of the house, to underneath the house, even into the second unit itself. The second warrant would be insurance against the possibility Smith was clever enough to store drugs beyond the boundaries of the unit in which he lived. Those drugs would be beyond the reach of the first warrant. They would, however, be within reach of the second.

There was a second reason for having two warrants, one for each apartment. The apartments were not easily identifiable as apartments 1 and 2, or units A and B. There were no identifying numbers or letters on either of them. A clever defense lawyer might argue the warrant served was not for the apartment searched. Having two warrants would prevent such nonsense.

It would be best, they decided, if two warrants were prepared.

<<>>

The Fourth Amendment to the Constitution protects residents of the U.S. against searches unaccompanied by a warrant.

> The right of the people to be secure in their persons, houses, papers, and effects, against unreasonable searches and seizures, shall not be violated, and no Warrants shall issue, but upon probable cause, supported by Oath or affirmation, and particularly describing the place to be searched, and the persons or things to be seized.

In law, a warrant is a written order from the judicial branch to the executive branch. Most commonly, it is a written order from a judge to a police agency to arrest a person or conduct a search.

In practice, at least in Prentiss in 2001, the police prepared three documents for each search warrant they requested: the unsigned warrant itself, an affidavit, and a description of the underlying facts and circumstances. Jones and Graves prepared two sets of three documents. They prepared the affidavits first.

In Mississippi, in 2001, *The Affidavit for Search Warrant* was a form with four numbered sections. The four sections required the requesting officer to explain the where, who, what, and why for the Search Warrant.

The first section, the "where" section, instructed the police to describe the location to be searched. It read:

> 1. That affiants have good reason to believe and do believe that certain things hereafter described are now being in or about the following place in the County: *(describe the place to be searched.)*

Ron Jones inserted a blank copy of the affidavit form into a typewriter, rolled the form to the appropriate location, then typed the following response to the first section, the "where" section.

> From the front steps of the Jefferson Davis County Court House, located on Columbia Ave., travel south on Columbia Ave. and go approximately .3 tenths of a mile to the intersection of Lafayette St. and Columbia Ave. Turn left on Lafayette St. and go to Mary ST. Turn right on Mary St. and goto first set of apt's on left.

The errors are in the original.

A similar, but not identical response was not long thereafter typed on to the second affidavit.

> From the Jefferson Davis County Court House, located on Columbia Ave., travel south on Columbia Ave. and go approximately .3 tenths of a mile to the Int. of Lafayette and Columbia Ave. Turn left on Lafayette St. and go 1.5 tenths of a mile to Mary St. Turn left on Mary St. and go to first yellow apt's on left.

The errors are in the original. Given the use of "apt's" as a plural for "apartments," it's likely the same person typed both affidavits.

<<>>

The second section of the affidavit, the "who" section, instructed the police to identify the occupant of the residence. It read:

> 2. That the place described above is occupied and controlled by:

In the first form, Ron Jones entered:

> Jamie Smith and / or Person Unknown

In the second form, he entered:

> Person (s) Unknown

While the police are required by the Fourth Amendment and by the State of Mississippi to be specific about the location of the search and the items to be seized, they are not required to be specific about the occupant. Since Jones and Graves expected to search only the Smith apartment, since they intended to make use of the second warrant only if necessary to locate drugs Smith might have stored beyond the boundaries of his apartment, they made no effort to learn the name of the occupants in the other unit of the Mary Street duplex.

Had they made such an effort, they would have learned that the apartment was occupied not by a drug pusher, but by a young mother who worked the graveyard shift at a chicken plant 1 hour and 20 minutes distant to provide for her infant daughter. They might have learned that the apartment was also occupied by a young man with no criminal record, a father who recently gave up his hometown job to be with and to care for his daughter throughout the night, while the mother processed chickens for scant wages.

<<>>

The third section of the affidavit, the "what" section, instructed the police to specify what items were to be seized. It read:

> 3. That said things are particularly described as follows: (describe thing or things to be seized, taking care to describe only those things which affiants have probable cause to believe and do believe are concealed at the place described above, and with enough particularity to insure that a uniformed officer will not seize one thing under a warrant describing another. Mere evidence is not a proper subject of a search or seizure. Certain items subject to a search and seizure include, in addition to the specific subjects mentioned in the Code, all contraband; instumentalities used in the commission of a crime; and books, writings, pictures, and prints adjudged in a proper proceeding by a proper court to be obscene.)

The response on each affidavit was identical, with the exception of punctuation and spacing.

> Drugs, Narcotics, and/or controlled substances illegal under the Mississippi Uniform Control Substance Law (41-29-101 et seq of the MCA of 1972 as Amended

This was the standard response for any drug raid. It would have been far simpler to simply type "crack cocaine", since that's what Randy Gentry told Ron Jones he had purchased from Jamie Smith. From the perspective of Ron Jones and Darryl Graves, however, it would have been foolish to be too specific. The more general description was not only adequate from a procedural standpoint, it was also wise from a cover-all-the-bases standpoint.

<<>>

The fourth section of the affidavit, the "why" section, instructed the police to specify why the search warrant should be granted. It read:

> 4. That possession of the above described things is in itself unlawful (or the public has a primary interest in, or primary right to possession of, the above described things), in that said things are:

The response to this section was effectively the same as the response to the "what" section, and identical on the two affidavits.

> The above items are unlawful under the provisions of the Mississippi Uniform Control Substance Law (41-29-101 et seq of the MCA of 1972 as Amended) and other applicable statutes.

Neither affidavit was signed. Mississippi did not require that Affidavits for Search Warrant bear a signature.

AFFIDAVIT FOR SEARCH WARRANT

State of Mississippi

County of Jefferson Davis

This day personally appeared before me, the undersigned judicial officer of said county, _____

RONALD W. JONES

known to me to be credible persons, who after having been first duly sworn, depose and say:

1. That affiants have good reason to believe and do believe that certain things hereafter described are now being concealed in or about the following place in this County: *(describe the place to be searched.)*
From the front steps of the Jefferson Davis County Court House, located on Columbia Ave., travel south on Columbia Ave. and go approximately .3 tenths of a mile to the intersection of Lafayette St. and Columbia Ave. Turn left on Lafayette St. and go to Mary ST. Turn right on Mary St. and goto first set together with all approaches and appurtenances thereto: of apt's on left.

2. That the place described above is occupied and controlled by Jamie Smith and/or Person Unknown

3. That said things are particularly described as follows: *(describe the thing or things to be seized, taking care to describe only those things which affiants have probable cause to believe and do believe are concealed at the place described above, and with enough particularity to insure that an uninformed officer will not seize one thing under a warrant describing another. Mere evidence is not a proper subject of a search or seizure. Certain things subject to search and seizure include, in addition to the specific subjects enumerated in the Code, all contraband; instrumentalities used in the commission of a crime; and books, writings, pictures and prints adjudged in a proper proceeding by a proper court to be obscene.)*

Drugs, Narcotics and/or controlled substances illegal under the Mississippi Uniform Control Substance Law (41-29-101 et seq of the MCA of 1972, as Amended

4. That possession of the above described things is in itself unlawful (or the public has a primary interest in or, primary right to possession of, the above described things), in that said things are: *(state briefly the use and intention for use of the specified things, citing the appropriate Code section or ordinance being violated and charging its violation, and a brief narrative account of the offense being committed.)*

The above items are unlawful under the provisions of the Mississippi Uniform Control Substance Law (41-29-101 et seq of the MCA of 1972, as Amended) and other applicable statutes.

AFFIDAVIT FOR SEARCH WARRANT

State of Mississippi

County of Jefferson Davis

This day personally appeared before me, the undersigned judicial officer of said county, _____

RONALD W. JONES

known to me to be credible persons, who after having been first duly sworn, depose and say:

1. That affiants have good reason to believe and do believe that certain things hereafter described are now being concealed in or about the following place in this County: *(describe the place to be searched.)*
From the Jefferson Davis County Court House, located on Columbia Ave., travel south on Columbia Ave. and go approximately .3 tenths of a mile to the Int. of Lafayette and Columbia Ave. Turn left on Lafayette St. and go 1.5 tenths of a mile to Mary St. Turn right on Mary St. and go to first yellow apt's on left.
together with all approaches and appurtenances thereto;

2. That the place described above is occupied and controlled by: Person(s) Unknown

3. That said things are particularly described as follows: *(describe the thing or things to be seized, taking care to describe only those things which affiants have probable cause to believe and do believe are concealed at the place described above, and with enough particularity to insure that an uninformed officer will not seize one thing under a warrant describing another. Mere evidence is not a proper subject of a search or seizure. Certain things subject to search and seizure include, in addition to the specific subjects enumerated in the Code, all contraband; instrumentalities used in the commission of a crime; and books, writings, pictures and prints adjudged in a proper proceeding by a proper court to be obscene.)*

Drugs, Narcotics and/or controlled substances illegal under the Mississippi Uniform control Substance Law (41-29-101 et seq of the MCA of 1972, as Amended

4. That possession of the above described things is in itself unlawful (or the public has a primary interest in or, primary right to possession of, the above described things), in that said things are: *(state briefly the use and intention for use of the specified things, citing the appropriate Code section or ordinance being violated and charging its violation, and a brief narrative account of the offense being committed.)*

The above items are unlawful under the provisions of the Mississippi Uniform Control Substance Law (41-29-101 et seq of the MCA of 1972, as Amended) and other applicable statutes.

ALTERNATE SCENARIO: THE WARRANTS
8:15 PM, Wednesday, December 26, 2001

The search warrants looked very much like their corresponding affidavits. They had the same first four sections for where, who, what, and why. They did not include the parenthetical instructions found on the affidavits.

Compared to the affidavits, the warrants included three extra sections, none of which required a response. The first additional section, Section 5, read:

> 5. The facts leading to establish the foregoing grounds for issuance of a Search Warrant are shown on a sheet "Underlying Facts and Circumstances" which is attached hereto, made a part hereof and adopted herein by reference.

The second additional section of the search warrant, Section 6, read:

> 6. This court, having examined and considered said affidavit, and also having heard and considered evidence in support thereof from the affiants named therein does find that probable cause for the issuance of a search warrant does exist. THEREFORE, you are hereby commanded to proceed at any time in the day or night to the place described above and to search forthwith said place for the things specified above, making known to the person or persons occupying or controlling said place if any, your purpose and authority for so doing so, and if the things specified above be found there to seize them, leaving a copy of this warrant and a receipt for the things taken; and bring the things seized before this Court instanter; and prepare a written inventory of the items seized, and have then and there this writ, with your proceedings noted thereon.

This section caused the warrant to be a knock-and-announce warrant. It included a requirement that the police make "known to the person ... occupying ... said place ... your purpose and authority." That's why the officers frequently shout "Police. Search warrant!" That announcement satisfies the legal requirement to make known their authority (they are the police) and their purpose (they intend to serve a search warrant).

Neither Mississippi nor the US Supreme Court, however, has yet defined any required delay between the announcement and a forced entry. Darrell Cooley made clear in his testimony that they allow only a few seconds to elapse between their announcement and their effort to breach the door.

> We usually wait a few minutes, a few seconds, not minutes, wait a few seconds then kick the door.

Nothing in fact requires the delay to be any longer than a fraction of a second. If the police intend to force entry, the application of force can be effectively simultaneous with the announcement. Police feel they gain substantial advantage catching suspects off guard. A rapid entry minimizes the time the occupants have to dispose of evidence. A delayed entry, on the other hand, could allow the occupants to arm themselves.

The seventh and final additional section of the warrant reads:

> 7. Do not interpret this writ as limiting your authority to seize all contraband and things the possession of which in itself is unlawful which you find incident to your search, or as limiting your authority to make otherwise valid arrests at the place described above.

At the bottom of the search warrant was a location for the signature block for the judge granting the warrant.

<<>>

Ron Jones and Darryl Graves had become increasingly impatient as Ron typed distinct information onto each of the two affidavits. They would expedite the process for getting similar responses onto the two search warrants.

Jones rolled a warrant into the typewriter and typed the responses for sections 1, 3, and 4. He did not at this point type any response to section 2, the "who" section. Instead, he removed the nearly completed warrant, took it to the copying machine, and made one copy. He then returned to the typewriter, rolled the original, nearly-complete warrant back into the typewriter, and filled in the response for section 2, the who section, as:

Jamie Smith and/or Person(s) Unknown

He removed that completed warrant. He replaced it with the copy of the nearly-completed warrant, but rolled it in slightly crooked. He filled in the response for section 2 as:

Person(s) Unknown

He removed the second warrant from the typewriter. It was identical to the first warrant in every detail except for the telltale misaligned response to section 2.

SEARCH WARRANT

STATE OF MISSISSIPPI

COUNTY OF JEFFERSON DAVIS

TO ANY LAWFUL OFFICER OF JEFFERSON DAVIS COUNTY, MISSISSIPPI

WHEREAS, _____ RONALD W. JONES _____

_____ known to me

1. That affiants have good reason to believe and do believe that certain things hereafter described are now being concealed in or about the following place in this County:

From the front steps of the Jefferson Davis County Court House, located on Columbia Ave., travel south on Columbia Ave. and go approximately .3 tenths of a mile to the intersection of Lafayette St. and Columbia Ave. Turn left on Lafayette St. and go approximately 1.5 tenths of a mile east, to Mary St. Turn right on Mary St. and goto yellow apt's on left.
together with all approaches and appurtenances thereto.

together with all approaches and appurtenances thereto.

2. That the place described above is occupied and controlled by: Jamie Smith and/or Person(s) Unknow

3. That said things are particularly described as follows:

Drugs, Narcotics and/or controlled substances illegal under the Mississippi Uniform Control Substance Law (41-29-101, et seq of the MCA of 1972, as Amended.

4. That possession of the above described things is in itself unlawful (or the public has a primary interest in, or primary right to possession of, the above described things), in that said things are:

The above items are unlawful under the provisions of the Mississippi Uniform Control Substance Law (41-29-101 et seq of the MCA of 1972, as Amended) and other applicable statutes of the MCA.

5. The facts tending to establish the foregoing grounds for issuance of a Search Warrant are shown on a sheet "Underlying Facts and Circumstances" which is attached hereto, made a part hereof and adopted herein by reference.

6. This Court, having examined and considered said affidavit, and also having heard and considered evidence in support thereof from the affiants named therein does find that probable cause for the issuance of a search warrant does exist. THEREFORE, you are hereby commanded to proceed at any time in the day or night to the place described above and to search forthwith said place for the things specified above, making known to the person or persons occupying or controlling said place if any, your purpose and authority for so doing, and if the things specified above be found there to seize them, leaving a copy of this warrant and a receipt for the things taken; and bring the things seized before this Court instanter; and prepare a written inventory of the items seized, and have then and there this writ, with your proceedings noted thereon.

7. Do not interpret this writ as limiting your authority to seize all contraband and things the possession of which in itself is unlawful which you find incident to your search, or as limiting your authority to make otherwise valid arrests at the place described above.

Witness my hand this, the __26th__ day of ___December_____ ___2001

_____
COUNTY JUDGE OFFICIAL TITLE

SEARCH WARRANT

STATE OF MISSISSIPPI

COUNTY OF JEFFERSON DAVIS

TO ANY LAWFUL OFFICER OF JEFFERSON DAVIS COUNTY, MISSISSIPPI

WHEREAS, _____ RONALD W. JONES _____

_____ known to me

1. That affiants have good reason to believe and do believe that certain things hereafter described are now being concealed in or about the following place in this County:

From the front steps of the Jefferson Davis County Court House, located on Columbia Ave., travel south on Columbia Ave. and go approximately .3 tenths of a mile to the intersection of Lafayette St and Columbia Ave. Turn left on Lafayette St. and go approximately 1.5 tenths of a mile east, to Mary St. Turn right on Mary St. and goto yellow apt's on left.

together with all approaches and appurtenances thereto.

together with all approaches and appurtenances thereto.

2. That the place described above is occupied and controlled by: Person(s) Unknown

3. That said things are particularly described as follows.

Drugs, Narcotics and/or controlled substances illegal under the Mississippi Uniform Control Substance Law (41-29-101, et seq of the MCA of 1972, as Amended.

4. That possession of the above described things is in itself unlawful (or the public has a primary interest in, or primary right to possession of, the above described things), in that said things are:

The above items are unlawful under the provisions of the Mississippi Uniform Control Substance Law (41-29-101 et seq of the MCA of 1972, as Amended) and other applicable statutes of the MCA.

5. The facts tending to establish the foregoing grounds for issuance of a Search Warrant are shown on a sheet "Underlying Facts and Circumstances" which is attached hereto, made a part hereof and adopted herein by reference.

6. This Court, having examined and considered said affidavit, and also having heard and considered evidence in support thereof from the affiants named therein does find that probable cause for the issuance of a search warrant does exist. THEREFORE, you are hereby commanded to proceed at any time in the day or night to the place described above and to search forthwith said place for the things specified above, making known to the person or persons occupying or controlling said place if any, your purpose and authority for so doing, and if the things specified above be found there to seize them, leaving a copy of this warrant and a receipt for the things taken; and bring the things seized before this Court instanter, and prepare a written inventory of the items seized, and have then and there this writ, with your proceedings noted thereon.

7. Do not interpret this writ as limiting your authority to seize all contraband and things the possession of which in itself is unlawful which you find incident to your search, or as limiting your authority to make otherwise valid arrests at the place described above.

Witness my hand this, the 26th day of December , 2001

_____

OFFICIAL TITLE

CITY JUDGE

UNDERLYING FACTS AND CIRCUMSTANCES
8:30 PM, Wednesday, December 26, 2001

Any search warrant issued by Jefferson Davis County requires the requesting officer to prepare a written summary of the underlying facts and circumstances leading to the need for the warrant. That summary, if properly completed, fulfills a constitutional requirement established by the 1964 Supreme Court decision in the case of *Aguilar v. Texas*. The salient portion of that decision follows:

> [T]he magistrate must be informed of some of the underlying circumstances relied on by the person providing the information and some of the underlying circumstances from which the affiant concluded that the informant, whose identity was not disclosed, was creditable or his information reliable.

Ron Jones rolled a blank sheet of paper into his typewritten and created the first Underlying Facts and Circumstances document. It read:

UNGERLYING FACTS AND CIRCUMSTANCES

I, Ronald W. Jones, P5, do hereby state under oath that I have received information from various sources that controlled substances are being stored in and sold from two apartments located on Mary St.

A C.I. personally known to me to have given true and reliable information in the past which has led to at least one arrest, went to said residence within past twenty-four hours and saw a large quantity of Marijuana being stored in both apartments located on Mary St .

I, Ronald W. Jones. also state under oath that I, personally surveillenced said apartment's and witnessed a large amount of traffic at unusual hours traveling to and from said apartments.

Said apartments is being occuppied by Jamie Smith a known drug dealer and persons unknown.

I therefore believe that other controlled substances are being stored in and sold from said apartments by Jamie Smith and/or person(s) unknown.

Errors are in the original.

Jones added a signature block for himself and for the judge. He would withhold his signature for the time being. He would be required to sign the document in front of the judge.

As he had with the warrant, Jones took the document to the copying machine and made a copy. There was no need, however, to re-insert either the original or the copy into the typewriter. Each would remain a perfect copy of the other, including the numerous typographical, spelling, and grammar errors. The most noticeable error was the misspelling of the word "underlying", preserved in all capital letters in the header of the document as UNGERLYING.

While the grammar and spelling were flawed, the structure of the document was disciplined, if not thorough or complete. In the introductory paragraph, Ron Jones declared that he received information from various sources about drug activity at the duplex. (In this alternate scenario, those various sources would be Darryl Graves and Randy Gentry.)

In the second paragraph, Jones described a controlled purchase by a confidential informant. (In this alternate scenario, that confidential informant would be Randy Gentry.) Jones declared that the confidential informant had observed a large quantity of marijuana in each apartment. (In this alternate scenario, that statement would be false. Randy Gentry never entered the apartment adjacent to Jamie Smith's, and could not therefore have observed a large quantity of marijuana within that apartment. Randy Gentry, Carroll Gentry, and Audrey Davis would each later affirm that Randy Gentry never entered the adjacent apartment.)

In the third paragraph, Ron Jones described his own surveillance. (In this alternate scenario, that surveillance would consist of Ron Jones and Darryl Graves driving past or near the Mary Street duplex.)

Ron Jones did not, however, include any mention of the controlled purchase. He mentioned only that the CI had observed drugs in the apartments. Had the purchase been mentioned, that mention would have raised questions about the status of the drugs purchased. Had they been taken into evidence? Had the CI been allowed to keep them?

The least troublesome of the alternatives, that the drugs were properly secured as evidence of a crime, posed problems for the prosecution. The evidence would require a chain-of-custody document, and that document would require disclosure of everyone in the custody chain, including Randy Gentry. The prosecution would have been bound by rules of discovery to inform the defense of the drugs purchased. That in turn would have led to questions about who had purchased the drugs, to questioning under oath of that person, to compromising a confidential informant, and to clouding the case against anyone arrested for selling the drugs.

<<>>

Having copied the Ungerlying Facts and Circumstances, Ron Jones and Darryl Graves had two complete sets of documents necessary for two warrants. The documents may not have been completely truthful, proper, and accurate, but the drug problem wasn't going to be getting any better unless someone made things happen.

UNGERLYING FACTS AND CIRCUMSTANCES

I, Ronald W. Jones, P5, do hereby state under oath that I have received
information from various sources that controlled substances are being
stored in and sold from two apartments located on Mary St.

A C.I. personally known to me to have given true and reliable information
in the past which has led to at least one arrest, went to said residence
within past twenty-four hours and saw a large quantity of Marijuana being
stored in both apartments located on Mary St.
I, Ronald W. Jones. also state under oath that I, personally surveillanced
said apartment's and witnessed a large amount of traffic at unusual hours
traveling to and from said apartments.
Said apartments is being occuppied by Jamie Smith a known drug dealer and
persons unknown.

I therefore believe that other controlled substances are being stored in
and sold from said apartments by Jamie Smith and/or person(s) unknown.

RONALD W. JONES, P5

SWORN TO AND SUBSCRIBED BEFORE ME, this 26th day of December, 2001.

DONALD G. KRUGER
MUNICIPAL COURT JUDGE FOR THE
TOWN OF PRENTISS, MISSISSIPPI

ALTERNATE SCENARIO: JUDGE KRUGER
9:00 PM, Wednesday, December 26, 2001

Prentiss Judge Donald Kruger had advice for those who were going to bring him search warrants to be signed: have the paperwork in order.

> This is what I expect and this is what I want. And if you don't have it right, don't bother calling me and coming over here.

> That's my policy. Every time we get a new cop I tell him the same thing: "Don't come to my house unless you got it right the first time."

In the words of Prentiss Public Defender Bob Evans, Judge Kruger was "as straight as they come."

If Judge Kruger had a fault, it was that he sometimes became more concerned about process than about substance.

<<>>

Donald Kruger had spent most the day after Christmas, 2001, with his family. The children and grandchildren made the sixty-mile drive down from Jackson for Christmas. The entire family had been together the previous day, and they had all dined together earlier that day. By evening, the children and grandchildren had returned home. Donald Kruger was spending a quiet and contented evening at home with his wife.

The phone rang around 8:30 PM. It was Prentiss Police Officer Ronald Jones. Jones explained he was at the police department, had some search warrants he wanted signed, and was about ready to bring them up. Jones asked Kruger if he would be available to sign them. Kruger confirmed he would be available.

Judge Kruger lived just a hop, skip, and a jump from the police department. By his estimate, the distance was just 300 yards "as the crow flies." Ron Jones arrived slightly before 9:00 PM. Kruger would remember that because he noticed that the Christmas lights were still on outside. The lights turned off automatically at 9:00.

Ron Jones handed Judge Kruger his two sets of three documents. Kruger read through each of the six sheets of paper. He was confused about the location of the duplex and the designation of the two units.

> I was trying to determine where the physical location of the property was. And I asked him -- I thought I knew where it was, but I wasn't for sure about it. And he explained where they were. And after reading this, I concluded that it was over there on Mary Street, as it says.

> We talked about right and left, I believe, or east and west, or some such language, and not apartment 1 and apartment 2. I asked him -- in trying to identify where he wanted to go, when I finally figured out where the place was, I asked him if that was the Tommie Speights' duplex over

there, and he said he didn't know. I knew she owned a duplex somewhere over in there, but I -- it was there in town.

Kruger was undisturbed that Jones had made no effort to learn who owned the building to be searched. He was undisturbed also that Jones made no effort to learn the name of the occupant in the second unit.

More troubling, Kruger was undisturbed that neither warrant clearly specified the location to be searched, either by street address or by apartment number. The Fourth Amendment commanded he be disturbed.

... and no Warrants shall issue, but upon ... particularly describing the place to be searched ...

Judge Kruger asked Ron Jones about the confidential informant. Jones explained that the informant was reliable, that one or two arrests had been made previously based on information provided by the informant. Jones did not identify Randy Gentry as the informant, nor did he mention that Randy Gentry had actually purchased drugs using money Jones had provided to him. Jones explained only that the informant had observed large quantities of marijuana in both units. Kruger did not pursue the issue further. That left unasked and unanswered any questions about the disposition of the drugs purchased.

Kruger asked Jones about his surveillance of the units. Jones explained that he and another officer had driven by or near the duplex, but offered no details. Kruger did not pursue the issue any further.

He said that they had been by there, that's true. I didn't exactly -- no, I didn't go into detail about it.

Having read the paperwork and talked briefly with Jones about the Ungerlying Facts and Circumstances, Kruger went through his routine of signing the warrants.

"Did you prepare the search warrants yourself?"

"Yes, sir, I did."

"Are they true and correct?"

"Yes, sir, they are," though they were not.

"Swear to them."

Ron Jones swore to them by signing the two identical copies of his Ungerlying Facts and Circumstances, thereby swearing under oath to documents that were not entirely true and correct. The drug war problem, however, was serious and demanded action.

Judge Kruger signed each identical copy of the Ungerlying Facts and Circumstances, based not on his independent assessment of their adequacy, but rather on Ron Jones' willingness to swear to them.

"It might have been hearsay information, but he swore to it, you know. If he hadn't sworn to it, I certainly wouldn't have signed anything."

Judge Kruger then signed each of the two warrants, despite their shortcomings and the suspicious nature of their documentation. The drug war, after all ...

The entire process took less than fifteen minutes.

ALTERNATE SCENARIO: THE BRIEFING
10:30 PM, Wednesday, December 26, 2001

With two signed warrants in hand, Ron Jones made the two-minute trip back to his office. There he made copies of the warrants. He would need to leave a copy at whatever residence he raided. He then began contacting others who would be involved in the raid. Ideally, he would be able to round up a team of ten officers, including himself, excluding Darryl Graves. He would use four to enter the Jamie Smith apartment, four more to secure it outside, and two others to secure the adjoining apartment, one in front and one in back. He would need nine other officers. He would manage to round up only seven, and barely that.

Ron called Stephen Jones around 9:30 PM. Stephen Jones was a fellow officer with the Prentiss Police Department. Despite their last names, Ron and Stephen were not related. Stephen agreed to help. It would take him around forty-five minutes to get ready and travel to the station.

Ron checked with the Jefferson Davis County Sheriff's Office. It is located in the same building as the police department. Sheriff's Department Deputies Allen Allday and William "Mike" Brown agreed to assist with the search.

Ron called Bassfield Police Chief Walter Earl Bullock. Earl in turn contacted Terrance "T.C." Cooley, Darrell Wayne Cooley, and Phillip Allday.

Terrance Cooley was on duty that evening when he received his call. He returned to the Bassfield Police Department and met Earl Bullock.

Darrell Cooley, after receiving his call, also met Chief Bullock at the Bassfield PD.

Phillip Allday, unlike all others contacted, was not actually a paid police officer. He was a non-uniformed volunteer officer. Based on the Mississippi Bureau of Narcotics Standards, as well as the Bassfield and Prentiss Department Standing Orders, volunteer officer Phillip Allday did not have jurisdiction to participate in the execution of any search warrant outside Bassfield city limits. He nonetheless joined forces with Earl Bullock and the others, thereby forming the eighth and final member of the search team.

<<>>

After assembling at the Bassfield Police Department, the Bassfield contingent made the 20-minute drive to Prentiss. It was around 10:30 before everyone had arrived and settled in for the pre-raid briefing.

Together, Ron Jones and Darryl Graves provided the background. As the officer who had secured the search warrants, Ron Jones was officially in charge of the raid. Darryl Graves would be advising. Not only did Agent Graves bring with him training and experience from the Drug Task Force, he was personally familiar with the subject of the raid. He had actually orchestrated a controlled purchased from the location before.

The target of the raid was Jamie Smith. He was a known drug dealer and he already had drug charges pending against him. He had been under investigation by the Task Force for several months. He lived in one unit of a yellow duplex located less than a mile to the southwest. The duplex displayed no address. Ron Jones would be in the lead car and would direct everyone to the residence.

A confidential informant had, within the last twenty-four hours, made another controlled buy from Jamie Smith. That purchase formed the basis for the two warrants they had in hand. The first warrant was explicitly for the Jamie Smith apartment. Should the search of the first apartment fail to turn up any drugs, the search would be extended to the perimeter of the duplex and to the crawl space beneath. The second warrant would be used as necessary, and only if necessary, for any search beyond the boundaries of Jamie Smith's apartment.

Darryl Graves sketched on the blackboard the interior of Jamie Smith's apartment. That sketch showed the front door and the back door, the living room in the front, the bedroom in the rear, and the kitchen and bathroom along the dividing wall with the other apartment.

There would be a fair number of people to control during the search. Jamie Smith lived in the apartment with his girlfriend, a teenage boy, and at least two younger children. It's possible that one or more drug clients might be in the apartment making a purchase. The people living in the adjacent apartment might come out to see what would be going on next door.

The raid would be conducted based on procedures used by the Pearl River Basin Drug Task Force, modified slightly to account for the duplex nature of the building and the shortage of officers available for the raid. They would be divided into three teams, an entry team, a security team for the Smith apartment, and a security team for the adjacent apartment. Ron Jones would lead the entry team. He would be joined by fellow Prentiss Police Officer Stephen Jones and Bassfield Police Officer Terrence Cooley.

The entry team would take with them a one-man battering ram. Ron Jones would use that ram to breach the rear door of the left-hand apartment. He would drop the ram, draw his weapon, and enter the residence followed by Stephen Jones then Terrence Cooley.

Entry would be through the rear door because the front porch had a confining railing. That railing would make it difficult to use the ram, dispose of it cleanly, and allow the remaining officers to enter the house quickly and smoothly behind Jones. It would also slow any officers on the porch from taking cover should shots be fired.

The security team for the Smith apartment would consist of Jefferson Davis County Sheriff Deputies Allen Allday and Mike Brown, plus Bassfield Chief of Police Earl Bullock. They would position themselves at the front of the left-hand duplex. Because of the number of people who might be fleeing the search team, the security team could have their hands full.

The two remaining officers would secure the front and rear doors of the right-hand apartment. Bassfield Police Officer Darrell Cooley would secure the front door and Bassfield Volunteer Officer Phillip Allday would secure the rear door. Should residents of that apartment attempt to investigate what was going on outside or within the Jamie Smith apartment, those officers would order the occupants to remain inside their home.

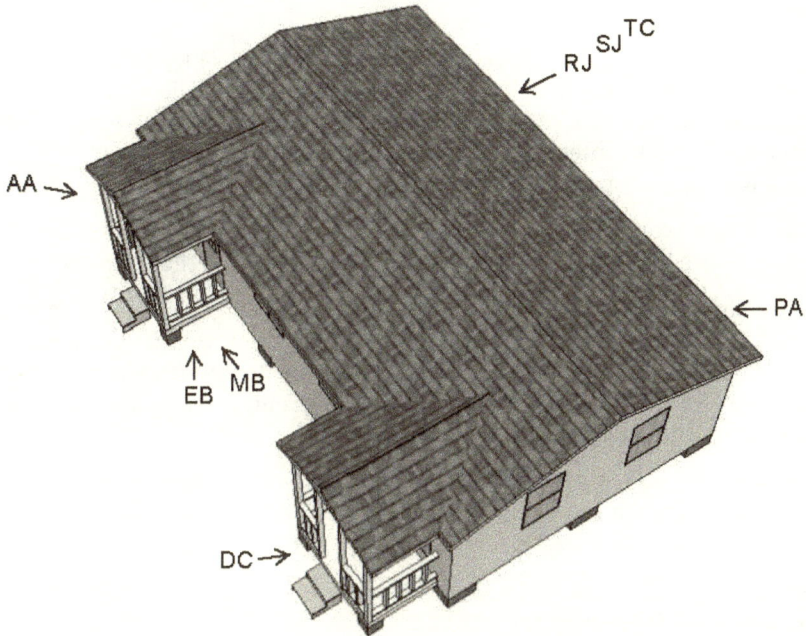

The warrant was a knock-and-announce warrant. As soon as the two teams were in position, Mike Brown would knock by banging on the exterior wall somewhere near the center of the building. He would not knock on the front door itself since that would put him in the firing lane of the entry team.

As Brown banged on the front wall of Jamie Smith's apartment, he would simultaneously identify the team as police officers there to serve a warrant. The banging and the identification would meet the knock-and-announce requirement of the warrant. It would also momentarily draw the attention of the occupants towards the front of the apartment, away from the rear entry door.

Upon hearing the knock-and-announce from the front of the duplex, Ron Jones would breach the rear door with the ram. He would then drop the ram, draw his weapon, and enter the apartment. Stephen Jones and

Terrence Cooley would follow, in that order. The three of them would order the occupants to the ground. One member of the entry team would open the front door from the inside so the security team could join them in the search.

Ron would travel to the site in Stephen Jones' patrol car. Stephen would drive. Ron would direct him to the site and carry the ram. They car would arrive first, without sirens wailing or lights flashing. They would park along one side of the yard, exit the car, head to the back of the building, and position themselves for entry. They would wait there both for the arrival of Terrence Cooley and for the knock-and-announce signal from the front of the building.

The two county sheriff's deputies, Allen Allday and Mike Brown, would travel to the site in a sheriff's squad car. They would follow the Prentiss patrol car and would arrive second, without sirens or flashing lights. They would park in the center of the yard, leaving plenty of room for car doors to swing wide and for people to exit quickly.

Mike Brown would position himself at the front of the building, near the center, where he could bang on the wall as he announced their arrival.

Allen Allday would position himself on the other side of the porch, somewhat away from the building, facing the front corner. That would allow him to bring fire onto the front of the apartment, if necessary, from a front quarter angle without threatening the entry team or the other members of the security team.

The Bassfield police contingent would travel in the Bassfield Police car. They would be the last to arrive and would park in the remaining yard space along side the sheriff's car.

Terrence Cooley would make his way quickly around to the back and join Ron Jones and Stephen Jones as the third member of the entry team.

Phillip Allday would make his way quickly around the back as well, to secure the rear of the adjacent apartment.

Darrell Cooley would take his position in front of the adjacent apartment.

Chief Bullock would join Mike Brown at the front of the building, near the center. From there, he would provide cover for Officer Brown as Brown banged on the wall and signaled the entry team to proceed. The two of them would then be in position to bring fire onto the front of the apartment from a third angle.

It was important for each person to know exactly where he and everyone else was going to be.

ALTERNATE SCENARIO: THE SHOOTING
11:00 PM, Wednesday, December 26, 2001

Inside the left-hand apartment of the Mary Street duplex, Audrey Davis and Jamie Smith were watching television. The children were asleep in the back bedroom.

<<>>

Inside the right-hand apartment, fourteen-month-old Ta'Corriana was sleeping on the bed in the back bedroom. The head of that bed was against the back wall, very near the solid rear door which was locked and chained. A large headboard blocked most of the rear window, though that made little difference: the rear window was already covered with blinds. The side window was completely covered with aluminum foil. The lights were out and the room was lit only by the soft glow of the television in the living room.

Ta'Corriana's mother was working far away at the Marshall Durbin plant in Hattiesburg, processing chickens.

Ta'Corriana's father was in the living room, sleeping, having succumbed while watching television. The living room light was off. The front door was locked. The outside screen door was wired closed with a coat hanger.

> The screen door was secured with a coat hanger because my daughter could open the door. The screen door would not lock by itself, so we kept it secured with a coat hanger tied from the inside.

The nine-pane window in the door was completely covered by dark red Venetian blinds. The large window in the wall was also covered by blinds. Between those blinds and the window was a large, dark drape spanning the window and extending to the floor.

> It was there to keep my daughter from standing up in the window because she had it bad about standing up in the window.

There was no way to see outside unless someone opened the door or moved aside a window covering.

Since his arrival there just weeks earlier, Cory Maye had been unnerved by all the people knocking on his door, trying to get in, day and night. His mother would later explain.

> Cory came back and said he that might be moving back to the house because he can't live over there with all that traffic going on like that next door. Day and night, day and night, and he said he can't hardly sleep, people knocking on the door, won't say who they are.

> He called me every day. He wanted to bring the baby and [her mother] and come home."

<<>>

Ron Jones directed Stephen Jones to the small yellow duplex, taking the very path described in the search warrant. They traveled 0.3 miles south along Columbia Avenue, turned left on Lafayette Street, and made a quick right onto Mary Street. The yellow duplex was there on the left.

No cars were yet parked in the somewhat grassy, mostly dirt yard in front of the duplex. Christmas lights glowed along the eaves. A light was on within the living room of one apartment. No other lights were on either in front or in back of the duplex.

It was a cloudless night, however, and a waxing gibbous moon hung high overhead. At 80% of maximum illumination, the moon reflected sufficient light onto Prentiss to provide reasonable visibility for those few working late outdoors.

Stephen Jones pulled his patrol car into the yard, along the right side of the yard. The car doors opened before he was at a full stop. Ron Jones was a bit slow getting out, impeded somewhat by the weighty and bulky battering ram in his lap. Once free of the car, the two Prentiss Police officers headed for the rear of the duplex.

<<>>

Jefferson Davis County Sheriff Deputies Allen Allday and Mike Brown arrived at the duplex close behind their Prentiss counterparts. Allen Allday parked in the center of the yard, far enough from the lead car so the doors would open without interference. He exited the car and took a position facing the corner of the building.

Mike Brown exited from the passenger side, moved forward, and took position against the front of the building, near its center.

<<>>

The Bassfield police car arrived almost immediately after the other two vehicles. It parked along the left side of the yard. Two Bassfield police officers sprang from the front and opened the rear doors for the two officers in the back.

Bassfield Police Officer Darrell Cooley took up a position in front of the right-hand apartment. He would discourage any occupants from coming out to investigate what was happening at the Smith apartment.

Bassfield Police Chief Earl Bullock joined Mike Brown at the front and center of the building. He would cover Brown as Brown banged on the wall and announced their arrival.

Bassfield Police Officer Terrence Cooley raced for the back of the building. He would join Ron Jones and Stephen Jones as the third member of the entry team. They should be just around the corner when he turned right around the back of the building.

Terrence Cooley was followed closely by Phillip Allday, the non-uniformed, volunteer officer from Bassfield. Allday's job was to cover the rear of the apartment adjacent to Smith's. He would discourage any occupants from coming out to investigate what was happening at the Smith apartment.

<<>>

Jamie Smith and Audrey Davis noticed the commotion outside their apartment. They pulled the curtains aside and saw police cars parked out front, shadowy figures running hither and yon. They knew they were going to be searched yet again, but were not particularly concerned. There had been no drugs in their place for quite a while.

<<>>

Ron Jones reached the back steps of the left-hand apartment. Stephen Jones was directly behind him. Terrence Cooley had not yet made it around the far corner. There had been no announcement from the front. Ron would wait a moment before breaching the rear door.

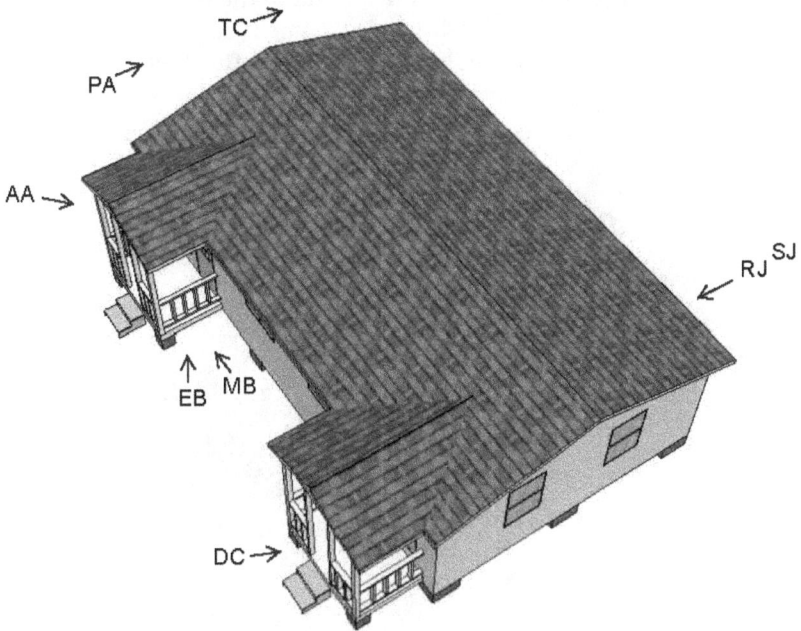

Though the moon shined bright above, Ron Jones would not be easily seen. He was dressed for concealment. He wore black pants, a black T-shirt, black shirt, and a dark blue jacket absent police insignia. He did not display even a badge that may have glinted momentarily in the moonlight.

Ron Jones was not, however, wearing a bulletproof vest. This unfortunate fact would become obvious but largely unnoticed once the autopsy report was published. That report would summarize the clothing Ron was wearing at the beginning of the autopsy.

His jacket was still on. No vest was beneath that jacket, nor mentioned at all.

> Clothing, valuables, and jewelry consist of one can of tobacco containing a perforating gunshot wound, black pants, blue jacket, blue belt with scabbard, black T-shirt, black shirt and blue and green boxer shorts. The clothing is removed prior to the external and internal examinations.

<<>>

Jamie Smith moved towards his front door. Jamie was well familiar with the search process. Tonight he would open the door to defuse the confrontation and to protect his property best he could. There was no need to have anyone breaking down his door.

<<>>

Terrance Cooley turned the back corner of the duplex and was startled by what he saw. Ron and Stephen Jones were not positioned as he had expected them to be. They were at the far end of the duplex, at the foot of the steps of what would be the left-hand apartment only if viewed from the rear. Terrence Cooley had assumed they were to enter the left-hand apartment as viewed from the front. He paused momentarily in confusion.

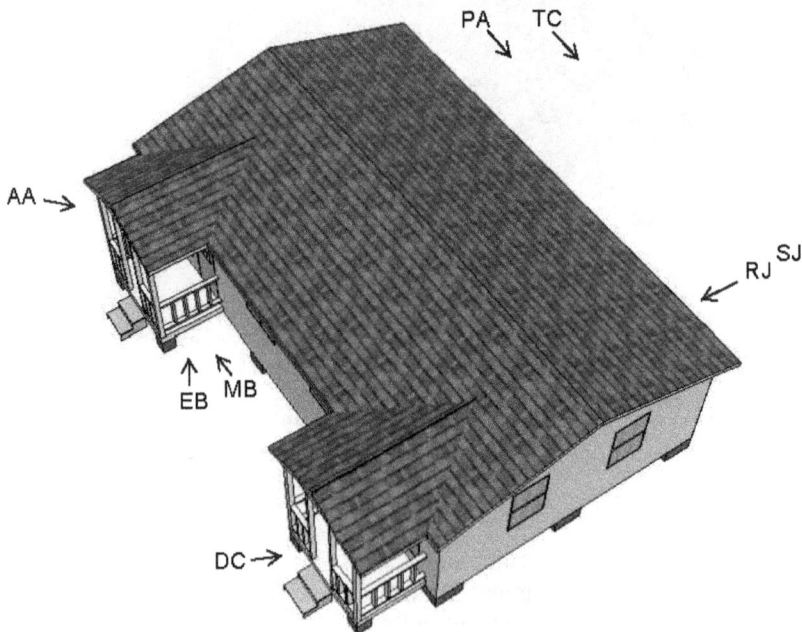

Phillip Allday arrived in the back of the building immediately behind Terrence Cooley. Allday had planned to race across the back of the building and position himself behind the rear door at the far side of the duplex. Ron and Stephen Jones, however, were there already. Phillip Allday paused momentarily in confusion.

<<>>

Mike Brown waited at the front wall just long enough to allow Terrence Cooley to join the entry team at the back. Brown then pounded on the front wall with the flat of his hand, announcing "Police, search warrant" as he did so. The announcement was largely drowned out by the pounding.

<<>>

Cory Maye sprang from his chair, jolted into a frightened state of consciousness by the banging outside.

<<>>

Ron Jones heard the banging from the front of the building just as Terrence Cooley appeared. Terrence Cooley hesitated, said something to Phillip Allday, then raced to join them at the foot of the stairs.

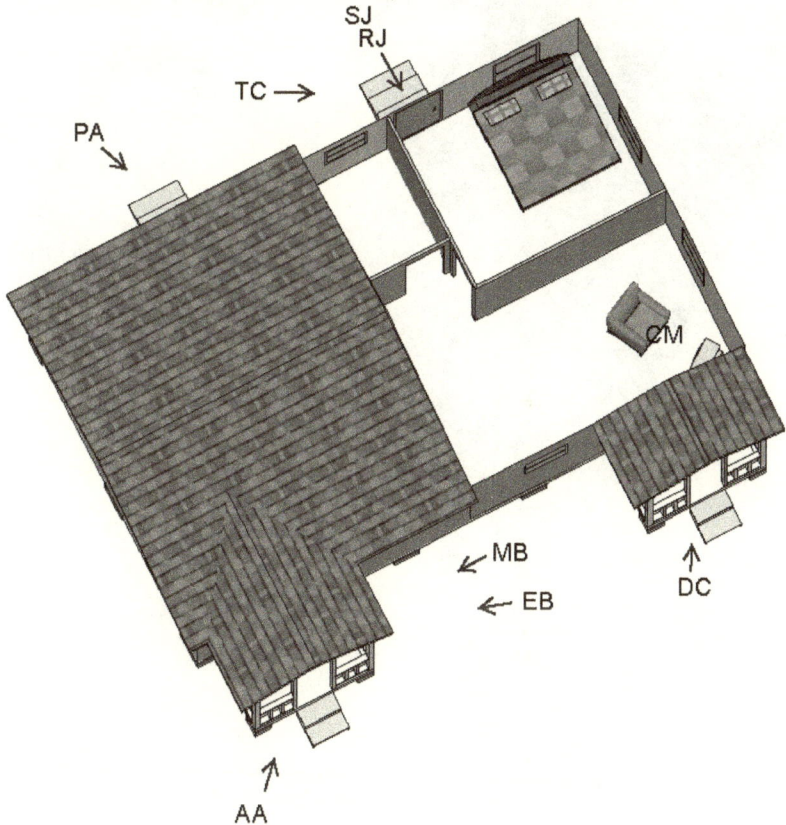

<<>>

Cory raced to the back bedroom. He had a gun there and he intended to retrieve it.

<<>>

Ron ascended the steps. Standing slightly sideward, he placed his left foot on the top step and braced his right foot on the step below. This placed his body in a slightly crouched position and at a slight angle to the door, left side forward.

<<>>

Cory grabbed his unloaded pistol from where he had left it, on the headboard shelf well beyond the reach of his daughter. That placed him directly next to the rear door. Ron Jones and the entry team were just beyond, ready to go.

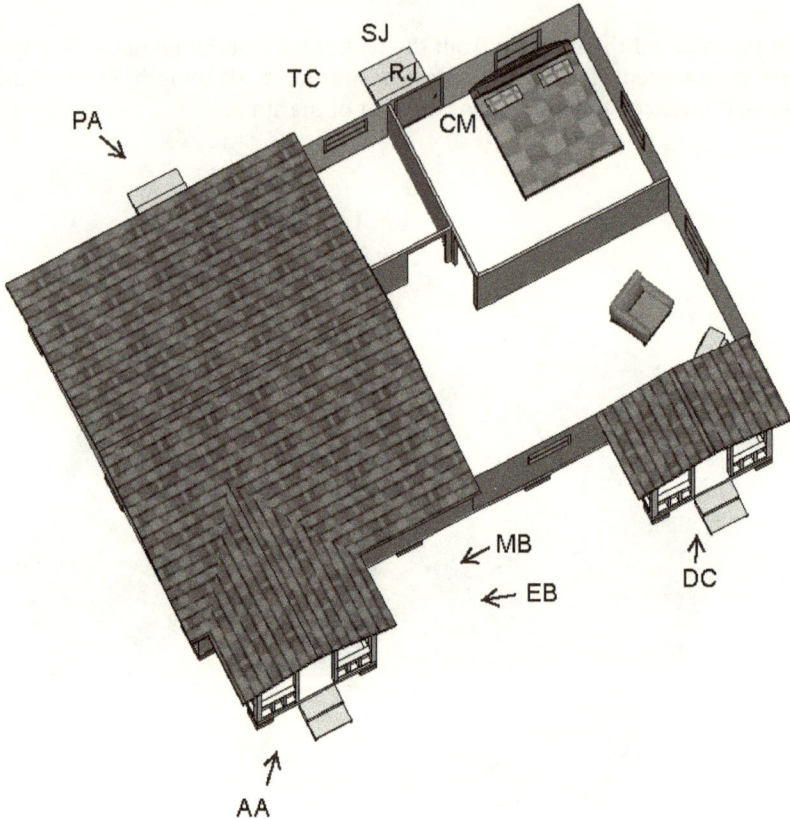

<<>>

Cory slammed a clip into his pistol.

Ron swung the battering ram backwards in a large arc.

Cory chambered a round.

<<>>

Using the force of muscle and gravity, Ron drove the one-man battering ram into the rear door, just beside the lock. The ram drove the deadbolt against the interior door frame, tearing the frame away from the wall.

<<>>

Cory jumped back, terrified. Someone was breaking through the door. He retreated, his gun pointed at the broken rear door.

<<>>

Ron swung the battering ram back for the second blow.

<<>>

Cory reached the foot of the bed. He dropped to the floor, leaving only his head and arms exposed.

<<>>

Ron unleashed the final blow to the door. The door frame and security chain gave way. The momentum of the ram carried Ron's left hand forward, into the doorway. The back of his index and middle fingers scratched along what remained of the door frame.

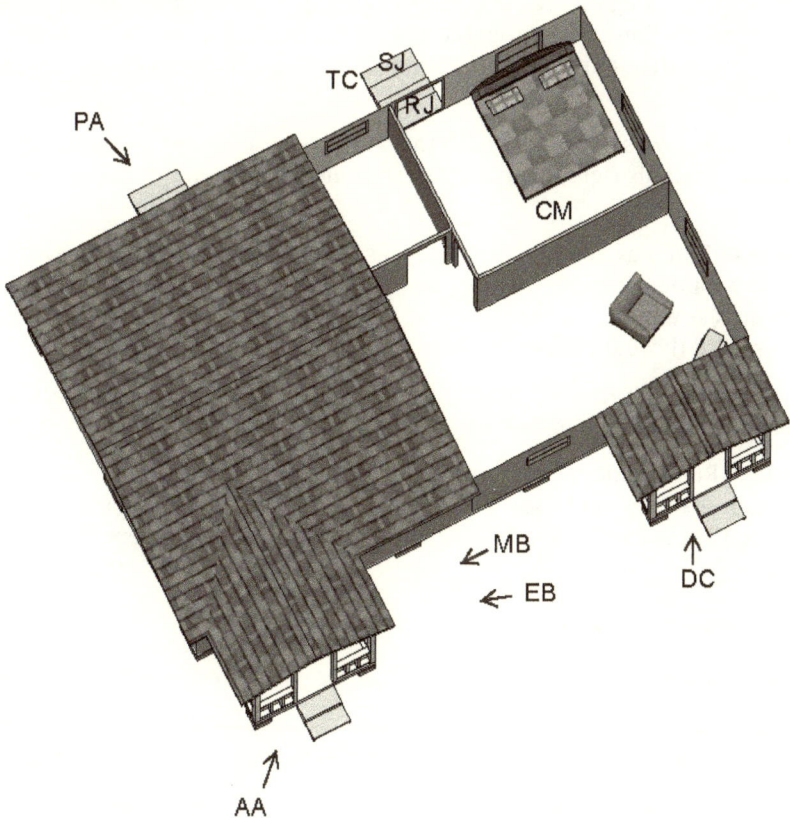

<<>>

Cory pointed his pistol towards the opening.

Ron dropped the battering ram to the ground. He reached for his pistol.

Cory turned his head away and fired. The pistol jumped with each shot. The first shot went low to the floor at a slightly upward angle. The second bullet traveled at a slightly higher angle, the third higher still.

<<>>

The third bullet whizzed harmlessly by Ron's ear. It would never be found.

The second bullet had already embedded itself into the shattered door frame to Ron's left. It would be found there and removed for analysis. Anyone bothering to insert a dowel into the bullet hole would see that the bullet had been traveling in an upward direction.

The first bullet had already wounded Ron Jones, and mortally so.

Because Ron had yet to reach the top of the steps, the first bullet hit his mid-section though it was traveling at an angle low to the floor. It passed first through Ron's Skoal tobacco tin. That caused it to rotate and change direction. It then burst into his abdomen leaving a hole slightly wider than it was tall.

Because Ron was not square with the door, because his left foot was further forward than his right, the bullet entered his left side and traveled towards his right.

Because Ron was slightly crouched, his upper body was tilted forward at approximately a thirty degree angle. Though the bullet was traveling upwards at ten degrees relative to the floor, it would seem to have traveled downward through Ron's torso once he returned to an erect position.

The bullet perforated his small bowel in four places. It pierced his aorta. It came to rest within him, at the back and right side of his abdomen.

Each of Ron's remaining heartbeats would pump a large amount of blood through the hole in his aorta. He would soon bleed out into his abdominal cavity. The medical examiner would find 7.4 pints of blood there.

<<>>

Ron Jones turned and headed down the steps. "I'm hit."

Stephen Jones took cover to the left of the steps; Terrence Cooley to the right.

Darrell Cooley raced from the front towards the back of the apartment.

Ron Jones made a small half circle at the bottom of the steps and disappeared alongside the apartment.

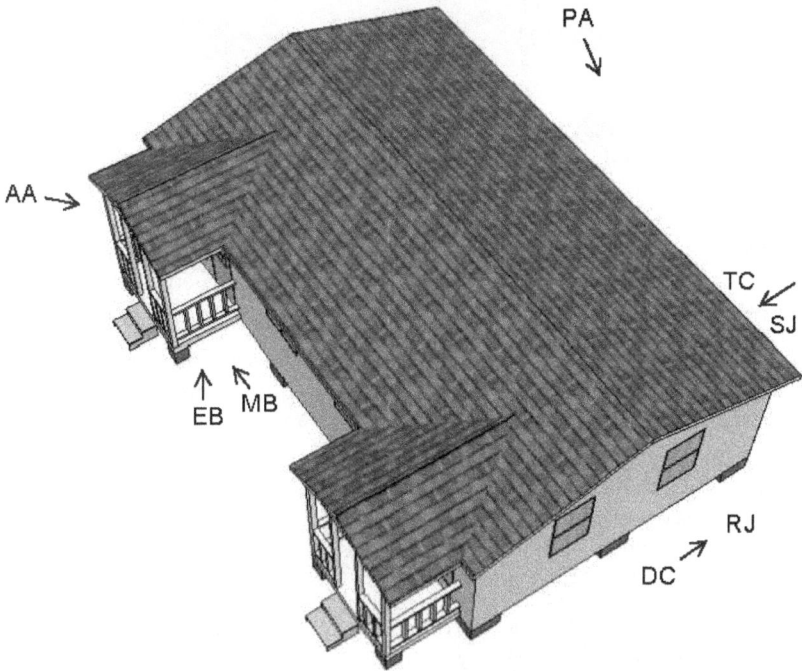

Terrence Cooley yelled into the apartment. "Police. Throw the gun out."

Cory Maye pushed his pistol towards the back door. He placed his hands on the floor above his head.

Stephen Jones: "Police. Throw the gun out."

Cory Maye: "I already have. It's on the floor."

<<>>

Darrell Cooley reached Ron Jones just as he fell to his knees. "Get me to the hospital. I've been hit."

Ron collapsed to the ground.

"Good Lord, help."

POSTLUDE

The night was cold and clear and calm. Conditions were ideal for sound transmission over a long distance. Had you been standing on the court house steps that night, when Cory Maye shot and killed Ron Jones, you might have been able to hear the gunshots from a mile distant. If you were inside the police station, you would have instead learned of the shooting over the police radio.

If you had rushed to the duplex, you could have arrived within minutes. Perhaps there, as you stood facing the yellow duplex on Mary Street, you would have seen Darrell Cooley and Stephen Jones struggling to lift the limp and seemingly lifeless body of Ron Jones into the back seat of a patrol car. Perhaps you would have seen Darryl Graves appear from somewhere to help them finish their desperate task. You might have then watched the patrol car race away, lights flashing, siren wailing, as if Ron's life depended on getting to the hospital quickly.

If you had walked to the back of the duplex and stood on the steps as Ron Jones had just minutes earlier, you might have heard an infant girl crying and screaming. At the instruction of the local law enforcement, she would remain unattended and uncomforted until her mother returned home from her night's work at the chicken processing plant.

Standing there, you might also have heard a scared and confused voice apologizing repeatedly, claiming he didn't know it was the police breaking through his door.

And had you laid there on the floor, in place of that scared and confused young man, you might have felt the boots of police officers who would vent their anger and their shame against a handcuffed citizen in their care.

<<>>

Cory Maye was transported to the jail in downtown Prentiss by Jefferson Davis County Sheriff Deputy Allen Allday. Terrence Cooley accompanied them.

> Sheriff Henry McCullum: "He was secured there, then he was transported by us, and along with the Mississippi Highway Patrol, to another location ... for his safety."

> Dorothy Funchess, Cory Maye's mother: "I went over there about four or five times, me and his father, and they would never let us see him ... because they didn't want me to see the bruises that he had on him. ... The first words out of his mouth, when he saw me, ... 'Mom,' he said, 'I don't know why they didn't say who they was when they came through the door that night, because things would never happen like they did.'"

<<>>

The autopsy was conducted by Dr. Stephen Timothy Hayne. Regarding the gunshot wound, Dr. Hayne wrote:

> A lethal, distant and consistent with reentry gunshot wound is identified over the lateral left abdominal wall.

When asked, only after the trial, about the meaning of "consistent with reentry", Dr. Hayne explained the term indicated the bullet, prior to striking Ron Jones, had struck something else.

Dr. Hayne reached his conclusion based on the shape of the entry wound, which he described as "slightly irregular in configuration suggestive of an irregular reentry gunshot wound." To him the irregular shape of the entry wound indicated the bullet had struck something prior to entering the body and was rotating as it entered.

<<>>

Jamie Smith and Audrey Davis left the town of Prentiss and the state of Mississippi. Word spread they were advised to do so.

No charges were filed against either of them.

During the trial of Cory Maye, neither would testify about what they knew of the events that night.

<<>>

The trial of *Mississippi v. Cory Jermaine Maye* began almost exactly two years after the shooting. Though her client was facing a death sentence, Rhonda Cooper met with Cory Maye no more than four times during that period.

<<>>

Rhonda Cooper's investigator realized the number written in ink on Ron Jones' palm was probably a phone number. He traced that number to Randy Gentry. Initially, Prentiss town officials acknowledged that Randy Gentry was indeed Ron Jones' confidential informant. Soon thereafter, they changed their position, denying that they knew the name of the CI. From that point forward, their official position would be that the CI's name died with Ron Jones.

<<>>

During jury selection, the State would use six of its nine peremptory challenges to strike African-Americans from the jury. None of the six were asked a single individual question. The State knew simply by looking at them that they should be excluded.

Only two African-Americans ended up on the jury. One of them was a county employee. She would be unwilling to give interviews after the trial, out of fear for her job. The other, when questioned by investigative reporter Radley Balko, provided disturbing insight into why the State accepted her as a juror despite her race.

Q "Do you think he did it? Do you think he knew it was a cop he shot that night?"

A "I couldn't say. Maybe he did, maybe he didn't. I couldn't say."

Q "You don't know if he was guilty or not?"

A "Some of what he said didn't make no sense. Some of it made sense. But I couldn't say."

Q "If you weren't sure, why did you convict him?"

A "I couldn't say."

Q "Did you feel any pressure? Were you intimidated?"

A "No."

Q "Are you sure? There's some talk that some of the jurors felt intimidated."

A "No. It wasn't like that."

Q "So you can't tell me if you think he actually did it or not?"

A "I couldn't say."

Q "Do you think he deserves a new trial?"

A "Oh, yes. He ought to get a new trial. Everybody deserves a chance."

Q "Is there anything else you want to tell me about Cory Maye and the trial?"

A "I don't remember a lot of it. I was on lots of medication. For my nerves. With the medication, I didn't hear everything. I didn't remember everything that was going on. So I couldn't say."

<<>>

During trial, Buddy McDowell asked carefully crafted questions of Dr. Stephen Timothy Hayne regarding the path of the bullet, never revealing to the jury that the bullet had hit something before striking Officer Ron Jones. Dr. Hayne answered those questions carefully, never revealing to the jury the bullet had hit something before striking Officer Ron Jones.

Buddy McDowell would never ask about the perforated tobacco tin found on Ron Jones body. Dr. Hayne would never mention it.

<<>>

During his closing argument, Buddy McDowell reminded the jury that Cory Maye testified he was lying on the ground when he shot at the doorway. Buddy then told them that Dr. Hayne's testimony gave them good reason to disbelieve all of Cory Maye's testimony.

I think that you do have to mainly get down to the fact about who you believe and who you don't believe. And the judge gave you that jury instruction with respect to how you can use your past and use your common sense and observe how the witnesses testified and what they had to say. And the reason for that is, you can believe all of what a witness said, some of what a witness said, or none of what a witness has said. ...

[Cory Maye] said, and this is a major thing, he said he was lying on the ground and he had that gun like this looking in the opposite direction when he fired. If you believe he's telling the truth about that, before you make your mind up about whether you believe he's telling the truth about that, look at Dr. Hayne's diagram. Think about what Dr. Hayne said in his testimony with respect to the angle of that projectile. Is Cory telling the truth about that? ...

Remember what the doctor said about the angle of the projectiles. Was he laying down flat and hiding? Or was he standing or kneeling and trying to hit what he was shooting at?

<<>>

Earlier in the trial, Buddy McDowell had Dr. Hayne mark the location of the entry wound on a diagram copied from Ron Jones' autopsy report. Dr. Hayne had created the original of that diagram during the autopsy to document several minor abrasions on Ron Jones' fingers. Buddy asked the court to admit that diagram as evidence. The diagram was admitted without objection.

"Dr. Hayne, I'm going to show you what appears to be a frontal and rear diagram of a male body. Can you identify that diagram?"

"I can. This is a illustration diagram taken at the time of the autopsy, and written on this diagram are the two small abrasions, scratches, located on the fingers of the left hand. And it indicates that it was on the decedent, Ron Jones."

"On the frontal view, could you indicate on therewith a pen approximately where the entrance wound was?"

"These were the two abrasions. Did you also want the entrance wound?"

"Right. On the frontal part."

"Label it sir?"

"Yes, if you would. We'd offer that into evidence, Your Honor."

The bastardized diagram was admitted as Exhibit Number 43. The jury would have it with them during their deliberations.

Use of that abrasion diagram was absolutely unnecessary, however, and therefore revealing. Dr. Hayne had already marked the entry wound on a separate, dedicated diagram and had added handwritten notes. Most of those notes were illegible. Some were understandable only when compared to the typewritten text of the autopsy. A few words were clearly legible though. Among those were "before striking officer" and "Ron Jones." The jurors would not be allowed to see that entry wound diagram. Buddy McDowell and Dr. Steven Timothy Hayne would use the abrasion diagram in its place.

<<>>

Well after the trial, for reasons not specifically related to Cory Maye, The Innocence Project, a national organization based in New York City, issued a press release reading in part:

> Based on evidence that Steven Hayne, who conducts 80% of autopsies in Mississippi, has committed fraud and misconduct that sent an unknown number of innocent people to prison, the Innocence Project and the Mississippi Innocence Project today filed a formal allegation to revoke his license to practice medicine in Mississippi.

Four months later, The Innocence Project issued a follow-on press release. It read in part:

> This afternoon, Mississippi Public Safety Commissioner Steve Simpson announced that the state is severing all ties with [Dr. Stephen] Hayne, who conducts 80% of all criminal autopsies in the state even though he is not properly board-certified and his work has been seriously questioned in a number of cases.   Simpson said Hayne will stop conducting autopsies immediately and will spend the next 90 days completing his pending autopsy reports -- which Simpson estimated to be a staggering 400-500 reports on autopsies that Hayne has not processed.

<<>>

At trial, the four officers involved in the raid told the jury that Cory Maye peeked out the window and had several minutes to hear their banging and announcements. That gave the jury reason to believe Cory Maye knew it was the police who were trying to gain entrance into his apartment.

If the alternate scenario presented in this book is correct, then Cory Maye did not peek out the window and had but seconds to respond to a surprising and terrifying threat.

If any alternate scenario similar to the one presented herein is correct, then the four officers conspired to convict Cory Maye using perjured testimony, and other agents of the State abetted them.

<<>>

After the trial, Cory Maye's family fired Rhonda Cooper. Bob Evans, the original public defender in the case, took over as Maye's appellate counsel. The Prentiss Board of Aldermen fired Evans for doing so. Bob Evans nonetheless continued to represent Cory Maye without hesitation or regret.

<<>>

In December of 2005, Radley Balko posted his first article regarding Cory Maye. Balko would write many more. His writing would come to the attention of Abe Pafford, a litigation associate who had joined the D.C. law firm of Covington and Burling LLP only a few months earlier. Despite Pafford's junior status, the firm decided to join Bob Evans, pro bono, in the effort to free Cory Maye.

<<>>

In September of 2006, Judge Michael Eubanks ruled that Rhonda Cooper did not adequately represent Cory Maye during the penalty phase of the trial. He overturned the sentence of death and ordered a new sentencing hearing. Mississippi declined to pursue the death penalty a second time. Cory Maye was re-sentenced to life without parole. Judge Eubanks found no other substantive flaw in the trial.

<<>>

Late last year, in November of 2009, the Mississippi Court of Appeals reversed Cory Maye's conviction and granted him a new trial on narrow grounds. The court ruled that Cory Maye should have been allowed to have his case tried in Jefferson Davis County. The defense had previously asked for and was granted a change of venue from that county, only later to have second thoughts. The appellate judges found no other substantive flaw in the trial.

<<>>

Not much has changed in Prentiss in the nine years since the shooting at the Mary Street duplex. Drugs are still a problem, the economy is still a basket case, and racial issues continue to divide the citizenry. The already sparse population has dropped by more than ten percent as people leave for greener, less troubled pastures.

Some things of course have changed, though their importance pales in comparison to all that Prentiss has lost. A memorial for Ron Jones sits in front of Prentiss Town Hall, and a portion of nearby U.S. Highway 84 is named in his honor. Road signs proclaim to those who pass that they are traveling on the Officer Ronald Wayne Jones Memorial Highway. It is small consolation for the loss of a dedicated police officer, a decent man, and a beloved son.

Perhaps next year, a new trial for Cory Maye will take place in the Jefferson Davis County Courthouse on Columbia Avenue, right in the heart of Prentiss. If so, the local populace will divide again along racial lines, as they always have. The prosecution will attempt to exclude blacks from the jury and the defense will try to stop them from doing so. Everyone will behave outwardly, at least, as if race isn't an issue. In some regards, things will be as they have always been in Prentiss.

In the new trial, however, Cory Maye will be represented by a well-funded, well-prepared team of talented attorneys. The State of Mississippi, on the other hand, will attempt to hold together a bruised and battered prosecution theory that has been unraveling ever since Judge Eubanks passed sentence.

> "All right. Then based upon the jury's verdict, I will sentence you to suffer death by lethal injection. All right. That will be the sentence of the Court."

This time, Cory Maye's defense team will take the offense. The State of Mississippi will mount a vigorous fighting retreat. It's not clear either side will be able to secure a unanimous vote from the divided citizenry of Jefferson Davis County, Mississippi.

The two factions may instead elect to call a truce under terms that allow each side to claim victory. I predict the State of Mississippi will offer Cory Maye a sentence of time served in exchange for a guilty plea to the crime of manslaughter. I predict Cory Maye will accept, and will walk free.

And I predict, sadly, that not much else will change in Prentiss, or Jefferson Davis County, or Mississippi.

ACKNOWLEDGEMENTS

I learned of the case of Cory Maye from the writing of Radley Balko. Balko is an award-winning investigative journalist who writes of criminal justice and civil liberties issues. He is, as of this writing, a senior editor for Reason magazine. He writes routinely for Reason and his own blog, The Agitator. His work has been cited by the U.S. Supreme Court and excerpted by the Mississippi State Supreme Court.

I have relied heavily on Balko's work. The quotations from Prentiss and Jefferson Davis County residents, found in the prelude and elsewhere in the book, are excerpted primarily from his writings. I downloaded copies of the trial transcripts and case documents from his blog.

No one deserves more credit than Radley Balko for bringing the case of Cory Maye to public attention.

I acknowledge also the work of Bob Evans. Evans agreed to work as Cory Maye's appellate attorney, even though Maye's family declined his services for the trial, even though the town of Prentiss fired him as their public defender for doing so.

I acknowledge as well the law firm of Covington and Burling for their pro bono effort to secure an acquittal for Cory Maye. Within that firm, I note specifically the work of Abe Pafford and Ben Vernia. Pafford learned of the Cory Maye case via the writing of Radley Balko and convinced his firm to assist in the case, despite his junior status. Ben Vernia argued the venue issue before the Mississippi Court of Appeals. The Court granted a new trial based on that issue and that issue alone. Vernia continues to represent Cory Maye even after forming the Vernia Law Firm, also of Washington, D.C.

I acknowledge the work of the folks at Reason.com for their support of Radley Balko as he investigated the case of Cory Maye. I acknowledge them as well for their role in the development of the online documentary *Mississippi Drug War Blues* that so clearly presents the case of Cory Maye.

NOTES

Despite a heavy reliance on those who have worked on this case before me, this book is an original work completed independently of those just acknowledged. No one has yet presented the trial testimony in a format palatable to general readership. No one has deliberated the testimony by means of a fictional jury. No one has provided a comprehensive, alternate scenario for the events as portrayed by the State of Mississippi.

Specifically, I am unaware that anyone else has publicly put forth the following possibilities:

That the raid may have been orchestrated primarily by Darryl Graves.

That Ron Jones met with Darryl Graves earlier in the day to discuss and plan the raid.

That Ron Jones and Darryl Graves may have together surveilled the duplex on Mary Street, and that the surveillance may have consisted of nothing more than a simple drive by.

That Darryl Graves may have remained behind at the Prentiss police department while Ron Jones led the raid, and that this behavior caused him to be unable to hear the three gunshots from within the Cory Maye apartment.

That Darrell Cooley may have never kicked or shouldered the front door to Cory Maye's apartment.

That Ron Jones and Darryl Graves may have planned to enter through the rear door due to difficulties associated entering through the front door.

That Ron Jones may not have been wearing his bulletproof vest.

That Darrell Cooley's testimony about removing Ron Jones' vest may be contradicted by Ron Jones' autopsy report.

That the clothing proffered by the State of Mississippi may improperly represent that worn by Ron Jones on the night of the shooting. More specifically that Ron Jones may not have been wearing a vest, and that had he been wearing a groin pad as shown in the proffer, he may not have suffered serious injury.

That Ron Jones may have entered the rear door of Cory Maye's unit due to his unfamiliarity with the duplex and issues of left/right confusion.

That the confusion between Terrence Cooley and Phillip Allday at the back of the duplex may have stemmed from the realization that Ron Jones was about the enter the wrong apartment.

That Ron Jones may have used a battering ram to breach the rear door, and this use explains his failure to have his weapon drawn.

That the abrasions on Ron Jones' fingers may have resulted from his use of the battering ram.

That the 35 degree left-to-right, front-to-rear track of the bullet within Ron Jones body may have resulted from the stance he assumed while using the battering ram.

That the fatal bullet may have traveled nearly parallel to the floor, or only slightly upward, and that it may have struck Ron Jones in the abdomen because he had not completely climbed the steps.

That Buddy McDowell may have had Dr. Hayne mark the entry wound on the finger-abrasion diagram to keep the entry-wound diagram from the jurors, and that he may have do so to keep the jurors from learning that the bullet could have changed its direction prior to entering Ron Jones' body.

Primary Sources

Many of the references have already been mentioned throughout the book.

I relied on the writing of Radley Balko, primarily from his blog *The Agitator* and from his writing for Reason.com. I learned of the case from his writing. I excerpted frequently from interviews he conducted during his several trips to Mississippi. I downloaded the trial transcripts and case documents which he generously made available from his blog.

I relied mostly on the trial transcripts and other case documents. I obtained my copy from Radley Balko's blog:

www.theagitator.com

They are now difficult to find there. They are more easily found at:

www.mayeisinnocent.com/index.html

I have made the trial transcripts and case documents available from my Skeptical Juror blog:

www.skepticaljuror.com

I relied heavily on the written appeal prepared by Bob Evans and the team from Covington and Burling: Brief of Appellant Cory J. Maye (October 28, 2008) in the case of *Maye v. State,* No. 2007-KA-02147-COA, certified and signed by Abram J. Pafford. I'll refer to it hereafter as the Brief of Appellant Cory J. Maye. That appeal is typically located with the trial transcripts and other court documents. You can search online using the search phrase "Brief of Appellant Cory Maye", with the quotation marks.

I relied extensively on the transcripts from a pretrial hearing on a motion-to-suppress submitted by Rhonda Cooper. Those motion-to-suppress transcripts are typically located with the trial transcripts and are therefore just as easily located.

I found the autopsy report to be particularly informative. It is typically located with the trial transcripts and other case documents and is therefore just as easy to locate.

Finally, I borrowed frequently from the excellent online documentary *Mississippi Drug War Blues*. Use the name of the documentary in any search engine to find copies. Select a site associated with Reason magazine, since they are responsible for the development of that documentary.

Modifications to the Trial Transcripts

I have taken editorial license with the trial transcripts to make the testimony more readable. My edits include:

- Exclusion of opening and closing statements.
- Exclusion of the judge reading the jury instructions.
- Removal of speaking crutches such as "All Right", "And", "Now", and "Okay" from the beginning of many attorney questions.
- Elimination of incomplete thoughts.
- Joining of multiple answers into a single answer, with concurrent deletion of the intermediate questions.
- Elimination of redundant or irrelevant questions and answers.

Because of the editorial changes made to the transcripts, the transcripts as presented in this book should not be cited as official or strictly accurate.

Introduction

The images of the Mary Street duplex used throughout this book are from a 3-D model I constructed using Google Sketchup. For reference, I used several photos of the duplex found online but not presented herein. I also used Google's Street View feature to view the residence. For the interior arrangement, I relied on the locations of the doors and windows. I relied also on graphics and interior photos presented within the online documentary *Mississippi Drug War Blues*.

Since I did not have the actual dimensions of the duplex, the model is unlikely to be perfectly scaled. The front porches in the diagram, for example, are probably more narrow than the real porches.

Jury Room: Mississippi v. Maye

The literary jurors in this book are pure fiction, the work product only of my own experiences within a jury room. There is one minor exception to this blanket statement. I took the first names of most of my literary jurors from jury pool members examined during voir dire but not selected for the actual jury. There is no correspondence between my depiction of a literary juror and that juror's namesake from the actual jury pool.

Testimony of Stephen Jones

Throughout the book, I refer to the witnesses based on their title and place of employment at the time of the shooting, rather than at the time of the trial or time of this writing.

Testimony of Terrence Cooley

Terrence Cooley went by the nickname T.C., and was frequently referred to as such throughout the trial. I have used Terrence or Terrence Cooley in place of all occurrences of T.C. I have done so as a part of my effort to ease the burden of tracking so many names appearing so quickly in the trial.

Testimony of Darryl Graves

Darryl Graves was called to testify twice, once by the prosecution and once by the defense. I incorporated his testimony as a defense witness into his testimony as a prosecution witness.

Beginning with Darryl Graves' testimony, I deleted testimony regarding "returns." A "return" is the paper on which the list of items removed from the residence is recorded.

Darryl Graves was the first to mention the Mississippi Bureau of Investigation. The officers who arrived from there worked more specifically for the Mississippi Highway Patrol, which fell within the Bureau's organization. Both organizations were mentioned at various points within the testimony. To ease the confusion, I referred to the organizations as the parent organization: the Mississippi Bureau of Investigation.

Testimony of Jim Stone

I did not have a copy of Cory Maye's statement to the police. I constructed the summary of what was said in that statement from secondary sources.

Deliberation of Jim Stone

I adapted the phrase "as if she's just swallowed a bee" from *Farewell My Lovely*, a Philip Marlowe novel by Raymond Chandler.

I did not have a copy of the jury instructions. I constructed a summary of them from secondary sources.

Testimony of Eric Johnson

I deleted many questions and answers regarding the window treatments. It was too confusing for me to understand and present, even after multiple readings.

Testimony of Dr. Steven Timothy Hayne

I excluded the testimony regarding Dr. Hayne's qualifications.

I did not have a copy of the autopsy diagrams as marked by Dr. Hayne during his testimony. I used instead the diagrams directly from the autopsy. I added a mark to the finger-abrasion diagram to indicate the approximate location of the entry wound.

Deliberation of Dr. Steven Timothy Hayne

I include below the diagram from Ron Jones' autopsy report depicting the entry wound. Much of the text is unreadable. It seems, however, that Dr. Hayne marked up the diagram during the autopsy, then later referred to that diagram as he wrote about the entry wound. The text discussing the entry wound follows the sequence of Dr. Hayne's comments on the diagram, if those comments are read from the top down.

By referring to the textual portion of the autopsy report, I believe I have been able to transcribe much of what was written on the entry-wound diagram. I added my typewritten transcription directly to the diagram and repeat it below with annotations:

GSW [gun shot wound]

76 cm [vertically from top of head to entry wound]

entrance [with two arrows pointing to depictions of the wound]

10 cm [horizontally from navel to entry wound]

1.2 cm [maximum height of entry wound]

1.1 cm [maximum width of entry wound]

360 deg [degree] abrasion [indicates entry rather than exit wound]

slightly irreg cw [consistent with] reentry

??? → ??? ??? ??? before striking officer

no tattoo   no smudge   no flame injury   no powder in wound

angle of trajectory

    1.   anterior to posterior ~ 30-35⁰ [front to back]

    2.   superior to inferior ~ 20⁰ [top to bottom]

    3.   left to right

Bullet coursed through adbom [abdominal] wall perforated small bowel x 4 [times 4, in four locations]

aorta → ??? ??? ??? ???

bullet cw [consistent with] 380 [.380 caliber pistol] received from st [state] patrolmen

Hemoperitoneum [blood in abdomen] = 3500 cc [7.4 pints]

exsanguination [complete blood loss] cw [consistent with] reentry penetrating gsw [gunshot wound] to abdomen

Ron Jones

Hayne 27 Dec 01

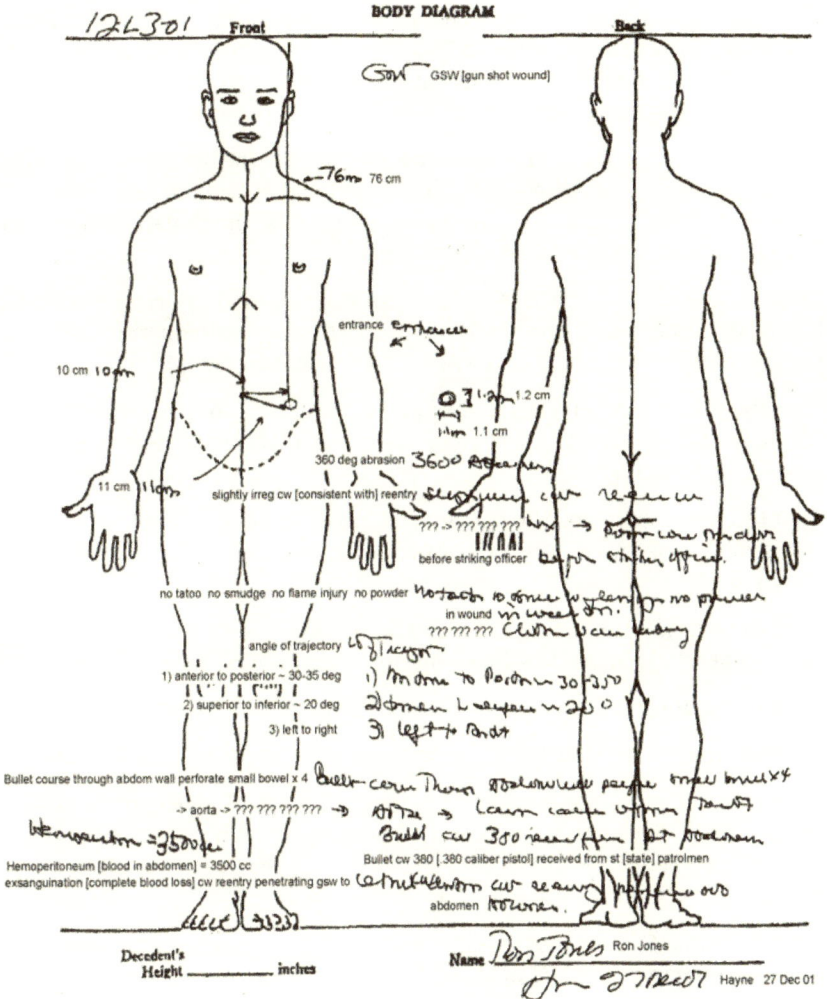

BODY DIAGRAM

Front   Back

GSW [gun shot wound]

76 cm

entrance

1.2 cm

1.1 cm

10 cm

360 deg abrasion

11 cm   slightly irreg cw [consistent with] reentry

before striking officer

no tatoo no smudge no flame injury no powder in wound

angle of trajectory

1) anterior to posterior ~ 30-35 deg
2) superior to inferior ~ 20 deg
3) left to right

Bullet course through abdom wall perforate small bowel x 4
→ aorta →

Hemoperitoneum [blood in abdomen] = 3500 cc
exsanguination [complete blood loss] cw reentry penetrating gsw to abdomen

Bullet cw 380 [.380 caliber pistol] received from st [state] patrolmen

Decedent's Height _____ inches

Name Ron Jones

Hayne 27 Dec 01

I suggest the State did not want the jurors to see the words "before striking officer." Those words argue against the significance the State assigned to the downward path of the bullet.

Interlude

For the quote about the three officers who were allegedly unable to hear the gunshots next door, see the Brief Of Appellant Cory J. Maye.

<<>>

I calculate that the volume of each gunshot, if measured from the center of the Jamie Smith living room, would have been 83 decibels, more than four times louder than normal conversation. That calculation assumes:

That the distance between the gun and the middle of the Jamie Smith living room was 24 feet at an angle of 105 degrees from the direction of fire. (I estimated that distance and angle using the three-dimensional computer model I built of the duplex.)

That the sound level at 24 feet directly behind the muzzle of an M60 machine gun is 133 decibels. (See "Database for Assessing the Annoyance of Small Arms", Technical Guide No. 135, published by the United States Army Environmental Hygiene Agency, June 1983.)

That the sound level at 105 degrees from the direction of fire is 5 decibels louder than the sound level at 180 degrees from the direction of fire. (See the equation in Section 2.1 of the Army document just cited.)

That the sound level of a .38 caliber pistol with a 3.5" long barrel, such as a Lorcin 380, is 10 decibels less than that of an M60 machine gun. (See the Army document just cited.)

That the wall separating the two apartments of the duplex was constructed of a double layer of ½" drywall on wood studs with batt insulation inside the wall.

That the sound attenuation of such a wall would be 45 decibels. (See the Wikipedia article on "Sound Transmission Class.")

Those assumptions allow the following calculation:

Gunshot volume in Jamie Smith Living room = 133 + 5 - 10 - 45 = 83 db

By comparison, normal conversation takes place at 60 decibels. A vacuum cleaner at 10 feet has a volume of 70 decibels. That's twice as loud as normal conversation. A garbage disposal at 3 feet has a volume of 80 decibels. That's four times as loud as normal conversation.

I calculate that the gunshot volume in the Jamie Smith apartment was more than four times as loud as normal conversation. Since the officers claimed they could understand conversation over their police radio, I conclude the gunshots were clearly audible.

Disagreements on this subject could be easily settled by controlled testing.

Alternate Scenario: The Investigation

A primary source for many of the details in this section is the Brief Of Appellant Cory J. Maye.

Not only did the autopsy reveal a phone number on Ron Jones' left palm, it revealed a second phone number on his left thigh. Both numbers were written in black ink.

Black ink was also found on the back of Ron Jones' left hand, and the front of his right thigh.

In my alternate scenario, I have Ron Jones meeting with Darryl Graves in Prentiss earlier in the day. I base that on Darrell Graves' testimony during trial.

> He asked me if I could come back to Prentiss. He had a search warrant
> that he wanted to run, asked if I could assist him.

That answer indicates not only that Graves had been in Prentiss earlier, but that Ron Jones knew Graves had been in Prentiss earlier. In other words, it indicates the two of them had met earlier in the day.

In my alternate scenario, I have Ron Jones surveilling the duplex during a drive by in the company of Darryl Graves. I base that on a passing comment by Judge Kruger during his testimony at the preliminary hearing.

> He said that they had been by there, that's true. I didn't exactly -- no, I
> didn't go into detail about it.

"He said that *they* had been by there."

Alternate Scenario: The Affidavits

The affidavits were modified after Judge Kruger viewed them. Apartment numbers were added to the upper left corner. Those apartment numbers are seemingly useless, given that neither apartment at the complex was labeled as being Apt #1 or Apt #2.

Apt #1 was added to the affidavit for the residence occupied by "Person(s) Unknown."

APT # 1

AFFIDAVIT FOR SEARCH WARRANT

State of Mississippi

County of Jefferson Davis

This day personally appeared before me, the undersigned judicial officer of said county. _____

RONALD W. JONES

known to me to be credible persons, who after having been first duly sworn, depose and say:

1. That affiants have good reason to believe and do believe that certain things hereafter described are now being concealed in or about the following place in this County: *(describe the place to be searched.)*
From the Jefferson Davis County Court House, located on Columbia Ave., travel south on Columbia Ave. and go approximately .3 tenths of a mile to the Int. of Lafayette and Columbia Ave. Turn left on Lafayette St. and go 1.5 tenths of a mile to Mary St. Turn right on Mary St. and go to first yellow apt's on left. together with all approaches and appurtenances thereto:

2. That the place described above is occupied and controlled by: Person(s) Unknown

3. That said things are particularly described as follows: *(describe the thing or things to be seized, taking care to describe only those things which affiants have probable cause to believe and do believe are concealed at the place described above, and with enough particularity to insure that an uninformed officer will not seize one thing under a warrant describing another. Mere evidence is not a proper subject of a search or seizure. Certain things subject to search and seizure include, in addition to the specific subjects enumerated in the Code, all contraband; instrumentalities used in the commission of a crime; and books, writings, pictures and prints adjudged in a proper proceeding by a proper court to be obscene.)*

Drugs, Narcotics and/or controlled substances illegal under the Mississippi Uniform control Substance Law (41-29-101 et seq of the MCA of 1972, as Amended

4. That possesison of the above described things is in itself unlawful (or the public has a primary interest in or, primary right to possession of, the above described things). In that said things are: *(state briefly the use and intention for use of the specified things, citing the appropriate Code section or ordinance being violated and charging its violation, and a brief narrative account of the offense being committed.)*

The above items are unlawful under the provisions of the Mississippi Uniform Control Substance Law (41-29-101 et seq of the MCA of 1972, as Amended) and other applicable statutes.

Apt #2 was added to the affidavit for the residence occupied by "Jamie Smith and/or Person Unknown."

Apt #2

AFFIDAVIT FOR SEARCH WARRANT

State of Mississippi

County of Jefferson Davis

This day personally appeared before me, the undersigned judicial officer of said county, _____

_____ RONALD W. JONES _____

known to me to be credible persons, who after having been first duly sworn, depose and say:

1. That affiants have good reason to believe and do believe that certain things hereafter described are now being concealed in or about the following place in this County: (describe the place to be searched.)

From the front steps of the Jefferson Davis County Court House, located on Columbia Ave., travel south on Columbia Ave. and go approximately .3 tenths of a mile to the intersection of Lafayette St. and Columbia Ave. Turn left on Lafayette St. and go to Mary ST. Turn right on Mary St. and goto first set together with all approaches and appurtenances thereto; of apt's on left.

2. That the place described above is occupied and controlled by: Jamie Smith and/or Person Unknown

3. That said things are particularly described as follows: (describe the thing or things to be seized, taking care to describe only those things which affiants have probable cause to believe and do believe are concealed at the place described above, and with enough particularity to insure that an uninformed officer will not seize one thing under a warrant describing another. Mere evidence is not a proper subject of a search or seizure. Certain things subject to search and seizure include, in addition to the specific subjects enumerated in the Code, all contraband; instrumentalities used in the commission of a crime; and books, writings, pictures and prints adjudged in a proper proceeding by a proper court to be obscene.)

Drugs, Narcotics and/or controlled substances illegal under the Mississippi Uniform Control Substance Law (41-29-101 et seq of the MCA of 1972, as Amended

4. That possession of the above described things is in itself unlawful (or the public has a primary interest in or, primary right to possession of, the above described things). in that said things are: (state briefly the use and intention for use of the specified things, citing the appropriate Code section or ordinance being violated and charging its violation, and a brief narrative account of the offense being committed.)

The above items are unlawful under the provisions of the Mississippi Uniform Control Substance Law (41-29-101 et seq of the MCA of 1972, as Amended) and other applicable statutes

The number added to the Jaime Smith affidavit provides further evidence of the confusion regarding which apartment belonged to whom, and which apartment was to be raided. Whoever added the apartment numbers seemingly labeled the Jamie Smith affidavit as Apt #1, then overwrote the "1" with a "2" as shown in the enlargement below.

Apt #2

Alternate Scenario: The Warrants

Apartment numbers were also added to the original warrants after Judge Kruger signed them. Apt #1 was added to the original warrant for the residence occupied by "Persons(s) Unknown." Though the number was added to the upper right corner of the document, rather than the upper left corner as in the case of the affidavits, the number seems to have been written by the same person.

APT #-1

SEARCH WARRANT

STATE OF MISSISSIPPI

COUNTY OF JEFFERSON DAVIS

TO ANY LAWFUL OFFICER OF JEFFERSON DAVIS COUNTY, MISSISSIPPI

WHEREAS, ___RONALD W. JONES___

_____ known to me

1. That affiants have good reason to believe and do believe that certain things hereafter described are now being concealed in or about the following place in this County:

From the front steps of the Jefferson Davis County Court House, located on Columbia Ave., travel south on Columbia Ave. and go approximately .3 tenths of a mile to the intersection of Lafayette St and Columbia Ave. Turn left on Lafayette St. and go approximately 1.5 tenths of a mile east, to Mary St. Turn right on Mary St. and goto yellow apt's on left.

together with all approaches and appurtenances thereto.

together with all approaches and appurtenances thereto.

2. That the place described above is occupied and controlled by: Person(s) Unknown

3. That said things are particularly described as follows:

Drugs, Narcotics and/or controlled substances illegal under the Mississippi Uniform Control Substance Law (41-29-101, et seq of the MCA of 1972, as Amended.

4. That possession of the above described things is in itself unlawful (or the public has a primary interest in, or primary right to possession of, the above described things), in that said things are:

The above items are unlawful under the provisions of the Mississippi Uniform Control Substance Law (41-29-101 et seq of the MCA of 1972, as Amended) and other applicable statutes of the MCA.

5. The facts tending to establish the foregoing grounds for issuance of a Search Warrant are shown on a sheet "Underlying Facts and Circumstances" which is attached hereto, made a part hereof and adopted herein by reference.

6. This Court, having examined and considered said affidavit, and also having heard and considered evidence in support thereof from the affiants named therein does find that probable cause for the issuance of a search warrant does exist. THEREFORE, you are hereby commanded to proceed at any time in the day or night to the place described above and to search forthwith said place for the things specified above, making known to the person or persons occupying or controlling said place if any, your purpose and authority for so doing, and if the things specified above be found there to seize them, leaving a copy of this warrant and a receipt for the things taken; and bring the things seized before this Court instanter, and prepare a written inventory of the items seized, and have then and there this writ, with your proceedings noted thereon.

7. Do not interpret this writ as limiting your authority to seize all contraband and things the possession of which in itself is unlawful which you find incident to your search, or as limiting your authority to make otherwise valid arrests at the place described above.

Witness my hand this, the __26th__ day of ___December___ ___2001___

Ronald G Nich

OFFICIAL TITLE

CITY JUDGE

Apt #2 was apparently added to the original warrant for the residence occupied by "Jamie Smith and/or Person(s) Unknown." I do not, however, have a copy of that modified warrant.

During a preliminary hearing, Judge Kruger made it clear that the apartment numbers were not on the warrant documents when he reviewed and signed them. He and Ron Jones never spoke of apartment numbers.

In the questioning repeated below, Rhonda Cooper makes it clear that original warrants signed by Judge Kruger were copied some time before the apartment numbers were added to them.

> Cooper: Well, those that I presented to you that's been marked, would you say those are copies of the originals?
>
> Kruger: They appear to be, yes, ma'am.
>
> Cooper: And the only difference being that your originals have apartment 1 and 2 on them, right?
>
> Kruger: Yes, ma'am.
>
> Cooper: When were those numbers placed on there?
>
> Kruger: I do not know that.
>
> Cooper: They were not designated as 1 and 2 when they were presented to you?
>
> Kruger: We talked about right and left, I believe, or east and west, or some such language, and not apartment 1 and apartment 2. I asked him, in trying to identify where he wanted to go, when I finally figured out where the place was, I asked him if that was the Tommie Speights' duplex over there, and he said he didn't know. I knew she owned a duplex somewhere over in there, but I -- it was there in town.
>
> Cooper: Okay. But my question to you, when those affidavits -- excuse me -- those search warrants were presented to you, they were not designated with apartment 1 and apartment 2, were they?
>
> Kruger: No, they weren't. I've testified to that, I believe.
>
> Cooper: No, I don't recall that, but it is your testimony now?
>
> Kruger: That apartment 1 and apartment 2 were not on the search warrant that I signed.

In my alternate scenario, the warrant documents were copied after Judge Kruger signed them, when Ron Jones returned to his office at police headquarters, when he met once again with Darryl Graves. In my alternate scenario, the documents are not modified prior to the raid.

If my alternate scenario is correct, the addition of the apartment numbers to the signed warrants may have been part of a conspiracy to cover up a raid poorly planned and poorly executed. The addition of the apartment numbers in that case could constitute tampering with evidence

Alternate Scenario: Judge Kruger

The quotes from Judge Kruger are from his testimony at a pre-trial hearing in the Cory Maye case.

In my alternate scenario, I have Ron Jones surveilling the duplex during a drive by in the company of Darrell Graves. I incorporate this in part based on Judge Kruger's testimony during the preliminary hearing.

> He said that they had been by there, that's true. I didn't exactly -- no, I didn't go into detail about it.

Alternate Scenario: The Briefing

I based the information about Phillip Allday's volunteer status in large part on the Motion for New Trial submitted by Rhonda Cooper, very soon after the verdict, on February 2, 2004.

I based the information about the pre-trial briefing exclusively on the trial transcripts, particularly the testimony of Darrell Cooley and Darryl Graves.

Alternate Scenario: The Shooting

The quotes by Cory Maye are from his trial testimony.

The quotes by Cory Maye's mother are from the online documentary *Mississippi Drug War Blues.*

I obtained the moonlight conditions for that night in Prentiss from the mathematically based search engine Wolfram Alpha, using the search terms "Prentiss MS December 26, 2001."

<<>>

Stephen Jones spoke of Ron Jones' clothing during the preliminary hearing. After being asked about his clothing that night, and after mentioning he personally was wearing a vest, he described Ron Jones' clothing without mentioning a vest.

> He was in his uniform, black uniform. He had a police jacket on, department jacket on, and his uniform shirt.

Darrell Cooley mentioned the vest twice during his trial testimony. First:

> I grabbed Ron as he was going down, rolled him up towards the house because I didn't know what was going on inside. Got him up close to the house, pulled his vest off and pulled his jacket back and pulled his vest off.

Later and more explicitly.

> I pulled his vest and his jacket off.

Unless someone put Ron Jones' coat back on him after he was pronounced dead, Darrell Cooley's testimony stands in conflict with the autopsy report signed by Dr. Hayne.

Ron Jones' vest was mentioned once again in a footnote to the Brief of Appellant Cory J. Maye.

> Jones' clothing was admitted into evidence during the two-day post-trial hearing in September 2006. ... Photographs of this clothing, displayed on a mannequin, were submitted with a post-trial proffer and are included in the appellate record. ... The photos speak for themselves: Jones' clothing on the night of the raid consisted of dark combat fatigues, a dark jacket with no police insignia visible from the front, and a bulletproof vest that contained no markings other than an oval "Extreme Armor" logo in the center of the vest.

A proffer is a preliminary offering, specifically with regard to testimony or evidence. It is a preview of what will be said or shown. With that proffer, the State was stating that, at the time of the shooting, Ron Jones was wearing the clothing as portrayed on the mannequin.

The photograph of that clothing is included within the online documentary *Mississippi Drug War Blues*. That photograph shows a vest worn beneath a jacket. The photograph also shows what appears to be a piece of body armor known as a groin pad. Had Ron Jones been wearing the body armor displayed on the mannequin, it's extremely unlikely he would have been killed. The bullet would have almost certainly been stopped by either the vest or, more likely, the groin pad.

As is the case with Darrell Cooley's trial testimony, the clothed mannequin proffered by the State of Mississippi stands in conflict with the autopsy report signed by Dr. Hayne.

<<>>

Anyone can demonstrate for themselves that a slight crouch can cause an upward traveling bullet to create a downward path in a body when the body is returned to the upright position. While standing crouched slightly with one foot forward, place a yardstick (or other elongated object) along your side at a slightly upward angle to the floor. Then stand upright and place your feet together while holding the yardstick securely against your side. The yardstick will be pointed downward, from front to rear.

For a graphical demonstration, see the online documentary *Mississippi Drug War Blues*.

Postlude

I obtained the weather conditions for that night in Prentiss from the mathematically based search engine Wolfram Alpha, using the search terms "Prentiss MS December 26, 2001." That source does not include wind conditions. I merely presumed the air was calm.

I based the police inattention to Ta'Corianna on a Radley Balko blog post. (The Agitator, March 18, 2006, "Cory Maye: The Vanishing of Jamie Smith")

One other item that doesn't paint the raiding officers in the most flattering light: The woman I spoke with also said that Cory's 18-month-old daughter Ticorrianna was left alone on the bed screaming, for hours after the raid. Audrey Davis apparently attempted to pick her up to calm her down, but was reprimanded by police at the scene, and told to leave her be. It wasn't until Chanteal Longino returned home from her night shift at the chicken plant in Hattiesburgh that anyone attempted to give the 18-month-old any consolation.

<<>>

The quotes from Sheriff Henry McCullum and Cory Maye's mother regarding his early incarceration are from the online documentary *Mississippi Drug War Blues*.

<<>>

Regarding the frequency with which Rhonda Cooper met Cory Maye before the trial, see the online documentary *Mississippi Drug War Blues*.

<<>>

Regarding the State's use of its peremptory challenges to exclude blacks from the jury, see footnote 51 to the Brief of Appellant Cory J. Maye.

> Ms. Cooper should have objected to the prosecutor's use of peremptory challenges to strike African-American and female jurors from the panel. Six of the State's nine peremptory strikes were African-Americans: [names withheld.] None of those women responded to a single question during voir dire, leaving nothing in the record to rebut the inference that the prosecutor struck them because of their race. In addition, the State used eight of its nine peremptory challenges to strike women, only one of whom responded to voir dire questions. Based on the record, then, Mr. Maye likely could have made out a prima facie case of purposeful discrimination on the basis of either race or gender.

<<>>

I excerpted the juror interview from a Radley Balko blog post. (The Agitator, March 18, 2006, "Cory Maye: Juror Interview")

<<>>

For more information regarding the prosecution-friendly work of Stephen Hayne and other medical examiners, see the writing of Radley Balko. A Google search using keywords "balko hayne" will lead to thousands of relevant hits.

<<>>

For information regarding the firing of Bob Evans as Prentiss public defender due to his defense of Cory Maye, see the letter Bob Evans wrote to Radley Balko. Use the search phrase "prentiss board of aldermen have fired evans" with the quotation marks.

Just found out this a.m. that the Town of Prentiss has "decided to go another route" pertaining to my position as town public defender. In other words, they have now made official what was intimated to me back in December and have fired me.

The explicit and sole reason given to me by the mayor was that my representation of Cory Maye was not to the liking of the aldermen. I guess it wasn't to the mayor's liking either since, to the best of my knowledge, he didn't veto their decision. Of course, I have no doubt that it's a politically popular decision among the Caucasians of Prentiss. But what in life is not, at least to some extent, political?

When apprised that this move was being contemplated, although I doubted that it would make any difference I requested the courtesy of being allowed to appear before the board to express my reasons for representing Cory. They did not deign to grant me this opportunity.

I have been Prentiss public defender officially (salaried) since February 1995 and unofficially for several years prior. During that time not one official complaint has been communicated to me about my performance. Of course, there have been many unofficial complaints about me "getting all those guilty people off."

What it boils down to is something that I have known and personally observed about members of the "unwashed masses" for many years: When the Constitution and Bill of Rights are applied to benefit others, the right to counsel, due process, fair trial et al. are "technicalities". Criminals get off on technicalities such as the 4th Amendment. Only when one of their asses is in a sling are these same documents "fundamental rights".

But what the hell. Four hundred a month ain't gonna bankrupt me. This decision, to me, is an indication that the "powers that be" actually believe that we can win Cory's appeal. That is a refreshing thought. I have always liked the adage "He who laughs last laughs best."

<<>>

I have not actually seen any of the signs proclaiming a portion of Highway 84 to be designated as Officer Ronald Wayne Jones Memorial Highway. I note, however, that the signs are mandated by Mississippi House Bill No. 974, signed into law on April 20, 2005.

House Bill No. 974

Section 2. (1) That portion of U.S. Highway 84 located in Jefferson Davis County is designated and shall be known as the "Officer Ronald Wayne Jones Memorial Highway."

(2) The Mississippi Department of Transportation shall erect and maintain appropriate signs along and approaching the segment of highway described in subsection (1) of this section.

www.ingramcontent.com/pod-product-compliance
Lightning Source LLC
LaVergne TN
LVHW011227080426
835509LV00005B/352